janey and me

j

g

V

Fo

First published in Great Britain in 2003 by
Fourth Estate
A Division of HarperCollins*Publishers*
77–85 Fulham Palace Road
London w6 8jb
www.4thestate.com

Copyright © Virginia Ironside 2003

1 3 5 7 9 10 8 6 4 2

The right of Virginia Ironside to be identified as the author of this work
has been asserted by her in accordance with the Copyright, Designs and
Patents Act 1988

The names of some of the characters in this book have been changed.

A catalogue record for this book is available from the British Library

ISBN 1-84115-750-3

Typeset by Palimpsest Book Production Limited, Polmont, Stirlingshire
Printed in Great Britain by Clays Ltd, St Ives plc

acknowledgements

Most of all, I would like to thank Jeremy Lewis for his encouragement and enthusiasm. First he gave me the confidence to write a memoir of my uncle Robin for the *London Magazine*, and then spent hours helping with this book. Tim Jeal gave me invaluable and sensitive advice, too. And Nik Cohn, for his invaluable godfatherly advice over the years. I would also like to thank my marvellous agent, Clare Alexander; my painstaking and sympathetic editor, Catherine Blyth; and to remember, with special thanks, the late Margaret Hewson, who was always so loyal and inspiring.

Finally, I must thank John Wright, my stepmother, Jean, and Kate, Sukie and Christian for their generosity.

prologue

A few days after my mother died, I took some of her things to a local antique shop in Kensington Church Street in Notting Hill where she occasionally sold unwanted china or bits of redundant furniture. There was a small Hindu carving she had plundered from a temple during her childhood in India, a folder of hand-painted Edwardian fashion prints bought for sixpence each when she and my father had lived in Leamington Spa during the war, an amber necklace given to her by one of her many admirers, but which she never wore because the colour was so unflattering.

Her death had been well publicized. Even people I hardly knew came up to me in the street, offering condolences. The papers produced a fanfare of obituaries, mourning the passing of a fashion guru, an icon; her name, they said, was synonymous with style and innovation. One eulogy was headed: 'Janey Ironside: Professor of Fashion, Royal College of Art, the woman who changed the face of English fashion in the sixties.' Every morning, the postman arrived with wads of letters from my mother's grateful and now madly successful students.

As I walked with my booty into the antique shop – thick with Victorian smells of dusty horsehair and cracking leather – the owner stared at me as if he had seen a ghost. He rose from his chair, steadying himself on a desk with his hand. He was ashen.

'Janey!' he cried out. 'But I thought you were dead!'

I look exactly like my mother. I am her beautiful daughter – 'beautiful Janey Ironside's daughter'. Guests at my house stop, embarrassed, when they see so many pictures of the person they think is me. But they're not of me; they're of my mother. Hanging on the walls are three portraits of her in oils, one lithograph, six drawings by my father and four drawings of my mother and me when I was a baby.

I am fed up with being called 'Janey' by accident, by her friends. When I stepped into the street with one of the people I'd been interviewing for this book, she said: 'I think I'm going your way. Do you want a lift, Janey?' Ancient, doddering people often come up to me, insisting we've met before, and don't believe me when I promise them it was my mother they'd met, not me.

Twenty years after her death, I'm often asked: 'Are you any relation of Janey Ironside?' and I found, in a yellowing press-cutting from the sixties, that my mother had been asked the same question in reverse. 'At forty-three, Janey Ironside has been taken as the sister of her grown-up daughter more times than she cares to remember. "Are you any relation of Virginia Ironside?" they ask.'

Having spent most of my life growing my hair, getting it permed in crazy curls or wearing it up, I'm now resigned to the fact that I look far the best with a short bob, exactly the same cut that my mother favoured for both of us, a look that I hated when I was a child, thinking it made me look like a boy.

When I listen to my own voice on the radio, I hear my mother speaking. And when I listen to recordings of my mother's slightly slurred voice on the wireless, I hear our identical expressions – '*Ghastly*', '*Frightfully* embarrassing', '*Hideous*', 'How *awful*', 'I can't *bear* it'.

Although I'm taller than my mother, and I don't suffer from the patchy skin-pigment disease that afflicted her, vitiligo, nor her middle-aged white hair (always dyed jet black), we share the same large breasts, short sight, right-footed bunion, tussles with alcohol, a direct kind of honesty that often takes no account of other people's feelings, and a tendency to depression. Builders shout at me, as they did to my mother when they saw her walking down the street: 'Cheer up, love! It'll never happen!' Like my mother, I keep my drawing-room tidy and polished; like her, I'm unable to relax.

And like her, I'm never quite certain who I am. Sometimes I've looked in the mirror and seen a solemn little eight-year-old child looking back at me; lately, I have seen the heavy features of my mother in middle age peering out, with desperate, imploring eyes.

After years and years of useless therapy, I've never been able to rid myself of my mother's oppressive presence.

I often wonder if I'll ever be able to exorcize her: whether, when I look in the mirror, I'll see not Janey staring out but, instead, myself.

one

TENT *A garment widening from the shoulders in the shape of a modified tent. Prone, in any case, to give a pregnant look, it is much favoured as a maternity dress shape.*

Janey Ironside, *A Fashion Alphabet*

For the first three days of my life, during the mini-Blitz of London in February 1944, I was put, for safe-keeping, under a large mahogany sideboard in the ground-floor dining-room of a private nursing home at 99 Cromwell Road.

One hundred and twenty linoleum-covered stairs above, my unhappy mother lay on a bed in a tiny room that contained a Victorian hand-basin, a pitcher and a small coal fire. She had given birth to me to the noise of shrapnel pattering on the roof and to the shuddering thumps of nearby bombs. She wasn't allowed downstairs to see me, and when she cried the nurses told her crossly not to be so silly.

As the sirens and buzz-bombs howled outside, and nearby

underground trains rumbled past every few minutes, rocking the building, I imagine my mother felt intolerably lonely. My father came to London on the second night of my existence, and walked back from the nursing home to his mother's house in Chelsea where he was staying. The black-out was illuminated, he wrote to my mother, 'by brilliant light from burning houses every step of the way. So romantic!' But the following morning he had had to get back to his job as a Camouflage Officer, a hundred miles away, in Leamington Spa.

They discussed what names to call me. Janey liked 'Virginia', which might have seemed a smart choice at the time, perhaps with echoes of Virginia Woolf. It would, my mother argued, be a far more suitable name than her own austere 'Janet', which she had changed to 'Janey' when old enough to decide for herself. Then there was 'Harriet', a sop to the same side of the family that christened my mother 'Janet' — dutiful, hard-working, middle-class professional Northern Irish relations, who my mother said were 'so mean there wasn't even a sherry cupboard for them to keep a key to'.

The last choice was 'Clementina', after my father's grandmother, whom I would meet once when I was tiny. Attended by a much-bullied lady companion, she sat crabbed, clutching a stick, dressed in a black Edwardian dress and hat, in her final quarters, a Gloucester Road hotel, just round the corner from the very nursing home where my mother was now staring gloomily at the ceiling.

In the end, I was christened all three — Virginia Harriet Clementina Ironside.

My mother had found herself pregnant in 1943, and she didn't like it at all. She felt awful, she looked fat and unattractive, or so she thought, and, lacking any maternal feelings, she didn't feel like painting a nursery or buying bootees or rattles. She was depressed all the time and it was lucky for me that on hearing the news of my arrival, her family, at least, was enthusiastic.

My mother's sister, Kitty, knitted a coat. 'It looks to me *enormous,*' she wrote from India, 'but perhaps it will be the right size by the time it reaches you. I hope it's a girl because it would be much more fun to dress and probably much easier to look after. I am afraid the Cashmere wool is rather peculiar, rather thin but beautifully soft to feel. Anyway you can always give it to some orphanage or something if it's not right.'

My mother's mother sent fussing letters from Kashmir, where my grandfather was Resident, advising weeks in Bournemouth and a course of Parish's food — 'Do take it, Janet, and also Calcium as it's a great help to your teeth to say nothing of the infant's bones' — warning her to keep out of draughts — 'You ought to put felt strips all round the doors and possibly windows too; it makes a huge difference' — and enclosing useful garments — 'Today I sewed up a skirt and smock for you in a perfectly good duster which may be useful. It is lined with an old "pettie" and has all been washed to get out dirt. I was given the pattern by an experienced Mama as being very useful and comfortable towards the end, and the smock will always do for housework afterwards.'

I can imagine the face my mother must have made as she unwrapped the parcel when it eventually arrived. 'Oh, God,' she would have said to my father. 'I couldn't possibly wear *that*! Oh, dear, it's so kind of mummy, but honestly — *look* at it! It's *ghastly*!'

All my mother could bear to wear, in public at least, was an elegant blue-grey brocade Chinese coat with bands of silk embroidery, which I still have, given to her by an ancient cousin of her mother's who had escaped death during the Indian Mutiny. My mother wore it with home-made silk trousers. When she wasn't doing the housework, which she hated, she didn't bury herself in the then fashionable baby books of the time by Truby King, preferring to read Dickens, Trollope, Somerville and Ross, Proust, Tolstoy, George Eliot — all recommended by my uncle Robin, an avid member of the London Library.

The week before I was due, my mother left Leamington Spa and came up to London to stay with my father's mother, Phyl, who lived in a tiny little house in Groom Place, off Belgrave Square, where my uncle Robin was also lodging at the time. Robin was my father's brother, a gaunt, emaciated flame of a man with glittering eyes. At the time, he was Assistant Director at the Tate Gallery.

When air raids started and shrapnel began to fall into the small courtyard in front of the house, Robin would bring out a cherished bottle of whisky, pour three slugs, and place them on the drawing-room table where they could be seen, like talismans, from the cramped positions that he, my mother and grandmother took in a tiny cupboard under the stairs. When the all-clear sounded, they had to be very nippy to seize and swallow the whisky before Robin could pour it back into the bottle. It was supposed to be kept for the times when bombs began to shake the house. Knowing her, I'm sure my mother was the nippiest of all three.

My mother must have enjoyed those few days. My uncle was amusing, clever and bohemian: my grandmother, funny and over-whelmingly kind. So to find herself suddenly in this grisly nursing home after a painful birth must have reminded her of being sent to boarding-school. Certainly, on first being shown her room, she immediately burst into floods of tears. There was now nothing to do but cry or read – and nothing to read except an old copy of *Vogue*, a few P. G. Wodehouses and a copy of *Elders and Betters* that Robin had brought round, written by his friend, the virtually inaccessibly surreal novelist, Ivy Compton Burnett.

After his visit, there was no question of my father ringing the nursing home. Had he done so, he would have had to call after 6 p.m. (cheap time), and leave a message with a nurse. My mother had to be consoled by daily letters, written in his small and florid italic hand. He tried to cheer her up by telling her domestic things, about the cat, about the chop he had had for supper, the apple sago, the dried egg, the spluttering gas fire, but it was his overwhelming passion for my mother that would have pleased her most of all.

> Darlingest Janey, I love you, darling snoopsit doopsit, to distraction and long for you to be back here with me and I want to see my little baby Pinny Bean again. With all my love darlingest heart, Christopher.

Had she managed to get out of bed to look out of the window, my mother would have seen, to her right, Gloucester Road underground station, and, to her left and opposite, long terraces of identical, huge Victorian houses. The windows would have been blacked out; in the window-boxes, spotted laurels and leggy geraniums struggled for survival against the traffic fumes; and in the porticoes of those huge, dank buildings, many of them turned into residential hotels for the retired, single, upper middle class, there might have hovered a nervous widow with hat, gloves and umbrella, on her way to a walk in Kensington Gardens. If my mother had had a periscope, she would have been able to see the corner of Stanhope Gardens, the street in which she had stayed, a few years previously, as a young art student – and the street in which, in another flat, at a later date, she would try to kill herself.

In the days after my birth, however, my mother had nothing to anticipate except, perhaps, a plate of boiled fish and potato, delivered by a grumpy nurse at six o'clock.

Finally, on the third day, my mother was pronounced well enough by the nurses to stumble down the stairs to visit me.

I can only imagine her thoughts when she peered under the sideboard into the crib. They were probably a mixture of horror ('Oh-my-God-what-have-I-done-now?'), acute anxiety about how on earth she was going to cope, and a slightly wistful sorrow that I wasn't a boy (though later she once said, rather creepily: 'Thank goodness you *weren't* a boy, darling, or I would have fallen in love with you'). But the overwhelming feeling must have been: 'Isn't she pretty! I simply must get back to Leamington and make a proper nightdress for her – and then I must cut her funny hair as soon as possible, pity about the scratch-marks on her face, oh God, I wish she'd stop screaming, poor thing!'

Then she would have added to herself, grimacing in a humorous, self-deprecating, hope-it-won't-rain-but-it-probably-will kind of way: 'I *do* hope she'll be *happy* and her life won't be *too* ghastly!'

two

GYM TUNIC *A sleeveless garment with a flat yoke from shoulder to above bust point, carried on by deep inverted pleats hanging straight to the hem. On growing schoolgirls worn with a tight girdle, this is a very ugly line devised as a decent garment for the gymnasium when physical exercise for girls became the fashion in the 1920s. However, transformed by British designer Mary Quant, and worn loose on a flat-busted girl, it can achieve great charm.*

Janey Ironside, *A Fashion Alphabet*

Clothes were always my mother's passion. Even in middle age, my mother could recall every design, every textile, and every stitch of everything she had ever worn in her life. One of the earliest photographs of her shows her wearing a Muslim girl's dress given to her, at two years old in India, by the Begum of Dehra. She remembered that the dress was a deep indigo blue, with scarlet, emerald, yellow and orange embroidery, and the little shoes were made of pale leather, the toes turned up with pompoms of pink silk.

Of her first party dresses in India, she wrote: 'One was made in yellow moiré silk with a fitted bodice and a full skirt. Two brown velvet bands crossed to the waist with a bunch of little artificial flowers at the end of each ribbon. With this I wore dark brown lizard-skin pumps with heels one inch high. The other was pink, round-necked and short-sleeved, with the bodice reaching to the hips – the skirt was made up of three flounces. I now realize it would have been quite pretty if it had not had to be too long to cover dreaded knee-length knickers.'

As a child, she was dressed in old-fashioned holland smocks, stitched in red, with over-buttoned and embroidered knickers, both reaching to her knees. Her little pyjamas were made of pure silk crêpe-de-chine, exquisitely hand-embroidered by the pupils of a convent.

My mother had been born into an exotic world of servants, status and respect – the world of Rudyard Kipling. She was my grandparents' first child, and arrived, in India, on 29 December 1917 in a bungalow in Lytton Road, Quetta, where my grandfather was serving as a magistrate. She was immediately handed over to a loving ayah, the Indian nanny, and spoke fluent Hindustani until she was six years old.

My grandfather, James Glasgow Acheson, had been a golden student, a scholar at Trinity College, Dublin. He entered the Indian Civil Service in 1913 and, only a year later, at twenty-two, was given his first job, as Governor of the gaol at Agra, home of the Taj Mahal. When he married Violet Field, my grandmother, their first home was in the gaol itself, where they were waited on by prisoners. It took Violet a few days to get used to the clanking leg-irons of their convict servants.

My mother had a retinue of servants, albeit rather peculiar ones. The man employed to push the pram into town when she was a baby was a 'delightful' ex-convict who had killed no fewer than four men. Later, he would play pram-pusher to her two brothers and her younger sister Kitty as well. When Janey was a little older, she had her own groom for her pony, and a personal launderer, who washed all her clothes in the morning and returned them, ironed, every evening.

By the time my mother was eight, my grandfather had risen to become Deputy Foreign Secretary, and the family lived in a Lutyens-designed bungalow on the outskirts of New Delhi, which was growing up around them. My mother shared lessons with the children of several families, including those of the Viceroy of India. Every summer was spent in the cool hills of Simla. She was secure and loved — at least until that painful parting which affected so deeply the many children of people who worked in India. At twelve years old, my mother was sent 'home' to school.

In the boat back to England, she had no premonition of the hideous contrast to her present life that awaited her; six years of more or less continuous unhappiness. She was billeted on her maternal grandmother, Madre, a sharp-tongued, amusing and bitter woman who lived in Fleet, in Hampshire, a 'kind of Anglo-Indian living graveyard', as my mother described it. The cold house they lived in was called Aram, which, though it meant 'rest' in Persian, my mother regarded as a very unsuitable name because Madre seldom gave her husband, or her, a moment's peace. Gone were the exuberance and colour of the Indian bazaars; instead there were the mean, grey shops of England. Smiling, fawning servants were replaced by one surly daily help. The skies were always grey; it rained constantly.

Far worse, my mother had to undergo a complete change of clothes. For school, the hated St Swithun's in Winchester, she was forced to wear a navy-blue, alpaca or serge pleated gym slip, black lisle stockings (not too fine) and a strange navy-blue felt pudding-basin hat. The gym slip, hideous over the girls' developing figures, was belted with a woven wool braid and the rule was that the slip should measure four inches from the floor when the wearer knelt down.

'Why *does* that awful Mary wear knitted woollen stockings the colour of her hair!' she wrote in her diary. 'With such an unfortunate carrot colour she ought to avoid repeating it like poison. And she wears a dreadful short gym tunic with her girdle round her hips and her horrid red mane hanging down behind.'

All her life, Janey dreaded the sound of pealing church bells because they reminded her of Sundays evenings in Fleet, sitting in a cold sitting-room and listening to the wireless with Madre. Her grandmother kept asking ridiculous questions about the crossword like 'What is a seven-letter African bird beginning with F?' when all my mother wanted to do was to go up to her room to mooch about, listen to records and imagine herself back with her family in India. She felt she had been cast out and abandoned.

Everything about her life seemed horrible. Even being a girl was beastly. She longed to be a boy, like her adored brother Jimmy, a pupil at nearby Wellington College. She couldn't see a single advantage in being a girl, 'unless one calls having a door opened for one, or being allowed to go first an advantage, which I don't,' she wrote, angrily. At fourteen, my mother was developing the gloom, pessimism and insecurity that was to dog her all her life.

It was her conviction that she was ugly that was partly to blame. As a child, my mother's almost Chinese eyes, huge, flopping mouth and shiny, dark, bobbed hair hadn't been considered remotely attractive. It was the delicate blonde and small-boned look that was then in fashion, and any self-confidence my mother might have developed about her looks as she grew older was cruelly eroded by Madre, who

me. age 16 at night

A self-portrait by Janey at sixteen

would say things like 'You're not going out in *that*, are you?' after my mother had spent hours adjusting and altering a dress to make it look more fashionable. 'You look like a monkey!'

The last straw came when she was sixteen, when a girl at school caught her across the mouth with a lacrosse stick, breaking one of her front teeth. From then on, she had to wear a plate. (At almost precisely the same age, swinging on two desks at school, I fell on my face, and one of my front teeth broke. My mother was far more upset about this than I was.) Janey felt this disaster was some test sent by God to try her. She feared that she was turning into 'a blighted person'. She was certain that she'd never ever look even reasonably pretty.

'If I hadn't such awful teeth and not quite so snub a nose, I could really be very attractive,' she wrote in her diary. Then, with a typical echo of Madre, she added, scathingly, 'If!'

There was only one consolation: shopping. When she was just seventeen, she was occasionally allowed up to London, where she could walk up and down Oxford Street and look into Peter Robinson, Marshall & Snelgrove and D. H. Evans. Once, she found two evening dresses at a guinea shop — one in pale yellow artificial silk with black spots and one in black lamé. Though they were cheap, she comforted herself with the fact that after she'd finished altering them, they'd look much more expensive. Another time, she found some green velvet and silver lamé at John Lewis, and saw some glorious velvet, deep, glowing blue-green 'with the most perfect lights in it', but when she heard the exorbitant price, so many tears rose to her eyes that she had to walk away quickly.

It was only when she was sent to finishing school in Switzerland for a few months, that same year, that Janey's view of herself began to change. With her sunburned skin and her straight black hair cut in a fringe and a bob, she was known either as *l'indienne* or *la petite chinoise* — and she began to realize that, if not exactly a beauty, she might just get away with being described as '*jolie-laide*'. When she got back to London, she touchingly wrote down in her diary every compliment paid to her.

'A man opposite me in the tube looked at me and whispered to the woman beside him, "Attractive, isn't she?" "Quite," said the woman coldly.' And she met an artist friend of her aunt's who said: 'I would love to paint you, you've got such lovely colouring.' 'First *I've* heard of it,' remarked Janey acidly, to her diary.

*

It was, however, at a party given by her parents, when they came over to London, that my mother had an experience which was to change everything. Her father had arranged a lunch at the Carlton Club to which he had invited his friend, the society portrait painter T. C. Dugdale. Seventeen-year-old Janey wore a clinging pink and black sprigged dress with pleated sleeves that she had bought for four guineas, and a droopy white hat with a pink rose. Her hair was done in a small, neat bun and with her high-heeled French shoes, she felt reasonably sure that she looked all right − in other words, grown up. Everyone grouped around a table with drinks, waiting for the guests, and when Mr Dugdale appeared, he greeted her parents. Then he turned to Janey, but as he was about to shake her hand, he stopped. He stared at her for several seconds. Finally he said: 'Good heavens! How beautiful you are! I must paint you!'

After the lunch was over, my mother remembered only those magical words: 'Beautiful − beautiful − beautiful!'

True, when she mentioned the fact that Dugdale wanted to paint her to Madre, her grandmother had simply laughed disagreeably. 'But he said I was beautiful!' said Janey. Madre, typically, responded scathingly: 'He must have been joking. *I* always look upon our Janet as the ugly duckling of the family!' And even her friends were rather confused. My mother remembered one girlfriend commenting, thoughtfully: 'Artists must like you, Janet. Though I've never made up my mind if you are ugly or beautiful.'

But no one could dampen her euphoria. The idea of being painted, being admired, transported my mother with delight. She was grown-up. She was in London. She was going to be painted by a fashionable artist who lived in Chelsea. She was beautiful.

The Dugdale portrait

At 11.30 on an autumn Tuesday, feeling nervous and excited, she turned up at Mr Dugdale's studio at 58 Glebe Place, clad in her 'glad rags' – pink frock, black shoes, floppy white hat. Mr Dugdale, wearing a blue painting overall, led her upstairs to his studio. She remembered every detail later – the Persian rugs on the parquet floor, the well-polished mahogany furniture, the three large windows, one of which filled nearly a whole wall.

Sitting her on the artist's throne, Mr Dugdale tried various poses and finally arranged her sitting on a chair with her legs crossed. Her hands rested on her lap, palms upwards, holding long gloves; her head was tilted a little to the left. While he painted, my mother ate chocolates and 'thought interesting thoughts about clothes'.

Before lunch, Mr Dugdale gave her a cocktail. She had already tasted the odd sip of alcohol at parties in India, but this was her first grown-up drink. Because she drank it on an empty stomach, it made her feel giddy and sick – but she enjoyed it. Over sandwiches and fruit off a tray prepared by the charlady, she listened, naïvely impressed, as the artist talked about everything from the Abyssinian question and the situation in Europe, to the châteaux of the Loire. Or he gossiped about all the people he knew, like the actors Dame Sybil Thorndike, Talmadge, Gordon Harker and the painter, Dame Laura Knight. It was a glimpse into a world she couldn't wait to inhabit.

The following year, she returned to India. My grandfather had been made Resident for Waziristan in Dera Ismael Khan, or DIK (known in the Indian Civil Service as Dreary Dismal Khan) and my mother

Janey in India, sitting by her father's knee. Her mother sits next to him on his right.

was dying to meet masses and masses of young men.

She led a frantic social life – once she was asked to a special evening given by the Maharajah of Cooch Behar – and her days were spent galloping in the hills, reading *Vogue* and eating sumptuous meals. She fell madly in love with a young man called Ian, but I know nothing about him because, after she was married, my mother tore every photograph of him out of the albums, destroyed every letter, and ripped up every page of her diary in which he gets a mention, no doubt due to my father's jealousy. Ian came back into her life just before she died. He got in touch and asked to come round to tea. He only had one leg, and my mother thought he was rather boring and not *nearly* as attractive as he used to be.

When she came back to London a year later, she rented a sunny back room in Stanhope Gardens, South Kensington, and signed up at the Central School of Arts and Crafts. Naturally, the course she chose was dressmaking. Even during her most miserable days in Fleet, she'd never lost that desire to 'look right' and at school, although she was forced to wear a brown beret with the initials of St Swithun's embroidered on to it, she always wore it in the French way, down on her face, and, apparently, looked marvellous. Now she took her obsession to such a degree and saved up so much of her money for clothes that she often didn't eat enough and fainted from starvation, much to the concern of her mother back in India, who begged her to spend more on food. My mother promised she would and continued exactly the same as before.

One day, she was travelling back from Holborn to South Kensington on the Underground when she noticed, sitting opposite her, the most attractive young man she'd ever seen in her life. Apparently her first thought was: 'That is the only person I ever want to marry'.

A week later, she saw the same man walking towards the Central School and a little while afterwards she spotted him at the New Year's Eve Chelsea Arts Ball at the Albert Hall — then a 'must' occasion. When she finally saw him in the art school itself, signing the register, she asked another student who he was. The answer, with a groan, was: 'Oh, you're not *another* — that's Christopher Ironside. He runs a drawing class here and *everyone* seems to be infatuated with him.'

Later that evening, at Holborn station, she spotted the gorgeous Christopher hanging about on the steps. She pretended not to notice but she was vain enough to hope for the next move — which came when Christopher, obviously just as attracted to my mother as she was to him, approached her and asked if he could ring her up. Their first date was a jaunt to Disney's *Snow White and the Seven Dwarfs*, followed by dinner at Quaglino's.

My father was tall, dark-haired and dark-skinned. On a hot day, he only had to pass from the shadow of one tree to another via the merest slant of sunlight to turn a deep shade of brown. Had he been rigged up with a dishcloth on his head, banded with rope, and let into the streets, I honestly believe that mobbing crowds would have refused to accept that he was not Rudolph Valentino himself.

There was some dispute about where his dusky looks came from. His mother, born Phyllis Cunliffe, used to whisper that we had a 'touch of the tar-brush', handed down from a distant great-uncle who ran a plantation in the West Indies. It was said that he had married an 'octoroon', a woman of Spanish and African blood, and I still have her slave bracelet.

The Cunliffes were really something. At least, they thought they were something. They had owned one of the first of the grand houses in the Little Boltons in South Kensington, a sumptuous place filled with servants and boasting a version of the earliest form of central heating in London. It was this house that probably made my father and me feel inextricably bonded with that part of London, which we both regarded as a kind of ancestral stamping ground. Now, I only live five minutes away, in Shepherd's Bush, but I still feel like a blighted villager who's been condemned to live outside the castle walls.

Because one Cunliffe became Lord Radcliffe, a high-powered legal eagle who wrote the Constitutions of India and Cyprus, and because another had been knighted, 'nobody ever got over it', said my father. 'I am afraid the Cunliffes were terrible snobs.'

All my father's relations said 'lorst' instead of 'lost', and anyone who said 'toilet' or 'settee' or, worst of all, 'leownge', was considered frightfully common. Idiotic as he thought it all was, my father had been marinated so long in the upper-middle-class system that although he wanted to treat everyone as an equal, he was never completely successful.

If a carpenter or plumber came into the room, my father would rise to his feet with exaggerated *noblesse oblige*, put out his hand and say: 'To what do we owe the extraordinary honour of this visit, my dear sir?' Or: 'My dear sir! How absolutely *splendid* to see you!' The workman would stand rather baffled, but usually charmed, by the effusive welcome.

By the time my mother met my father, he and his brother Robin were sharing a bed-sitter in Exhibition Road. Always passionate about drawing, Christopher had enrolled at the Central School of Arts and Crafts and the moment he finished the course he was offered a job teaching there.

Robin, after a couple of years at the Sorbonne and then studying the history of art at the Courtauld, had got a job at the Tate as Assistant Keeper in 1937, eventually becoming number two under its director, John Rothenstein. Every night, Robin used to return from work, walking from South Kensington Station in a long black overcoat and black hat and carrying a briefcase, umbrella and a small brown paper bag. This contained a whipped-cream walnut which was eaten on his arrival home with almost ritual solemnity. After dinner, he would write and paint far into the night.

Although my father didn't have the wild imagination to make an artist, he was a superb draughtsman. He could draw everything, from sheep's back hooves to ornate palaces, nude figures, charging bulls or filing cabinets. Ask him to draw a railway-station waiting-room and he would immediately put it down on paper, with the correct moulding on the ceiling, the broken bulb hanging down from a wire, the timetables in their oak frames on the wall behind the padded benches. He would draw the station-master with his head peeping around the door, with exactly the right moustache and the right cap. He knew precisely how everything worked and was put together, and could pin it all down – beautifully – on paper.

Before she met Christopher, my mother had very clear ideas about what the man of her dreams should have to offer. It could be looks. At sixteen, she had written: 'If I marry I *hope* I marry someone nice-looking. Think of the shock when you are out of love and one day you look over the breakfast table and see, instead of the Adonis you have been imagining, a fat, red-faced elephant with sandy hair and eyebrows.' Or it could be money. At seventeen, she wrote: 'Hursley Park was the most glorious place, lovely old trees and rolling green park land, and then we caught a glimpse of the gardens, lovely clipped lawns with great rhododendron bushes and a little blue lake. I so wish I had been born into a place like that, never having to buy cheap clothes and feel inferior. I would marry a man who wasn't too repulsive who would offer me grounds like those, beauty like that.'

Certainly her husband would have to be someone that she had chosen herself. At eighteen, she wrote: 'I sat opposite a revolting young man in the train home. Fat, white and sandy with pimples and a poky nose. He stared at me throughout the journey. When I finally got out he sprang forward to get my suitcase and handed it to me and nearly carried it out but I said: "Thank you" and firmly grasped it. As I took the handle his hand touched mine and I felt the white warmth of it through my glove and thought I would be sick on the spot. Then I thought: supposing I had been a Victorian girl and my parents had arranged a marriage for me with a young man like that, what would I have done? His touch would have made my flesh creep.'

Christopher had no money at all, but he was only a couple of years older than her and he couldn't have been more glamorous. Fat, white, pimply or sandy he was not. Along with hundreds of others, Janey and Christopher got engaged just after war was declared in 1939, and were married at the Register Office in Marloes Road — where I myself was to marry in 1970. My mother wore a black and white print with square shoulders and a full skirt worn with black peep-toed shoes. Christopher nervously broke matches into little bits.

Madre, who sat with other relatives in the waiting-room, announced through pursed lips that 'Marriage is like a besieged fortress. Those outside want to get in and those inside want to get out.'

IRONSIDE : ACHESON.—On Sept. 22, 1939, in London, CHRISTOPHER IRONSIDE to JANET MARY ACHESON, daughter of J. G. Acheson, C.I.E., I.C.S

Janey and Christopher after their marriage. Notice the sandbags – and Madre lurking in the background.

three

NEW LOOK *In 1947, French designer Christian Dior brought out a collection which turned the fashion world (hitherto restrained by Government wartime regulations) upside-down. He introduced a sloping-shouldered, tight-waisted, full-skirted outline. The skirts, which were approximately 7 inches from the ground, had a hemline even in daytime of sometimes up to 20 yards. The look was completed by small hats of veiling or flowers, very high-heeled ankle-strapped shoes and long elegant umbrellas. His sloping shoulder and sleeveline in one with the bodice created a new type of cut, involving an underarm gusset to allow movement.*

Janey Ironside, *A Fashion Alphabet*

A couple of weeks after my birth, escaping the nursing home and the bombs, I was taken back by my mother in a basket to our house in Leamington Spa. Much to everyone's relief, both my father and his brother had been spared from actually fighting in the war. While my uncle was safely employed at the Tate Gallery, in charge of evacuating hundreds of old masters from London to Upton in Gloucestershire, my father had applied to the Ministry of Home Security Camouflage Unit, and was posted to Leamington Spa as a Camouflage Officer.

For the inhabitants of the sedate spa town, the invasion of a bunch of artists in their midst must have been a complete shock. My father said that the camouflage people were generally regarded as 'a group of maniacs'. But the task of these maniacs was crucial: to disguise Britain from the enemy. Every so often, my father would go up in a plane to take aerial photographs of sensitive targets that the Germans might have their eye on, like factories and aerodromes, and then, with the aid of paint, netting, seaweed and sludge – the residue of oil from ships' tanks, which was used to darken all kinds of surfaces, from roofs to runways – the camouflagers were commissioned with the task of transforming them, using their knowledge of colour, shadows, angles and dimensions, so that from the air they would look like innocent fields of sheep, residential housing estates, or pieces of forest or scrubland.

Every day, my father turned up at the Leamington Ice Rink, which had been converted into a giant studio, and joined the other artists slaving away over enormous turntables on which they had constructed models of factories and aerodromes, lit by ever-moving moons and suns attached to wires, trying out different ways of painting them to make them invisible to enemy aircraft. The models were made to look as if they were being seen from four miles away and lamps were provided with colour filters to simulate different weather conditions.

The Camouflage Unit teemed with men who would become huge artistic cheeses in the years after the war. They were the painter Tom Monnington and the architect Hugh Casson (both future Presidents of the Royal Academy); Richard Guyatt, the graphic designer (future Rector of the Royal College of Art); Eric Schilsky, the sculptor, and Edward Wadsworth, whose later semi-abstract woodcuts were made on the black and white 'dazzle' theme that arose from his experience as a camouflage designer. The painter and lithographer Julian

Trevelyan and the artist Edward Bawden worked in camouflage units nearby. But the key figure was Robin Darwin. He was secretary of the Camouflage Committee and a man who would play a consistently powerful role in both my parents' lives.

Robin de Vere Darwin was born in 1910, the great-grandson of Charles Darwin. He had been educated at Eton and Cambridge, and studied at the Slade School of Art. At Eton, he not only acquired an excellent education, but further developed what was already a hugely grand and charming manner, which made it easy for him not just to hob-nob with but sometimes even to patronize the great and the good. His illustrious family had imbued him with a confidence and certainty that fuelled a driving ambition. Added to this, he was a big man, both in height and in breadth. He cut a preposterous figure in Leamington, and caused great amusement when, off-duty, he would set out in an open Rolls-Royce, wearing a wide-brimmed hat, to sketch the countryside. On one occasion, when he was out with the sculptor Leon Underwood, this mildly bohemian behaviour caused him to be arrested as a spy.

My mother and father had begun their married life in a house in Lansdowne Crescent, where they lived with their tortoiseshell cat and two lodgers, also camouflage artists, who had been foisted upon them by the authorities. Janey bought food for them, cooked for them, made their beds and washed up after them − everything that was still expected of a woman in those early years of the war. One of the lodgers demanded that he be given his egg ration individually so that he could use the yolk for painting in tempera but my mother, desperate for different ingredients to add variety to wartime meals, rightly refused.

After a spell of 'war work' at Lockheed's Hydraulic Brakes, and a brief period in the Records Section of the Camouflage Office, Janey took on voluntary work at a home for evacuees whose billeters couldn't cope with the nits, scabies, impetigo and bedwetting of unhappy East End children, whom she entertained by getting them to pose for portraits.

'Do me now, Mrs Iminside,' they would beg, as my mother sat, stifling in the antiseptic air of the children's home, with a sketch-pad consisting of thin sheets of paper, drawing these sad children, many of them with their heads shaved to prevent nits and all dressed

The back of an evacuee's coat, by Janey

in the most unsuitable cast-offs. Tiny boys wore huge grey shorts held up by string; adolescent girls with bosoms burst out of floral dresses suitable for nine-year-olds. My mother always emphasized the clothes in her drawings: she actually drew one poor evacuee from the back, fascinated by the line of her oddly tailored coat.

During her pregnancy, and relieved of war work, my mother made clothes — first, dolls' outfits for Harrods' toy department and then dresses for herself, flowing garments in earth colours *à la* Augustus John's Dorelia, which suited my father because when he came back from work he painted and drew her endlessly.

Tiny scrap as I was at the time, I still remember Leamington with affection. It's something about the smell. When I returned, at fourteen, for a visit with my father, I breathed in the dank, fetid air of

Janey, drawn by
Christopher, pregnant and
gloomy

the canals as if I were a Bisto kid, because it reminded me of dark, rank waterway paths that I was wheeled along as a baby. And yet these watery memories are inextricably linked with a feeling of melancholy. I had been born between two deaths. Four years before my birth, in the autumn of 1940, my mother had received a telegram informing her that her pilot brother, Jimmy, who had been posted to Norfolk in Coastal Command, was, at only twenty years old, 'Missing, believed killed'.

My mother had been half in love with her dashing, left-wing brother – he'd caused terrible anxiety in the family when, as a boy at Wellington, he'd announced that he was a Communist. He used to motor over from his posting to spend weekends with her, driving her about in an open-topped sports car and taking her from pub to pub. After she died, I found a large suitcase stuffed with his letters. And a year after I was born, my mother received another blow. Her sister Kitty had died, also at twenty years old, of a brain tumour at the Military Hospital at Secunderabad in South India, where she was serving in the Women's Auxiliary Corps.

My mother must have felt desperately alone and unhappy. Since I experienced severe post-natal depression when I had my own child, I wouldn't be surprised if my mother hadn't suffered in a similar way. Certainly, I was rather shocked when she told me, years later, that she used simply to dump me in my pram at the bottom of the garden for hours on end 'so I couldn't hear you screaming' – not the action of someone basking in the glow of maternal contentment.

Life as a housewife and mother in wartime, blacked-out Leamington Spa seemed dreadfully bleak to a beautiful, bereaved and talented young woman. One colleague wrote: 'Her creativity

Janey, Christopher and me in the garden at Leamington Spa

even shone in the unutterable boredom of the Camouflage Records Section.' Although she was indefatigable when it came to cooking and looking after the house, she absolutely loathed housekeeping. When I later asked her what she thought might happen to us when we died, she replied: 'Well, I suppose if we don't go to heaven, we go to hell. That probably means we have to spend all day and every day washing up.'

She became completely fed up with queuing, scrimping and saving, mothering, caring for lodgers and provincial artistic life in general. Three years in Leamington Spa was enough. She longed for the bright lights of London, café society, Quaglino's, the Café Royal, the Gargoyle Club in Fitzrovia, black-market booze, famous people – a life that my father used to describe, in a jaded, weary voice, as 'Faster! Faster!'

I was two years old when we moved to London. But before we could find anywhere to live, we needed somewhere to stay, and for a few months we lodged in a huge, ramshackle Victorian house on Haverstock Hill in Belsize Park, North London. It belonged to other members of the camouflage community, the illustrator Mary Adshead and her husband Stephen Bone, son of the war artist Muirhead Bone.

I couldn't stand Haverstock Hill. Although the Bones only came up to stay in their house briefly and infrequently, I was petrified by their bohemianism. A lot of cheerful stews were brewed in their jolly family kitchen, and their scary children went about barefoot like gypsies, shouting at each other. It was all chaotic and dangerous. The house was also infested with flies and spiders (or, as I called them, 'bozzie-bees and podos') to which I had an almost phobic reaction. Knowing already that my mother would probably be unavailable when I cried, it was my father I summoned for help. He remembered my constant screaming: 'Christopher! Christopher! There's a podo in the bath!' or 'There's a bozzie-bee in my room!'

To this day, I am filled with a dreadful gloom whenever I go anywhere near North London. Naturally, I now pull myself together and grit my teeth as I drive up Fitzjohn's Avenue or Rosslyn Hill from Swiss Cottage, but the very mention of 'Hampstead Heath', 'Belsize Park' or 'NW1' arouses in me frightening spectres of lentils, collages, pottery, corduroy trousers, poetry readings, bad jazz,

Freudian analysis, dirty nappies, free love, cheap red wine and people who say terrifyingly relaxed things like 'Oh, just leave the washing up!'

The only good thing about our stay in Haverstock Hill was the fact that my mother's parents, who had then become Sir James and Lady Acheson, had come back to London and were staying with us. My grandfather's post as Resident in Kashmir meant he virtually ruled over three and a half million people in an area the size of England and it must have been an unnerving contrast for him and my grandmother to arrive at the Bones's squalid house in post-war London straight from their palatial Residency in Srinagar. When I went to Kashmir recently, I found the Residency. Set in a huge park, it was a vast half-timbered pile now converted into a government tourist emporium. In what had been my mother's bedroom, men with dark faces and little moustaches were selling honey, scarves and painted papier-mâché boxes.

It says something for my grandparents' gutsy characters that, having come from this life of luxury, groaning with food and staff, they knuckled down and made the best of things. My grandmother was an enormously practical woman. She had run the Residency to accommodate weekly events: Red Cross sales, auctions, purdah and garden parties with clock golf and tennis given for British soldiers of all ranks. She had also been made Chief Commissioner of the All-India Girl Guides, and in Hampstead she soon bustled around, making friends with the people in the local Jewish delicatessens and finding ways of getting meat on the sly.

Every day, my grandparents went out to look for somewhere for us all to live and found, on a twenty-year lease, a stuccoed Victorian house in Neville Street, off the Fulham Road in South Kensington. It was perfect – particularly because it was back in my father's old stamping ground. It had a pillared porch, a stone balustraded balcony and sash windows, a basement, a coal hole and, even though it was almost completely filled with two enormous scabby plane trees and a gasping privet hedge, a garden.

But just after the house had been acquired, my grandfather was suddenly summoned to Germany on distasteful denazification duty. So my mother, my father and I all moved into Neville Street and my father's mother, Phyl, now a widow after a second marriage, moved into the ground floor and basement.

Houses in Neville Street today sell for millions, but post-war they were miserably run-down affairs. At the top of the road was a street called Foulis Terrace, which I never liked, simply because of its name. Adjoining Foulis Terrace was Onslow Square. Now a land-scaped private garden full of benches, plane trees, lawns and signs written in gold seriffed letters which announce 'No ball games', then it was a bomb-site full of rubble, willow herb, stray dogs and poisonous-smelling bonfires built by local ragamuffins. I wasn't allowed to play with these children because they were, according to my mother, 'common', and since I was so excruciatingly shy, I would hardly have known what to do had I been allowed to join them. I walked past, clutching on to my mother's hand, hoping they wouldn't notice me and shout something horrible at me in their cockney accents.

Upstairs from the hall in our house, the kitchen led off a small landing. It was furnished with an Ascot water-heater; a marble-topped wash-stand; a sink with wooden draining boards that became rather soggy after washing-up, like skin after a bath; a shelf on which butter paper and bowls of dripping were stored; a table bought for half a crown in Leamington; a couple of bentwood chairs and an ice-box. This consisted of a small cupboard with a lead-lined cavity at the back which had to be filled with slabs of ice which, when I was older, I begged from the fishmonger down the road.

The linoleum in the kitchen was laid by my ever-practical mother, made up from spare bits and pieces left over from my great-grand-mother's smart house in the Little Boltons, which had been ruined by bombs. Upstairs, there was a wonderfully large T-shaped drawing-room with a worn parquet floor and three sets of long windows which led on to a balcony overlooking the street. My mother hung white cotton curtains, and furnished the room sparsely with odd pieces of rather good Victorian tables and chairs, and pictures that my parents had picked up for virtually nothing in Leamington Spa. For heating, we had coal or gas fires in every room, consisting of broken columns of hollowed ceramic tubes, and on each landing burned a grey Aladdin stove, permeating the house with the smell of paraffin.

A little further up the stairs were my parents' bedroom and mine adjoining, and just above was a tiny bathroom in which was the only lavatory in the house (beside which hung rolls of Bronco lavatory paper) and a terrifying geyser with a roaring pilot light which growled and shouted whenever you turned on the hot tap.

This room was painted — by my mother, who thought it fashionable — a deep, angry, red gloss. The ceilings were red, the walls were red, the pipes and boxed-in wires, all red. My father commented, rather gloomily, that it 'looked like an abattoir'.

Our luxuries were twofold: the use of a laundry and a charlady. Each week, my mother filled in the laundry book — all our sheets, towels and pillowslips had little red numbers, 411, embroidered on them — and I often helped her to count the pillowcases and the sheets.

Once or twice, a rogue sheet or nightdress appeared, which my mother examined distastefully. I would discover some alien number embroidered on it, say in green. 'Oh, well-spotted!' said my mother. 'You *are* clever, darling!' Then I helped her gingerly to fold it back into the basket. It was something, my mother explained, that belonged to 'other people', a group from whom we had to be protected by never sharing our combs and, when going to the lavatory on trains, always laying sheets of lavatory paper along the seat before sitting down.

I enjoyed helping my mother make the beds every week. They were top-to-bottomed — so our top sheet was used as the bottom sheet for the second week. Nearly all our sheets were sides-to-middled — that is, when they wore out in the middle, my mother cut them in half and skilfully machined the two outer edges together, leaving the frayed bits to be tucked in under the mattress. As in other families at the time, everything was darned and patched; very little was thrown away, or not until it had been made into dusters and worn to shreds. Familiar phrases were ones you rarely hear now, like 'Make-do-and-mend', 'Second-best' and 'It's as good as new!'

The problem was that nothing *was* new. Fulham Road, now a chic stretch of coffee shops, restaurants, boutiques and trendy jewellers, was then full of repair shops — shoe repairers, electrical repairers, furniture repairers, pen hospitals, doll hospitals. There was always someone available to enable you to eke a few more months out of any gadget or article you possessed.

We had no car, no television and only one big radio. The doors were always closed in winter to keep the heat in, the lights always turned off whenever we left a room. If the toast was burned, as it frequently was, it was scraped over the sink and eaten. Mould that developed on cheese was simply cut off, and if the pork smelled a bit peculiar, it was just washed thoroughly and cooked for a rather longer time than usual. Nearly every meal consisted of 'remains' cooked up in some ingenious way with Bisto to make them edible, followed by a pudding like semolina, junket or ghastly quivering things known as 'moulds' to which we added top of the milk as a substitute for cream.

It seems incredible to me, as I sit here typing on my word-processor, stifled by central heating, listening to the whirring of a dishwasher in the background, that when I was small a man used to come round every evening on a bicycle with a long lighted stick to ignite the gas lamps in our street. There was still a working granary in Old Church Street which I passed on my daily walk down to the river to feed the seagulls. Rag-and-bone men drove by at weekends with their carts and nose-bagged horses, shouting their strange styl-ized cry: 'Ragnboooone!' and the roads were covered with steaming piles of horse manure.

A couple of times in the autumn, rough men who looked like troglodytes, with blackened faces and long flaps at the back of their black hats to protect their necks, lugged sacks of coal from lorries, which they would empty into our cellar with a rattling series of thuds, leaving a haze of bitter-smelling black dust over the coal-hole after they'd gone. On dark, foggy evenings, we collected it with the aid of a torch, a shovel and a brass coal-bucket.

It is hard to describe the bleakness of the London landscape. Nearly everyone was thin and white. Their teeth were often bad, their hair was, like mine at the time, only washed once a week, and everyone smelled, it being long before the days of deodorant. We were living in post-war London, where, as George Orwell wrote, austerity ruled and everything smelled of 'boiled cabbage and sweat, of grimy walls and dirty clothes'. Cyril Connolly called this period between 1940 and 1950, appropriately, the 'drab decade'.

So drab was it that it was hardly surprising that my mother, though happier to be in London than provincial Leamington, remained stifled and miserable. Money was still extremely tight, she was working her fingers to the bone and looking after a fractious child in a wretched grey city that looked like one huge bomb-site. Worse, everyone in the street, in their worn, dingy clothes, looked horribly unattractive and not at *all* beautiful.

Early on in my life, I tried to clarify our mother-and-daughter roles – at least, that's how it seems in hindsight. My parents, according to some liberal credo of the day, had decided that from the moment I could speak I should call them 'Janey and Christopher' rather than 'Mummy and Daddy'. I called my father 'Christopher' until the end of his life. But I have a clear memory, when I was about two, of standing in my bedroom and holding my mother's left hand. My mother's hand was memorable. It was white; on the fourth finger was a bishop's ring, a purple emerald set in a gold band, and her nails were long, pointed, hard and painted deep, silent-movie red. My father was also in the room.

'Daney,' I said – I could never get my mouth round the word 'Janey'.

'Yes, poppet?' came the voice from above that white hand.

'I am going to call you "Mummy".'

'*Really*?' said Janey. Both she and Christopher laughed, amused and startled adults, as they looked at my serious face. 'How sweet! Well, if you want to . . .'

Perhaps some part of me hoped that were I to call her 'Mummy' she would transform into someone more Mummy-like. She might ruffle my hair, go red with pride as I tricycled madly down the street, or she might run screaming with fury in Onslow Gardens to slap any street-urchin who dared to shout at me.

It was a good try. But her initial demand for me to call her 'Janey' was the more honest. She was 'Janey'; she was never 'Mummy'.

Part of the problem was, I think, that my mother had never forgotten the thrill of being called 'beautiful'. She not only craved an outlet for her own creativity – the role of mothering didn't begin to satisfy it and she never really got the hang of it – but she needed flattery and attention to keep going, and she needed beautiful things to stimulate her and to keep her feeling alive. It was naturally a fashion event that gave my mother the opportunity to start to emerge from her cocoon of drudgery.

For years, fashion had been a vague no man's land but nine days after my third birthday a revolutionary style heralded Europe's recovery from the war. The French designer Christian Dior showed a collection which was christened the 'New Look'. It became an immediate success.

His new silhouette was fragile, impractical and very attractive. Ignoring disapproving mention of shortages, he introduced a slim, sloping bodice with a new smooth cut to the shoulders, a small waist, boned and canvassed, and an immensely full skirt, which flared out to end only seven inches above the ankle. His models wore flirtatious little hats trimmed with flowers and veils, ankle-strap shoes with high, fragile heels, and long, slim parasols. Their hair was transformed from the heavy rolls of wartime into feathery curls.

My mother was enchanted and immediately ran herself up an entirely new wardrobe. She trawled the shops and managed to buy a lot of surplus black-out stuff from the war, some spotted material for a top, ankle-strapped shoes and artificial flowers and veiling for a hat. With the outfit she created, she looked so extraordinarily glamorous and chic that people started to say that she ought to be become a model.

At thirty-three, my mother was thrilled with the idea. I was never sure what my father felt about this project. He probably hummed and haa-ed and raised his eyebrows and said: 'Well, if you want to give it a go . . .' Secretly, I imagine, he hoped the whole idea would go away.

My mother spent days machining and stitching, sometimes staying up till four in the morning and waking my father to pirouette around him, saying: 'What do you think this looks like, Christopher? A bit shorter? Or a bit longer? Is it too baggy at the back? I can't see in the mirror,' as my father groaned, looked at the clock and said: 'For God's sake, Janey, do you know what time it is?'

When she had run up several outfits, she asked a neighbour, a professional photographer, to take some photographs for a portfolio.

I had been sent across the road to play with my one friend, Sally Ann Hopkinson. Sally had a cheeky, dimpled face and short, straw-coloured hair held in place with a ribbon. She was looked after by a tiny bent little nanny with a beard. That afternoon we played in her nursery with her dolls and went down to tea in the dining-room. Tea at Sally's was a proper meal, prepared by Sally's mother, a scatter-brained, talkative and enormously warm-hearted woman who lived for bridge. As usual, we had bread and butter and sandwiches, filled with scrambled egg and mustard and cress, followed by a wonderfully sticky chocolate cake, washed down with milk. It was a real treat compared to the orange squash and digestive biscuit that Sally was handed when she came to play with me.

When I returned home − being careful to escape the attentions of the man who delivered the *Evening Standard* and had a habit of grabbing little girls and trying to kiss them − I rushed up the stairs, calling: 'Mummy! I'm back!'

There was silence. The door of the sitting-room was closed. Remembering my mother was being photographed, I tiptoed past, but my mother called out to me to come in.

The sitting-room was in darkness, lit only by one candle on a small table. The long white curtains were pinned closed, and I could just make out the silhouette of a strange man who was standing by a camera mounted on a tripod. My mother was sitting on a chair, wearing a small hat and a tight black dress. The man was good-looking and smiling. I remember very clearly the feeling of dislike I had for him. I flinched.

To my dismay, the drawing-room, normally a cosy haven, had changed into a foreign country. The carpet was rolled up. Furniture had been moved into strange places against the walls, leaving gaping spaces of parquet. A picture that my father had painted of my mother had been taken down and now rested on the floor against the wall, facing it.

My mother had changed, too. She sat with her skirt slightly pulled up, her ankles crossed, her head on one side, looking at me from under dark lashes. She was smiling in a funny way I'd never seen before. I looked from the man to my mother and from my mother to him. I was dimly aware that something was going on between them, something of which my father would disapprove. Where was Christopher, anyway? When would he come back from work?

'Do take some photographs of Virginia,' my mother said to the man, with a slow and burning smile, looking straight into his eyes. He moved from his camera to turn on the light.

I tried to slink upstairs, but my mother called me back.

'Don't go away, darling! Do come and be photographed too, sweetie!'

'I don't want to.'

'Oh, dooooo, please . . . it'll only take a minute . . .'

'No.'

'Oh, darling, come on, don't be so silly!'

Then my mother half-rose, grabbed my arm and taking a hand-kerchief from her bag, spat on it and wiped some piece of smut from my face. 'But darling, you're looking so pretty, and you're wearing

Me, taking part in my first modelling session

that lovely Black Watch suit I made, oh, *do* pull up your socks, oh dear, look at your knees, just let me put a comb through your hair . . . no, now where should she sit, David, no, not like that, oh, if you have to keep your arms crossed . . . do at least smile, darling, cheer up, it'll be a lovely photograph . . .'

From behind his camera, David said: 'That's gorgeous, Janey. Now, look over towards the mirror, chin up a bit, lick your lips, that's it . . . Virginia, can we have a smile? Please? Just a little one? Right! Let's have the lights off again . . .'

We were in blackness again. Then the flash exploded, the camera clicked. I maintained a sullen, resentful and rather frightened silence.

When I was small, I couldn't bear to leave my mother's side. I screamed when she went away, I clung to her when she returned. I was a nervous and solitary child and dreadfully shy. I refused to be parted from my comforter, which was made from a piece of one of my mother's cast-off felt hats. It was black and soft and reassuring and I rubbed it against my upper lip as I sucked away at my thumb, until a lump of hard skin appeared between the knuckles.

Both my parents, when exasperated with my tears, would snap at me: 'Stop whining!' and now I have to sympathize with my young and vibrant mother, full of new ideas, having to cope with a child she must have seen as maddeningly demanding. It was not that she was cruel – she hated to think of me as unhappy – more that she was simply born self-absorbed, and perhaps needed to be in order to survive. So, realizing that I had to have someone around to give me more time than she could, she employed what was then known as a 'foreign girl'.

Although au pairs are commonplace today, in 1949 they were a rarity. If a woman wanted to have a career, couldn't be bothered to look after her child, or was emotionally incapable, she would usually employ a starched nanny. Nannies were, however, expensive: foreign girls were cheap. Our first foreign girl was a sweet young woman called Nicole, an undernourished Parisienne whom I loved dearly. She left after a year and I never heard from her again. The next foreign girl, Edith, was an undernourished German from a refugee camp, discovered by my grandfather abroad.

I adored Edith. She was an affectionate, human-being sort of person, who adored me back. She had a big, rosy face and braided fair hair and she was full of smiles and hugs and laughter. I never whined for long with Edith around. I never wanted to. Soon I was flourishing, secure and happy. But all too quickly, after only one year, Edith's time with us came to an end and she left, never to be heard from again until, in the mid-seventies, she appeared, plump and jolly, with buck teeth, accompanied by a bristly-haired German husband and two plump and bemused teenagers. We had nothing to say to each other.

Next was a Swiss girl called Marlise. I hated her because she told me off for sucking my thumb and teased me for being a baby because of it. Since Edith had gone back to Germany, I had become insecure and unhappy once more, and my only consolation, thumb-sucking, seemed a vital means of emotional survival. I was horrified at the idea of giving it up. To my relief, after two weeks Marlise announced she was leaving, because, she said, she 'could not live in these primitive conditions'.

'What on earth do you mean?' asked my mother.

Marlise shrugged her shoulders and looked meaningfully around the kitchen.

'How dare you,' said my mother, coldly. 'Just because the bloody Swiss were neutral during the war and never had to give anything up, you have no idea what the rest of Europe went through. We are lucky even to have a house and a kitchen.'

'Do not think that attacking my country is going to make me change my mind,' replied Marlise. 'My friend works in Golders Green with a family who have everything modern, and I am going to find a family like that.'

My mother told her to get out at once. However, looking round the sparsely furnished house she had defended so staunchly, with its Aladdin stoves and old ice-box in the kitchen, she did feel rather depressed.

At least there were no more foreign girls after that.

Nothing came of my mother's plans to become a model. I suspect my father became prickly and uneasy about the whole idea, having probably felt the same kind of threatening rumblings as I did on the afternoon of the photograph session. But she wasn't daunted. She would get involved with fashion in some other way.

She began to design and make clothes for friends – my parents still moved in arty circles, many of the old camouflagers having moved to London – and she tried to sell her ideas for children's clothes to retail outlets. Other people were enlisted to look after me after school while she worked.

Sally across the road was always a good bet, but I couldn't see her every day and even the affectionate Hopkinsons were no substitute for home. But once, when my parents wanted to go out in the evening, and my grandmother Phyl had another engagement, they suggested I stay the night with her. I packed my things and went, but after supper, in my nightdress and dressing-gown, I became so unhinged with anxiety and fear that Mrs Hopkinson kindly took me to the window so that I could see my house, just across the road. Seeing the light on in my parents' bedroom and watching them moving about, just returned from their dinner party, only increased my agony, and I had to be bundled home, pottering tearfully across the road in my slippers and clutching the little suitcase I had so excitedly packed earlier that afternoon.

I was happiest being left with my grandmother, whom I loved very much indeed. Being a theatrical type — she looked like Margaret Rutherford, with chins rolling down her neck, and had she not been prevented by her parents from a longed-for career on the stage, she would have been a great star — she made each of my visits into a huge treat.

'Now!' she might say, as I came into her sitting-room downstairs, putting a finger to her lips to make everything seem exciting and mysterious. She would then shut the door, sit down on her plump, red sofa and pat the seat next to her. 'We have to make a *big* decision this afternoon, and I need your help.' Heads bent together, we were already in the thick of a great conspiracy. Wafts of her favourite scent, Apple Blossom, would overwhelm me. 'This afternoon, we could do one of two things. We could make a picnic and take it to the park.'

'Yes?'

Me and my grandmother on a
seaside holiday

'Or we could make some sugar biscuits and then . . .'

'Yes?'

'Read *Rainbow*!' With a flourish, she would then produce the comic from behind a cushion, like a conjuror.

It was entirely for my benefit that she took *Rainbow*, *Tiny Tim*, the *Beano* and *Sunny Stories*, and she devoted the whole of the bottom of her bureau to children's toys and games. She would never allow these upstairs, simply because, she said, they 'lived downstairs'. Another treat was a gramophone with little wooden doors, on which, with metal needles that lived in a tiny round box, we played 'The Laughing Policeman', 'Nellie the Elephant' or, a favourite of hers, since she always fancied Danny Kaye, 'Little White Duck'.

Sometimes she played or sang the theme from *The Third Man* – she was a great fan of Joseph Cotten – and conducted it as she did so. 'Tumti tumti *ta* ta-*ta!*' Occasionally we took evening picnics in the park, taking sandwiches of bread and butter with sugar or, as a treat, bread and butter with hundreds and thousands; or we might have tea on the roof gardens of Derry and Toms and look at the flamingos. When I was older, she took me to see Joyce Grenfell, Flanders and Swan, the Crazy Gang.

Like a lot of middle-aged ladies, she was excessively interested in murder. It was the time of Haig, Neville Heath, and Craig and Bentley. She was particularly fascinated with John Christie, who had killed and holed up several young women in his house in Paddington. One day I met her coming in from the street, carrying her umbrella and wearing gloves and a hat with a small net over it.

'Where have you been?' I asked.

She looked very solemn and struck a theatrical pose. 'I have, my darling, just been out to walk past 10 Rillington Place, home of John Christie,' she replied.

I thought her fascination rather strange – until, years later, when staying in the West Country, I couldn't resist walking past 25 Cromwell Street in Gloucester after the Fred West murders had been discovered, just for the shudder.

Although she was something of a snob, Phyl always became friends with her charladies or nannies. She shared my father's *noblesse oblige*. That phrase 'her servants adored her', into which are packed so many ironies, applied to her. Whenever we went into a shop together, the assistants' faces lit up as she addressed them all by name, winked, and made flirtatious jokes – and once, to my embarrassment, she took the hand of a particularly grumpy green-grocer at the bottom of the street and insisted on his dancing a polka with her. 'I don't think *he'll* be giving me any more scowls in future,' she said briskly as we made our way home with a paper bag full of plums.

She was adamant, however, that 'one' should never live north of the park or south of the river, she considered the Royal Family extremely vulgar and tasteless, she talked of people's 'profeels' rather than their 'profiles', she always went 'motoring' and instead of 'because' she said 'becorz'. And she could never quite forget that she no longer had the retinue of servants that had featured in her childhood. She often announced that she would get a book or some left-over cake 'sent up' to us. This involved putting the book or the dish on the chest in the hall, for one of us to take up to our part of the house.

Sometimes, of course, it was my father who looked after me.

My mother had already been told, before she married, that '*every* girl is infatuated with Christopher', but she was unprepared for and probably unpleasantly surprised by my own infatuation with my father.

What with all these surrogate parents, and my mother having so little time for me, it was natural that I should look to him for security and comfort. I adored him. To me, he was the perfect man, being handsome, funny, kind, utterly reliable, bright and inventive. He, also, adored me.

In the late forties he worked for a company called Cockade in South Kensington, which specialized in the design of graphics and exhibition interiors. Robin Darwin, the perennial string-puller, had helped him to get the job, and he worked alongside other old camouflage friends, Dick Guyatt and Hugh Casson. Every evening, I waited for him in my tartan dressing-gown, milk and biscuits and a pack of cards in my hands, ready to play Beggar my Neighbour.

It was on my father's shoulders that I watched George VI's funeral in the Mall, and any time there was a marching band or a pageant, for which my father had a passion, we would leave my mother at home and be there with our Brownie camera and periscope, constructed out of a couple of hand-mirrors, cardboard and glue. At weekends, he took me to Kensington Gardens and we walked together up the Broad Walk, dominated by the original huge plane trees. Sometimes we went to Kensington Palace, which housed a splendid toy museum, or, on lowering, grey Sunday afternoons, we might crouch by the Round Pond, net in hand, to fish for minnows which I kept in a small tank at home. (My father helped me arrange the plants and various stone arches in a classical Poussin-like landscape, but unfortunately the minnows always developed white parasites and died.)

In the summer, we might go rowing on the Serpentine – in those days you could row for hours and even picnic on the little islands. Sometimes he took a sketch-book and did roughs for future landscapes. Afterwards, we would have a cup of tea, out of thick white cups and saucers, at the café, now the Serpentine Gallery.

If it was raining, we went to the Science Museum and looked at the Children's Section downstairs, where we watched a wooden bird endlessly pecking at a glass of water, and the panorama of Lighting through the Ages, which had buttons to press, and, in glass cases, various models of little donkeys attended by natives, walking round and round. After much winding they would pull up tiny buckets of water from a well. Failing that, there was always the Natural History Museum, where we gawped at the dinosaurs.

Every night, when I went to bed, my father brought me up my supper, usually a boiled egg and the buttered top crust of a loaf, and just before I went to sleep he would come up again and either read me tales from Andrew Laing's *Pink Fairy Book* or invent stories for me about little men who could become big or small at will, or about goblins who lived under the floorboards. He always left me with a terrifying cliff-hanger, sometimes so frightening that after my lights had been turned out, I had to scramble out of my warm bed in my nightdress and lean over the staircase, yelling 'Christopher! Christopher!', begging him to come back and tell me what happened next.

When I could read, it was Noddy and Big Ears and Milly Molly Mandy that enthralled me — my mother tried, and failed, to interest me in Kipling's Mowgli stories — or I would count the cigarette cards that my father diligently collected for me from his huge packets of Woodbines. He smoked fifty a day, which he bought in enormous boxes. I might listen on headphones to a radio programme on the crystal set my father had helped me to make.

Just before going to sleep, I would check that the toys were in order on the eiderdown — a penguin, a duck, a golly and two dolls, one called Dirty Dolly and one called Clean Dolly (a fact which has caused many a therapist I consulted when I was an adult to stop and ponder). Then I would watch the shadows on the ceiling cast by a Price's nightlight, kept in a saucerful of water on my bedside table.

*

Later in life, I discovered that my mother had wanted more children. It may have been that she realized that I needed company. But my father, recognizing that Janey's talents, although considerable, did not lie in the mothering line, put his foot down. The upshot was that, even when I started school, I felt extremely lonely.

I recently met the mother of Roger Lloyd Pack, the actor, who was one of the tearaway Neville Street kids.

'Oh, you were a poor child!' she exclaimed when talking of the old days.

According to her recollection, all the children in the street were always in and out of each other's houses, like one big, happy family — but I was never allowed to come and play.

'Your mother', she said carefully, 'was a very nice woman. But very distant. I remember once I was on the train and she was sitting opposite me. She knew who I was and I knew who she was, but she never returned my smile, and we walked, only a yard or so apart, all the way back to Neville Street. It was only when she was going up her steps that she gave me a slight acknowledgement.'

Sally was my only companion, and before too long she was sent to boarding-school, where she made new friends whom she brought back during the holidays.

I remember many nights standing, lonely in the dark, peering through the crack in the long white curtains of our drawing-room, seeing the lights on in Sally's room across the street and occasionally watching enviously as I saw the silhouettes of Sally and another strange girl's figure against the light in her nursery.

four

DUFFEL-COAT *A warm coat of heavy cloth, with collar cut in one with fronts or separately cut but sewn so that the effect is a shawl, i.e. without revers. The front is fastened with toggles. The 'fashion' origi-nated in the Navy, when duffel-coats were worn as protection against the elements, and became very popular immediately after the Second World War when surplus duffel-coats were sold very cheaply. The orig-inal colour is off-white but as 'fashion' coats they are sold in a variety of colours.*

Janey Ironside, *A Dictionary of Fashion*

'A rtists don't make much money,' said Christopher. Because my great-aunt's day-school was free, because we were so badly off, because my father and his brother had both been to the same school before the war, and because it was round the corner from us, I was sent there at the age of two and a half.

It was called Miss Ironside's School. But my great-aunt was a progressive teacher and had taken a Froebel training course, which favoured teachers being addressed by their Christian names, so it became known to parents and pupils as Rene's. It was housed in another large, pillared Victorian building at 2 Elvaston Place, off Gloucester Road.

There were two Misses Ironside. Rene, the headmistress, was the colder and thinner of the two sisters; Nellie, the jollier, prettier and dumpier. They were the daughters of an Aberdeen doctor and had been brought up highly principled: emphasis on consideration for others was combined with the work ethic. Rene's habit of pursing her lips at the merest whiff of pleasure resonated with my mother's Presbyterian Northern Irish background.

Originally, Rene taught the children, cousins and friends of a family called Holland-Martin, but since Mr Holland-Martin was rolling in money, his wife suggested he should finance a proper school. So Rene opened Miss Ironside's and the pupils came flocking. Disapproving of anything that wasn't 'improving', Rene organized the education; Nellie, trained in domestic science, saw that the sash cords were functioning, organized the food, mediated in the rows in the kitchen and did the accounts.

Incredibly advanced in the days when my father and his brother had been pupils there, this school was something of an anachronism by the time I arrived there in 1946. It was steeped in the Arts and Crafts movement, with an emphasis on good italic handwriting done with Osmiroid pens, Dalcrose Eurythmics for the young ones, which involved dancing about pretending to be flowers *à la* Isadora Duncan, and a complete resistance to uniforms, science or religion of any kind.

Rene and Nellie lived on the premises, with their bedrooms on the top floor − occasionally, if you were feeling very ill, you might be sent to lie down on one of their hard oak beds. There were 150 children, three lavatories, no fire drill, no health and safety rules, and none of the teachers had any qualifications at all. No teasing was allowed − nor was it possible, because there was always a teacher present, even at break in the classrooms, when we drank our free milk through straws.

Despite Rene's principle that there were to be no punishments, the very phrases 'Rene's coming!' or 'I'm afraid I'll have to report you to Rene' transfixed the pupils with terror. If you were reported to Rene, you were sent to the large sitting-room on the ground floor, where Rene worked at papers, and she would ask why you had been sent down to see her. After you had stammered out the reason, Rene pierced you with a look full of the cold horror of one appalled by the unspeakable betrayal of trust that had just been committed. Then she would say a few words like: 'Well! That didn't become you!' or 'I hope you won't have to be sent to me again!' Naughty pupils often left the room in tears of shame.

I only learned of this second-hand, because I was incapable of being anything other than good. So good was I that once, when a teacher forgot to set us any prep, I put up my hand to remind her, to the fury of everyone else in the class. Only children tend to be good, because of the imbalance in their families, but the fact that my great-aunt ran the school made it even more difficult to be anything other than saintly. The headmistress was not just some feelingless idiot whom I could regard callously as most pupils regard their teachers. She was part of my family.

At the beginning of each day, Rene waited in the tiled hall to say good morning to every pupil. You could never slink in quietly. You had to look her in the eye when you said good morning, too. She stood sternly, perfectly erect, dressed in a tartan, powder blue or burgundy suit. Underneath, she wore a blouse with a high, frilled Edwardian collar, fastened with a brooch made of some Scottish semi-precious stone. She wore lisle stockings, and shoes with a thin strap with a button. Old-fashioned diamond earrings hung from the long lobes of her ears. Even my mother quailed in the presence of Rene.

The teachers at Rene's were an eccentric bunch. My history teacher, Miss Irwin, who lived in a nearby Gloucester Road hotel, was so passionate about ancient history that virtually all we ever learned was how to write our names in hieroglyphics. Both the maths teacher and the geography teacher were alcoholics and the French teacher was suffering from the early stage of Alzheimer's. We were taught public speaking by an elocution teacher called Miss 'Po-cock', and harmony by Cyril Cork, a man with a very long Adam's appley neck, no chin and Brilliantined hair. He taught us how to read music and got the whole class composing simple tunes on manuscript paper.

And then there was my father, who taught art every Friday morning – in return, I imagine, for my being educated free. Since he was so glamorous, every girl in the school was in love with him. I always felt extremely irritated if he praised any other girl's picture; eager not to show favouritism, he naturally said very little about my work.

Home was lonely; school was full of my family playing oddly formal roles. It was all the wrong way round, it seemed to me.

The two star teachers in the school, however, were Mrs Kelvin and Miss Staynes. Mrs Kelvin was an Austrian refugee, working illegally as a piano teacher, who lived in the school with my great-aunts, in a tiny bedroom with a little cooker on which she brewed gruel. She lived, slept and taught in one room. She had a fine, handsome face, swathes of white hair pulled into a bun, and long, baggy skirts to hide dreadful, swollen legs. I was one of Mrs Kelvin's star pupils – because my mother's cousin was Sir Michael Tippett, it was always thought a few musical genes might have found their way to me – but I hated my lessons with her because, although fundamentally warm-hearted, her occasional rages frightened me so much.

'Please, please can't I give up music?' I begged my parents regularly. My mother, completely unmusical and sorry to see me so unhappy, was on my side. My father sympathized but kept saying: 'Well, I gave it up when I was your age and never ceased to regret it. Give it till the end of the term and see how you feel then.'

It was only later that I discovered that Mrs Kelvin was concert-pianist material, and had been taught by Theodor Leschetizky, who had himself been taught by Czerny, who was taught by Beethoven.

Some Saturdays, Mrs Kelvin would buy tickets for the Sir Robert Mayer children's concerts at the Festival Hall, often presided over by Sir Malcolm Sargent. I loathed these expeditions, which involved giving up a whole Saturday morning, and a freezing walk over Hungerford Bridge. All I remember is the creaking facetiousness with which Sir Malcolm tried to interest the children in classical music.

'Can you hear the elephants in the background?' he would say – at which some bassoon honked a few notes which were received by a ripple of sycophantic laughter from teachers while all the children stared glumly at each other, wishing they were back at home reading their Enid Blytons or practising on their yo-yos. 'And then we have a peaceful passage . . . I think you can imagine the stillness of the pond and perhaps a fawn peeping round a tree and the chirruping of a little bird in the background . . . Cecil . . . a bird, please . . . ?'

At this, some musician stood up at the back and blew a few peeps on a piccolo to the same ripple of laughter. My shoulders became more and more hunched and I stared miserably at my watch.

It was Miss Staynes, who taught English and Latin, who I loved most of all. I was amazed, on the first day of one spring term, to see a Gogomobil, a bubble car with a motorbike engine, parked outside the school door. I was even more amazed to find that its owner was my new class teacher. She was only twenty-eight years old, wore a big black hat over lustrous chignoned hair, a belted leather jacket, a stole and a long black velvet skirt. Apparently she had been appalled to find she was expected to work alongside all these ancient people dressed in grey, but was reassured by Rene saying: 'We have no quarrels between the staff because we have no staff-room.' The only place the staff ever met was on the stairs.

Miss Staynes laid down firm rules on essay-writing. 'Never say anything is "nice" and never say, at the end of a story, that you woke up and it was all just a dream.' She impressed us all one day as she kept her cool when one of our class, a girl who was mentally ill, approached her bearing a knife and intoning the words 'Something is wrong . . .'

'Nothing is wrong,' said Miss Staynes. 'Please sit down. It is your turn to translate.'

Many of Rene's pupils had illustrious parents – Juliet Mills, daughter of John; Tessa and Susan Price, daughters of Dennis; Tracey Pelissier, stepdaughter of Carol Reed, who directed *The Third Man*.

Then there was Jane Birkin, who became an actress and married Serge Gainsbourg. I used to talk to her at the 49 bus-stop on our way to school.

But our most famous pupil was Rose Dugdale, a year or so older than me. Everyone adored this generous, clever and dashing millionaire's daughter, who was full of life and laughter. She ended up falling for a member of the IRA and, with him, invaded the Irish home of Sir Alfred and Lady Clementine Beit (oddly enough, friends of my uncle Robin) and tied them up before stealing a quantity of old masters.

And yet, however unusual the girls were, I felt certain that their home lives were more secure than mine. Nannies, grannies or mothers were always on hand to pick up the children in the afternoon. My classmates looked forward to going home at the end of the day, while I never quite knew what would be up when I arrived back at Neville Street. My mother might be in − or out. I might be picked up by the nanny of another friend to go to tea, a plan that would have been arranged behind my back.

If my mother and Christopher went out in the evenings and Phyl wasn't in, I panicked. Often they left me with a Universal Aunt, from an agency that provided babysitters, and I stood on the doorstep in my dressing-gown with my milk in my hand, screaming 'Please don't go! Don't go!' until my parents were just specks turning the corner into the Fulham Road.

My insecurity expressed itself in tastes not shared by my friends at school. My favourite poem was 'The Fairies', which started 'Up the airy mountain, down the rushy glen' and my favourite line in it was 'They stole little Bridget for seven years long'. When I was about seven, I was overcome with a compulsion to paint a strange watercolour of the Elfin King, spiriting a child away in the night. I had recurrent nightmares, the worst being one in which a burglar came into my bedroom. In my dream I had shouted for Christopher, the burglar had raced away and Christopher had told me: 'Don't move, stay there. I'll find him.' I remained rooted to the spot, looking out of the window into the garden where I could see my father hunting behind the plane trees. Then there was a tap on my shoulder . . .

I once spent a whole week in tears, convinced that there had been a mix-up at the nursing home where I was born and that I wasn't, in fact, my parents' child. This anxiety might well have been a result of a general feeling of formality and melancholy that pervaded Neville Street and recently I was relieved to be told by a friend that I wasn't the only one who felt rather spooked by the atmosphere at home. She said that whenever she came to tea and my mother was there, she experienced a most uncomfortable feeling, as if a poltergeist were present. It was as if Janey was an island, completely separate from everything else. She had a chilling aloofness, and the house felt like an abyss or a vacuum when she was around.

One weekend, I took this friend into the sitting-room where my mother was resting in the dark. She suddenly felt terrified. 'It was as if she was a disturbing force,' she said later. 'Even though, of course, she was always kind and sweet to me. Perhaps,' she added, reflectively, 'it was something to do with your reaction to your mother that made everything so sinister.'

I can't help wondering now if it was my mother who cast a shadow over our house or whether it was I, like some bad seed, who was already, even at seven years old, building up resentment towards a parent I felt didn't love me enough.

The air of unease in our home was compounded by the fact that faint stirrings of an interesting, wild and dangerous life were emanating from an area only a few hundred yards from our home. Rodrigo Moynihan and Elinor Bellingham Smith, both artists, were established at 155 Old Church Street. Anthony Devas — a glamorous society painter — and his wife lived around the corner. Augustus John's studio was only down the road. Laurie Lee, the poet, was a couple of streets away. They formed a roistering set, renowned for getting drunk, rowing and having affairs with each other. The Queen's Elm, the pub in which they congregated, was virtually at the bottom of our road, yards away from the Chelsea Arts Club.

The Elm was stuffed with actors, artists, writers and a variety of intellectual layabouts, who all hung out there in the evenings and on Sunday mornings. My mother would have given anything to lead a raging social life, and longed to hob-nob with painters and intellectuals, sipping rough red wine, listening to stories about the Spanish Civil War, smoking cigarettes and flirting on a bar stool. She would have liked to nip down for lunch at the Chelsea Arts Club and perhaps steal an afternoon of sex with Anthony Devas. (Later she succeeded, and a portrait that Anthony did of her in 1952 was used as an advertisement for chocolate.)

Sometimes she might suggest to my father that they go down to the Elm on a Sunday morning for a drink. He always refused, and I could see the disappointment in her face. She had no choice but to stay at home; in those days it would have been thought very strange for a woman to go to a pub on her own, even had she dared.

DIFFERENT...

for her, AERO – the milk
chocolate that's
different!

BY ROWNTREES

For a new experience in delightful full-cream milk
chocolate that melts in your mouth in a moment.

The portrait by Anthony Devas

Once, just after lunch, my mother gave me a shopping list. I had to get a tiny bottle of olive oil – only available then at the chemist; some yoghurt from Bunce's, the corner dairy – which delivered our milk on a horse-drawn cart, full of metal churns; and some bacon from Oakshotts. 'Tell him to cut it thin, won't you, darling?' she said. I hurried into the hall, past a collection of my grandmother's bridge-playing friends – all middle-aged women with legs that were either very fat or very thin – and ran down to the corner.

The Queen's Elm was just closing across the road as I went into the grocer's. While I waited, I looked dismally at the supplies of Spam and corned beef and examined the modern Dutch cheeses, wrapped in a casing of red wax, and the most exotic new meat, mortadella, slabs of pinky-grey reconstituted god-knows-whatery, interspersed with white circles of fat. On various tables were pyramids of tins of peas and carrots and packets of suet, tapioca and currants.

When I had got the shopping, I looked back at the Queen's Elm. A man with a red, bruised face and stained cravat round his neck was lurching unsteadily on the pavement. Worse, staggering up from where she had fallen on the pavement, was a dishevelled, yelling woman whose knee was bleeding. I could almost smell the beer, wine and smoke, and hear the roaring debauchery that spurted from the pub doors. I imagined it full of bacchanalian orgies, bearded men with open-necked shirts shouting poetry and insults, with bosomy girls sitting on their knees doing all sort of horrifyingly Hampsteady things. I hurried home. I thought it no wonder that my father had a pathological hatred of pubs.

The problem was that while Christopher seemed on the face of it like a wild, carousing sort of hell-raiser, inside he was nothing of the sort. Yes, he was an artist, he was cynical and amusing and clever, with extraordinary charm — the sort of man that any sensible matron would have taken one look at and then told her daughter that he wasn't 'husband material' and that he must be 'mad, bad and dangerous to know' — but the truth was the exact opposite.

It was his father, Reginald, who had been the rake. He was an extremely attractive society doctor (my father rather scathingly described him as '"allegedly" attractive'), a partner to Sir George Hastings, an even more fashionable London doctor. (It was said that Dr Hastings was abortionist to the gentry — 'So naturally he eventually got knighted,' said my father, cynically.) Being dashing, socially presentable, upwardly mobile and a good provider, Reginald appeared irresistible to my grandmother, the young Phyllis Cunliffe, and after they were married my uncle Robin was born, followed, a year later, by my father. They had taken a house in Sidney Place in South Kensington — plus servants and nanny, of course — and there was suddenly a terrific epidemic of Spanish Flu, a boon to every doctor, since it killed more people than had died in the war. So there was my grandfather, much sought-after, with a brass plate on his consulting rooms and a flourishing practice.

My grandfather may have been irresistible to women, but my grandmother's misfortune was that he found women irresistible, too, and therefore the marriage was, unsurprisingly, extremely unhappy. Matters came to a head with the great peppermint cream débâcle.

The family had always kept dogs — and always chows. One day, my grandmother found a peppermint cream embedded in the fur of one of them. Clearly my grandfather, being a mean man, would never have given the dog sweets. So, she deduced, the sweets must have been given to it by a lady. This peppermint cream became, to my grandmother, like the discovery of a blonde hair. Reginald had been visiting a lady with this dog. When a private detective was put on his trail, the peppermint-cream-giver was discovered — one of a long string of mistresses.

After they were divorced, my grandfather became involved in various scurrilous goings-on, prescribing illegal drugs and, eventually, he fell into bankruptcy. He was struck off the medical register for a while and then bundled off to Buenos Aires in disgrace as a ship's doctor.

When he died in 1959, my father was rung with the news in the middle of the night. He put the phone down, turned over and went back to sleep.

'He was a fairly dreadful person who simply wasn't interested in his children one bit,' commented my father, later. 'As a father, he never contributed anything at all. He never came with us on holidays, never took us to the cinema, never took us out. His death caused neither rejoicing nor sadness.'

In response to his father's rackety life, Christopher always disapproved violently of any kind of extra-marital romantic activity at all. Even as a single man, had a dancing girl turned up and offered herself to him, he would not have thrust a rose between his teeth and gone tangoing off with her to the Ritz; rather, he would have become covered in embarrassment and rung for a cab to take her home.

The very word 'bohemian' made my father screw up his eyes in horror, and pucker his lips as if he had eaten a bowl of sugarless stewed plums. The nearest he got to bohemian was to wear a donkey jacket to work, or sometimes a duffel-coat, to wear his hair a little bit longer than most and to sport a red spotted handkerchief in his pocket. Beyond that, bohemian was out.

Even on festive occasions, there was very little letting-down of hair in our household. We never celebrated New Year, and birthdays, if they were remembered (my parents celebrated my own birthday on 4 February for about eleven years until they remembered I had been born on 3 February), were usually over by about nine in the morning, after a few presents had been opened.

Except for the odd times when my mother put her foot down and we had Christmas at home, we even had to spend most Christmas days at my school, with Rene and Nellie.

I always got a very good stocking, which my parents packed tight with all kinds of bits of nonsense – metal puzzles, magic drawing books, an ocarina, a glass animal. Crackers were pinned to the top. I woke early and took it in to open on my parents' bed. My father and I struggled over the puzzles, and my mother got up first to put on the kettle. After breakfast, all the big presents were laid out on the sofa. I had the most, of course, but I was almost as excited to watch my parents opening theirs as I was to open mine.

In the autumn of 1951, I had begged my mother to teach me how to knit. She bought me some huge needles and I chose thick, lime-green wool to make Christopher a scarf for Christmas. I knitted in bed when he thought I was asleep, and often had to stuff it down underneath my blankets hurriedly when I heard his step on the way to the lavatory. In the end, the scarf was about seven feet long.

As for my mother, knowing she adored marzipan, I saved up my pocket money to buy her some marzipan animals I had seen in a sweet shop.

When my parents took their presents from the sofa, my father slowly opened mine, with all the usual rolling of eyes and: 'What *can* this be? I'm completely baffled! It isn't a jersey . . . a flying saucer . . . Oh look! It's a scarf! It's *exactly* what I wanted!' He put it around his neck at once, delightedly admiring himself in the mirror.

My mother had already opened her present while all this was going on and stared at the marzipan animals in confusion.

'Well, go on, eat one!' I said.

'I'll eat one after lunch. Otherwise I might spoil my appetite,' she said. 'Thank you *so* much, darling.'

After telephoning Phyl to wish her a happy Christmas – she usually spent it with her brother in Sussex – we walked up Queen's Gate to the school, carrying, in a brown carrier bag, a bottle of wine that my mother had wrapped in Christmas paper as a present. In the school sitting-room, Rene offered everyone a thimbleful of sherry.

That year, my grandfather and his new wife were there as well.

After his return from Buenos Aires, he had got a job as a private anaesthetist. One of his patients was a hideously unattractive million-airess called Dolly. She had a high forehead, wriggly hair, hard lipstick and a wizened face. She was shrill, stupid and little bit mad. The moment this wealthy creature woke up from an operation, she saw the stunning good looks of her anaesthetist, my grandfather, staring down at her and she decided to marry him. He spent the rest of his life in a mock-Tudor house in Esher, was kept on an extremely tight rein with a very small allowance and never allowed up to

London except in the company of her chauffeur, who dogged his every move.

Now my grandfather was no longer dashing and good-looking, but fat and bald, though he still had an uncomfortably flirtatious way with him. He kept offering me cigarettes and calling me a 'little sauce-box' — a description that could hardly be less appropriate; at seven years old, I was always dumb with shyness. At one o'clock we made our way to the school dining-room in the basement. The cold light of the silent South Kensington day filtered in through the barred window on to the same oak trestle table I sat at every school day of my life, engrained with fat and the smell of old cabbage. We sat on the same long oak benches. There was nothing to drink as accompaniment to the chicken — then a special treat — except tap water in an earthenware school pitcher.

'Oh, what about the wine?' said my mother, pretending she'd just remembered it and hadn't been craving a glass for the last half-hour — and only then was it grudgingly produced.

Later, over coffee in the sitting-room upstairs, my grandfather stuffed a ten-bob note into my hand, telling me 'not to spend it all on ice-cream, you cheeky monkey!', while Rene presented me with an improving book on Norman architecture.

As soon as we could politely leave, we rushed home. Even Christopher agreed that it had been '*Ghastly!*' As we walked, I fingered his scarf, examining the loopy stitches.

'Do you like my present? Is it warm?' I asked him, fishing for a compliment.

'It's just *wonderful*, particularly in that freezing dining-room,' said Christopher, who had nobly worn it throughout the Christmas lunch.

'And when we get home, you can eat one of your marzipan animals, mummy!' I said to my mother. 'Which one will you choose first? The rabbit? Or the chicken?'

My mother laughed. She looked down and squeezed my hand. 'I love my animals!' she said. 'I love them so much I don't think I am ever going to eat them. I am going to keep them and look at them for ever and ever!'

I felt, suddenly, terribly disappointed.

My uncle Robin, always popping in and out of Neville Street, was the only person who could offer my mother any kind of entrée into the intellectually racy world she so longed to frequent. A close friend of Cyril Connolly, Kenneth Clark and John Rothenstein, he moved in artistic, literary and generally grand bohemian circles. It was he who had persuaded Angus Wilson to send his stories in to *Horizon* and thus start his literary career.

After nine years at the Tate Gallery, Robin had given it all up in 1946, driven by arguments with the Board and internal creative demons to live in penury and devote himself to writing about art, and painting minutely detailed romantic pictures, even though he had never received any formal training. As a writer, he revived interest in the Pre-Raphaelites almost single-handedly and even, it is said, coined the term 'neo-romantic' in one of his many essays. With some money left him by a distant relation, he managed to buy the lease on a minuscule, cold and wretched flat in Clarendon Street, a row of tiny peeling Victorian houses in a little road behind Victoria railway station.

Amusing, charismatic and clever, Robin derived much of his income from the patronage of rich friends who believed in his talent. He was courted by the rich, off-beat upper classes and helped by friends like Sir Edward Hulton, the publishing millionaire. When the novelist Ian Fleming died, Robin was commissioned by his wife, Anne Fleming, the society hostess, to design a four-foot obelisk as a memorial to him in Sevenhampton churchyard.

I remember Robin best at lunch. He would ring the bell very late, maybe at four in the afternoon. My father would open the front door and I would hear Robin groaning — about the taxi, the cold, or his new, uncomfortable false teeth. As he came up the stairs, an intense, gaunt, sepulchral figure, with feverish eyes and sometimes a slightly grubby stiff collar — though he often still wore his pyjamas under his black jeans — he would cry, in a melancholy way: 'I'm late, I'm late, I should not have trifled at the gate!'

My mother cooked him a boiled egg and he sat at the end of the dining-room table, either groaning 'Oh no, oh no!' in a half-facetious, half-poignant tone or remaining in complete silence, slowly eating his egg between sighs, for about an hour. Then he would start talking to my father about art, how to draw things. It was partly the fact that he was self-taught that made Robin's pictures so original, and he wore his lack of training proudly, as if it were a credit. But it did mean that sometimes he was stumped when it came to drawing a broken lute or a sylph.

Robin was an immensely attractive presence, a dark flame of eccentric life that flared into our lives like an alarming genie from a bottle. I can still see his taut, yellowish skin, stretched over high cheekbones, watch the liveliness in his eye, hear his voice and his laugh, though I can't distinguish what he's saying. He talked as fast as an Italian, but in English, in perfect sentences. Because of his addiction to Dr Collis Browne's Chlorodine, he was probably high most of the time, but brilliant too. (He had been recommended this over-the-counter medicine by the eccentric Oxford academic, Maurice Bowra. It was then alleged to contain opium or some such thing, and Robin used it to prolong painting sessions throughout the night. It certainly had an effect on his obsessive behaviour and on the bizarre and dark imaginative scenes he created in his work.)

As a child, I used to find Robin's paintings rather creepy. He often used a magnifying glass to work, and it is almost possible to see the very weave of his painted silk drapes, the skeletons of leaves, or the tiniest veins on the hands of the haunted figures which appeared, to use Robin's own expression, 'under the spell of some charming but vaguely dreaded hallucination'. The titles of his pictures were as mysterious and evocative as the paintings themselves. One was 'A Picture to Prove that the Greeks only Painted with Three Colours', another, 'Street Entertainer playing Threatening Music to a Cinema Queue'. There were also 'Wounded Man in Bed-sitting Room', 'Crowd Awaiting a Portent', 'Famous Statues Visiting a Museum of People', 'Patients Suffering from Waxy Insensibility' and 'Visitor to a Museum Posing on a Vacant Plinth'.

'Matthew, Mark, Luke and John', a painting of mine which was stolen, showed Robin dying on his iron bed in Clarendon Street, an Aladdin heater by his side and at each corner of the bed the four angels, all turning away to hide their eyes. His pictures were like dreams seasoned with black jokes, and even his most romantic works were threaded with threat and destruction — a wounded deer hiding in the trees of a sylvan forest, a scorpion nestling in the grass under the feet of two nymphs.

Unfortunately for him, he was an obsessive. He could never let a picture go. I remember us all laughing when, over the usual boiled egg, he told us how he had been staying in Ireland with the Beits, for whom he had done a picture of their drawing-room many years before. In the middle of the night he was overtaken by a compulsion to repaint some piece of drapery that he felt needed improvement. He was standing on a chair, touching it up with the aid of a torch, when Sir Alfred appeared, a poker in his hand, having heard the sinister rustling of Robin's brushes.

When he came round, he brought an excitingly disturbing influence. His stories of the parties he had been to, the people he had met — and admired or despised — the way he could dismiss people my mother would have given her eye-teeth to have met, all these served to make Janey less and less satisfied with her lot. The feeling of her straining against the leash of her marriage was almost palpable as, glass in hand, she listened to Robin talking casually of his rich and intellectual friends. He frequently arrived late at night, bearing under his arm several black volumes from the London Library by Milton or Baudelaire and leaving with another collection thrust on him by my father, consisting of garish paperbacks covered with illustrations of daggers and screaming women, by Erle Stanley Gardner or Rex Stout, his favourite detective writers, which Robin devoured with as much enthusiasm as the classics.

When he left, in a whirl of late taxis, high drama and intense anxiety, I felt both bereft and relieved.

*

It was quite clear that Robin was the only person who could offer my mother the tiniest chink through which she might escape, if only for a few moments, into the glamorous world that she was convinced was partying and dancing outside the dreary confines of 15 Neville Street. He could hardly introduce her to his wide circle of friends without Christopher's acquiescence, and Christopher dreaded meeting anyone remotely fashionable, so Robin suggested my mother accompany him to Viva King's Sunday tea parties.

Viva, the wife of an eccentric British Museum curator who had taken to drink, was a London socialite who lived in Thurloe Square. Since the parties were given in the afternoon, my father could hardly disapprove, particularly as the cakes were from Floris and the tea was always China, served in cups and saucers. Grumpy and shy, I was later dragged along with my mother, feeling the chaperone I probably was, and while I looked at Viva's collection of Victorian musical boxes, my mother was introduced to friends of Robin's, like Ivy Compton Burnett (rather a disappointment; apparently she only talked about the servant problem) and her friend Margaret Jourdain, who had seen eighteenth-century ghosts in Versailles.

Norman Douglas might have been there, or Nina Hamnett, an old alcoholic painter who had once been very beautiful and a member of the Picasso/Gide/Modigliani set. I remember being scared when I saw her sitting on a chair, with long greasy hair, her stockings ragged, and rather smelly. I hung around my mother, pulling at her sleeve and whispering: 'When are we going home?'

Whenever my mother went out to parties or dinners, her friends, who could still get nothing from the shops except government-prescribed, square-shouldered short-skirted styles of garments, would beg her to tell them where she bought her beautiful clothes. When she told them that she made them herself, they asked: 'Oh, Janey, would you make something like that for me, too?'

So my mother bought an ancient tailor's dummy with a stained white cotton torso and a handle that cranked it from size ten to size sixteen, and started making clothes for friends. But without a social life she would have no clients, so occasionally she would overcome my father's resistance and throw a cocktail party at home.

I liked these parties. My parents were on their best behaviour and they both looked wonderful, my glamorous father with clean hair, clean shirt and a clean red-spotted handkerchief sprouting from his jacket pocket, my mother in a full scarlet felt skirt topped, perhaps, by a black high-collared shirt. Social life made her sparkle, and, scented and made-up and knowing she looked lovely, my mother actually seemed nicer than usual.

Since he was extraordinarily adept socially, it was curious that my father hated these occasions so much. When the bell rang to announce the first guest, he would groan 'Oh Gawd!' before getting up, bowing and smiling as the first guest entered the room and saying: 'How *lovely* to see you!' He offered them Martini or vermouth or 'gin and ton' while I handed round Smiths crisps, pickled cocktail onions and green olives stuffed with bits of red pepper.

I would answer the bell to people like the architect Hugh Casson. 'Duckie!' he'd say. 'Is this the right day? Is your mum here? And your old man?' Then he would hug me far too tightly and for far too long – particularly embarrassing because we were about the same height – while his tall, elegant wife, Reta, stood by, looking on with a world-weary smile on her face. She was used to his compulsive philandering.

After they had divested themselves of duffel-coats and stoles, the bell might ring again and I would race down to welcome someone like Diana Holman Hunt. 'My *dear*, am I too *early*? Or too *late*? I'm sure I'm too *something*!' she might say, in a tittering, drawling voice and with a rather flirtatious, lopsided smile. The granddaughter of the painter Holman Hunt, she was an old flame of my father's and now a great friend of my mother's as well. She was willowy, thin and extremely attractive. 'Now don't ask how I *am*, my duck, or I might give you an *organ* recital! Hee hee hee!'

After regaling everyone with funny stories, laughing at their jokes, involving himself in a bit of argumentative cut and thrust, but never letting it get out of hand, asking everyone about themselves, filling their glasses and apparently enjoying himself like billy-o, when the door banged after the last guest, my father would sink, groaning, into the sofa, saying: 'Christ, thank Gawd! At last! I thought they'd *never* go!'

One visitor to our house who was always welcome, however, was Robin Darwin — generally known to everyone by his full name. He seemed to galvanize both my parents and in his company they even seemed happy together. For much of the time at home, Janey could appear rather depressed, harassed and sad, and though I was small I realized that there was a lack of warmth between my parents. They joked together, they talked, but they never touched each other, and sometimes there were long, cold silences between them that made the house feel dead and unlived-in. But once Robin Darwin arrived, and after a drink, my mother changed into a flirtatious, giggly and amusing woman, sitting on the sofa with her legs tucked under her, making sophisticated and ironic contributions to the conversation that had both my father and Robin Darwin rocking with laughter and admiration.

When he'd come to the end of his stint in Camouflage, Robin Darwin had joined the Ministry of Town and Country Planning – where he briefly found my father a job – and then, for a short while, he had been made head of Newcastle College of Art. But his eye had always been on a bigger prize: the Royal College of Art in London.

He had had it in his sights ever since he had written a report on it when, after Newcastle, he joined the Council of Industrial Design. When he'd gone to tea at the College, to meet the then principal, Percy Jowett, in 1947, he'd been struck by how low the morale was. It was said that most of the staff had never even met each other. Robin suggested that the College should be made a 'magnet for talent'. In his report, he also proposed that, along with the old Schools of Painting, Engraving, Sculpture and Design, there should be new Schools: Ceramics, Textiles, Typography, Silversmithing, Metalwork, Jewellery, Light Engineering, Furniture, Graphic Design – and Fashion Design. As a result, he replaced Percy Jowett in 1948 and started empire-building.

Robin Darwin was becoming quite a powerful figure. He was also gaining a reputation as a benign bully. If he was on your side, he was a loyal friend; if not, he could be ruthless. As a child, however, I found him irresistible. Whether I was in my school clothes or my dressing gown, he always treated me as an adult and laughed at my jokes on the rare occasions that I dared to open my mouth. Both my parents enjoyed his frequent six-o'clock visits. He would always have a 'gin and ton, and not too much ton' and he would stand in his greasy pin-stripe double-breasted suit from Savile Row, with his back to the fire and his huge tummy sticking out, his great black Stalin moustache covered with bits of crumbs, exuding an intimidating air of grandeur. He had a loud, booming voice and often told such outrageous stories and laughed so much that he had to take off his black spectacles and wipe them with the handkerchief that poked out of his top pocket. Slightly older than my parents, he seemed like a paternal influence, always eager to hatch some scheme that would involve them, or suggest some job he thought might suit Christopher, adding that he would 'see what he could do'.

When he was around, I was always allowed to sit quietly on a chair and listen. I remember him telling my parents how depressing he'd found the Royal College building when he arrived. He said that it was painted a cold grey and that when he went into his offices he found two aged stewards playing a game of shove-halfpenny. When he got into his room, which was, of course, coloured the same cold grey, there on his desk he saw an oblong green book. It was called an Attendance Book, and when he asked what it was for, the senior steward told him, respectfully but sorrowfully, that he was expected to enter daily his times of arrival and departure. 'Can you imagine it, Christopher?' he expostulated. 'Of course I threw it into the waste-paper basket!'

There was no room for all the new Schools that he wanted to set up, so he had to find buildings in the area. The Common Room was at 21 Cromwell Road, and the Fashion School was at 20 Ennismore Gardens, round the corner in Knightsbridge. The Sculpture School was housed in some curious outhouses in Queen's Gate, which Robin Darwin dubbed the Drill Hall.

Over the following months, when he came to visit us, he was high on his new achievements. I remember him saying: 'Christopher, I think we need to have a proper ceremony at the end of the year, give a sense of gravitas to the place, don't you? We'll call it Convocation. Now, what I need are good ideas. Come on, Virginia! I want everyone working on this!'

Between the three of them, they flannelled up Convocation, introduced the idea of a College beadle and got all the professors wearing gowns embroidered with special symbols; they drummed up a 'traditional' fanfare blown by heralds in ermine-trimmed jerkins, and generally invented an illustrious, fictional history. It was in Neville Street that it was decreed that the beadle should carry the 'College Yardstick', which featured a silver phoenix at one end and a gloomy old dodo at the bottom end. It was known in our house as the Holy Poker.

Until Robin Darwin's arrival, the art-school serpent had enjoyed a long history of eating its own tail, with art teachers teaching art to students who became art teachers, in a drowsy continuum of stagnation. He set out with clear and simple aims — to break that pattern and establish professional standards of design competence within the art-school world and feed into industry the quality of design talent it so clearly lacked.

One of his first acts was to get rid of virtually all the old staff. A few weeks after he took over, the students laid wet concrete on the steps of the RCA building and, using an improvised dodo's claw, imprinted its footprints in it, going away towards the street. He instituted a new College emblem – a phoenix rising from the ashes. The phoenix consisted of all Robin Darwin's old chums from Camouflage. Although hardly any of them had any experience of teaching, he picked them for their professional attainments. Hugh Casson was dragged in. So were Julian Trevelyan and his wife, Mary Fedden. Rodney Burn arrived. Dick Guyatt was made head of Graphic Design. Robert Goodden, also from Camouflage, was made head of the Silver and Jewellery School.

Naturally, Robin Darwin, the amiable patron, offered my father a job, too – teaching life drawing in the Painting and Sculpture Schools – which he accepted eagerly. And, next, it was Janey's turn.

The Head of the then School of Embroidery was a Mrs Gibson, who had been there since 1936. Robin gave her the boot and, although she complained to her MP, Mrs Gibson stayed booted. In her place, Robin established Madge Garland as Professor of the new Fashion School. A childhood friend of Cecil Beaton, her first job had been as a merchandise manager for Bourne and Hollingsworth; she later became a fashion editor at *Vogue*.

Robin Darwin proposed that Janey should stop making clothes for friends and apply to become Madge's assistant.

Although, in 1948, the ready-to-wear industry and the retail chain stores had established completely new patterns of purchasing in the fashion industry, and it was beginning to be recognized that fashion designers would soon be needed to supply the mass markets, the fashion scene was still dominated by Paris, where couture designers reigned supreme, well backed financially by their rich female clients.

Couture was synonymous with class and money, and at fashion shows the audiences dressed, even at 9.30 in the morning, as if they were going to a cocktail party, with white gloves, hats and paste brooches. They sat on tiny gilded chairs and smoked cigarettes in long holders. If there was any music, it would be the tinkling of a cocktail piano.

Professor Madge Garland's ladylike presence fitted perfectly into this world. She ran the Fashion School in the big Edwardian house in Ennismore Gardens along finishing-school lines. Her office was more like a drawing-room than an office, and was furnished like a couture salon, with expensive, elegant antique furniture and pink velveteen curtains falling from an elaborate pelmet. The walls were painted shrimp pink and pale grey, and the carpets were yellow.

Madge was never to be seen without a hat, and her clothes were from Digby Morton, Michael, Balenciaga or Balmain, with wedge shoes by Ferragamo. Since she always wore Dior's little white gloves and never went out without an elongated rolled umbrella, this look became a kind of uniform for all her pupils. They wore their accessories with green, red and black felt skirts, black jumpers and chiffon scarves.

A student who came in with a crooked seam on her stocking or dirty nails would be in for a rebuke from Professor Garland. Even though some of the students were from working-class backgrounds and unlikely to have the social or academic skills of people like Madge, they were set compulsory improving readings from the classics like Jane Austen or Aldous Huxley and were expected to write monthly essays in reaction to them.

*

Cecil Beaton

Madge Garland in her office

When she returned from her interview with Madge, Christopher and I were agog to hear what had happened to my mother. She looked flushed, shaky, and immediately settled on the sofa, tucking her legs underneath her, demanding a large vermouth.

Entering the Fashion School, with its atmosphere as rarefied as an intellectual soirée, my mother said that she had felt extremely nervous. She had met Madge before at the odd dinner party, and had even made her the occasional dress, but when she arrived in Madge's boudoir of an office, she had rarely felt so churned-up, so home-dressmakerish or gauche.

Madge sat behind her desk, immaculate in a tight-bodiced, full-skirted cotton dress from Horrocks — the most prestigious firm making mass-produced dresses at that time — a large straw hat, dark glasses, and short white gloves. The sight of her terrified my mother so much that her lips stiffened and came apart with a 'guk' sound when she had to answer a question.

'I see you realize that separates are the coming thing,' Madge had said, looking favourably on my mother's mustard-coloured wool skirt and waistcoat with a white shirt. My mother nodded wisely, although she had no idea that separates were the coming thing and had only made her outfit in that manner because she liked it.

My mother paused in her story to ask for another drink.

'What happened then?' I asked.

My mother looked rather nervously at Christopher's back as he poured out the vermouth.

'Well, despite all my "guks", she actually offered me the job,' she said.

'And?' said Christopher, turning round.

'I accepted.'

*

I already knew what it was like to have a mother who was rarely around, but to have a mother with a proper job, a 'working mother' – that was very strange. It made me feel even more of an outsider. Certainly none of the mothers of the children at Rene's had jobs – and Sally's mother over the road had never worked a day in her life, as far as I knew. Mothers didn't work in the fifties. They stayed at home and baked cakes – at least, that's what I imagined.

Although my father may have had forebodings about my mother accepting this job, he may well have thought that were my mother more fulfilled, we all might feel a little happier.

The problem was that because she was entirely inexperienced, not only did she have to work extremely hard to learn the art of being Madge's dogsbody, but during the season she had to take various trips to Paris with Madge and groups of students to see the fashion shows. While she was feeling 'that unmistakable frisson of pleasure at the sight of clothes', and the shows of Dior and Givenchy were making her 'quite ill with envy', and she went round shops like Prisunic and Galeries Lafayette in search of cheap wooden-handled cutlery pinned with brass, brown pottery cooking dishes and clever, amusing toys for me – these were BC, or Before Conran, days – I became angrier and more unhappy.

Around seven to eight years old, my satchel bouncing on my bottom, I hated coming home on my own, taking the 49 bus from school to Stanhope Gardens and then walking down Queen's Gate, a street of unutterable gloom and boredom, lined with immense plane trees. Now and again, it was almost impossible to find my way back, so dense was the bitter, yellow smog that used to envelop London in the fifties, and I had to shuffle gingerly from tree to tree with my hands outstretched, hoping that I would find a reassuring trunk. When I turned down Onslow Gardens and finally reached home, it was often to an empty house. I longed for someone to pick me up from school and be pleased to make my tea and listen to my anxieties.

I began to resent the Fashion School. It became like another, more favourite, daughter, a daughter that my mother loved and wanted to spend as much time with as possible. I particularly loathed it when my mother insisted on my appearing in the College's annual fashion show.

She had got it into her head that nothing could be more enchanting and smart than the sight of her and me parading down the catwalk together, dressed in identical blue-and-white-striped nylon dresses, designed and made by a student. Janey would wear a pink rosebud at the neck of hers, and I would carry a long-stemmed rosebud.

I recoiled at this plan, and looked to my father for support.

'It'll only be for an afternoon,' he said. 'Janey has got her heart set on it – man was born to sorrow as the sparks fly upwards, these things are sent to try us . . . it's not worth making a fuss.'

I felt exceptionally shy as, on the day, I waited behind the scenes of the big first-floor room of the Fashion School. I was surrounded by glamorous models, all shouting at each other, snatching hairbrushes, wriggling in and out of dresses, even swearing. No one took any notice of me, and I felt very frightened of the turbulent bustle that raged around me. A spotlight of grey bleakness surrounded me as I pressed myself against the wall and tried to make myself invisible.

My mother, completely involved in pinning, cursing missing buttons, pointing out wrong shoes and adjusting hats, had no time for me at all, except when she spotted me skulking in the corner and rushed across to check me over, see that my dress was hanging correctly and rub a spot off my cheek with a spit-wetted hand-kerchief. Her eyes focused only on the dress; they never scanned my miserable, frightened face. I could almost feel the absence of myself in the pupils of her eyes; it wasn't that she wasn't looking at me, more that when she looked at me, I didn't exist. When she examined only my looks and clothes, I felt as if I had no self and no soul. I was just a vacuum.

Nothing had prepared me for the ordeal of actually walking down the catwalk with my mother. As the audience cooed their embarrassing 'oohs' and 'aahs', clapping and whispering 'Isn't she sweet!', and as I heard the patronizing, affectionate laughter that bounced off the walls, I felt like a kitten in a pet shop, with passers-by tapping on the glass. Worse, the shyer I became, the more my eyes filled with nervous tears, the more my bottom lip trembled and the tighter I clung to my mother's hand, the more everyone tittered.

What made the whole thing even more excruciating was that my mother had also insisted that I model beachwear with her in the sports section. My mother was too attractive, too naked; I, flat-chested, holding a bucket and spade and wearing a matching yellow bathing suit with black spots, found the scenario repellent, and shrink from recalling the confused sexual undertones of the whole affair.

A piece in the *Daily Express*, under a picture of us both, commented: 'Daughter Virginia, a chic moppet with her mother's black urchin fringe and bright-as-a-boot button eyes, modelled young-idea clothes designed by RCA students.' Another cutting

Me modelling at a dress
show with everyone
thinking how sweet I am

revealed that 'Janey Ironside and her daughter caused much interest, and delighted laughter, when they walked together down the gangway in similar beach models at the fashion parade given by the School of Fashion Design. What was important was that both looked charming and suitably dressed.'

My mother may have felt charming and suitably dressed, but I felt resentful and miserable and as suitably dressed as a chimpanzee at a tea party.

five

THE BUYER   *To a nervous fashion designer the word 'buyer' has almost the same spine-chilling sound as the word 'Boney' had to children during the Napoleonic wars. Buyers are at the moment the Ugly Sisters of the fashion scene, wicked, venal, spoiling all design-Cinderella's fun — even looking the part. 'She looks like a buyer' is almost the most cutting thing that one can say about anyone in the fashion world.*

Janey Ironside, *Fashion as a Career*

The story always was that my mother gave up working at the Fashion School because I was becoming so unhappy. I suspect that the truth was that she found the imperious Madge too difficult to work with but, if the story is correct, then I imagine it was my father who put the pressure on. Sadly, any hope of seeing more of my mother when she decided to work at home was short-lived, because she chose to become what she would have called 'that dreaded phrase — a little dressmaker'.

A dressmaker was a 'jewel', a 'treasure', a secret only to be shared with dearest friends, and above all to be kept unaware of her true value. A sad, grey figure with indigestion and bad breath, hunched over the sewing-machine in the nursery, eating hasty meals brought up to her by cross and hoity-toity housemaids, or working in her own tiny, badly lit parlour, she made beautiful party dresses for Mama and the girls, let out Sir's waistcoats, repaired tablecloths or sides-to-middled sheets, all as part of a day's work at an incredibly low rate of pay.

Little had changed in attitudes towards dressmakers when, in 1951, my mother set up her business at the top of our house.

Above the bathroom were two more rooms – one used by my father as a studio to paint in. This was a wonderful place, smelling of turpentine and oils, full of canvases, easels, palettes, squeezed tubes of Burnt Umber and Chinese White, grey twists of old putty rubber and drawing pins and bits of charcoal ground into the boards on the floor. The room next door was large enough to become my mother's work-room. She moved in a trestle-table, a hand sewing-machine with an electric motor added, two hard wooden chairs with bottom-shaped seats and the dressmaker's dummy. Finding business rather slow, she put an advertisement in *Vogue* and was inundated with work.

Suddenly she had to advertise for staff. The tiny room became packed with Italian and Indian seamstresses, while Yugoslav and Irish outworkers traipsed in and out; the house hummed to the sound of an increasing number of sewing-machines.

Nine women worked, hunched over a tiny gothic gas fire, in a room no more than fourteen feet square; with only one lavatory in the house, it was more of a sweatshop than a workroom. Heaven knows what Health and Safety would make of it now. The only emergency equipment, had there been a fire, was a huge white strip of canvas coiled up in a metal case, in my father's studio. There

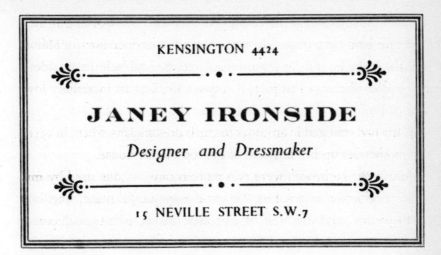

KENSINGTON 4424

JANEY IRONSIDE

Designer and Dressmaker

15 NEVILLE STREET S.W.7

Janey's card

were no instructions available as to how it should be used.

With so many women of so many different nationalities squashed up in one room, rows broke out. One lunch-time, my mother went upstairs to find a stony silence. There had been a terrible argument, about food and smells, between the Neapolitans, who had brought in garlic sausage and goat's milk cheese, and the Indians, who had brought spiced vegetables and rice. Each worker was sitting in silence, each with a home-made paper national flag in front of her. My mother took one look, said that if anyone didn't like working there, they could leave, and went downstairs with trembling knees. Next time she looked in, the flags had vanished and they were all listening to *Mrs Dale's Diary*.

Our dining-room table was converted into a cutting table by balancing a huge piece of plywood on the top, and throughout the house clothes in various stages of made-upness were draped –

brides' dresses hung in our cupboards; cocktail gowns were thrown over the stair-rails; page-boy outfits lay on the beds; skirts, suits and coats were laid out on sheets on the floors. Everywhere we sat, there were pins; pieces of cotton and stray sequins attached themselves to our clothes, and in each room lingered the smell of oiled machines and freshly cut fabric.

I could never go into the sitting-room when I came home from school because my mother was inside, supervising fittings. Often I felt like an intruder in my own home. I made my own tea — chocolate Nesquik and milk, a roll that I heated up in the oven with butter and Marmite, and often a tablespoon of vinegar to relieve the appalling headaches I suffered. I then tiptoed past the sitting-room with my tea, which I ate, if there was room, with the girls upstairs. They must have blanched at the sight of my buttery fingers but I knew better than to touch any of the expensive fabric that lay around. I picked up the pins from the floor with a giant magnet on a string and then went to my bedroom to do my homework, crouching in front of the gas fire, with my cat Sooty sitting on my back.

Behind the closed doors of the sitting-room, curtains were drawn all day to prevent peeping Toms spying on ladies in various stages of nakedness. My mother's customers were invariably incredibly grand and they would have been amazed if she had told them that she was the daughter of Sir James and Lady Acheson. To them, she was simply their 'wonderful little dressmaker', and my mother's self-esteem, never very high, took a fearful battering as she danced attendance on princesses, ladies, countesses, baronesses and duchesses. Even Ernest Hemingway's last wife, Martha Graham, was a visitor to the 'little dressmaker' in Neville Street.

At first, my mother lacked any business sense or assertiveness. She would nod when a customer announced 'I think it should be just a quarter of an inch shorter' when the agreed length of a ten-yard-wide skirt had just been finished exquisitely by hand – half a day's work. Sometimes a customer would arrive, saying 'I paid £10 a yard for this material, so could you charge me less for making the dress? Otherwise it is going to be *so* expensive!'

But quite soon my mother developed a healthy disrespect for many of her 200 or so clients, whom she once dismissed as 'lots of rich, fat middle-aged women holding their tummies in, using me as an economy, always asking me to copy clothes they'd bought at some couture house for quarter the price'. When she was asked later why little dressmakers were becoming thin on the ground, she answered, with feeling, that it was because their lives were so awful. Work could be endless, she said, with no time for fun or holidays, and it usually took place in an unhealthy atmosphere of steam and fug.

It soon seemed obvious to her that it would be far more economic to become a designer of mass-produced garments and to give up this punishing work-load. Unfortunately for me, her special interest was in childrenswear.

Nowadays many children – and adults – say: 'Virginia, you were so *lucky* to be wearing fashionable clothes!' At the time, other children's parents, when they saw how I was dressed, would coo: 'You look just like a little French girl' or 'Oh, she's straight out of a Monet!' But I didn't want to look straight out of a Monet. I wanted to look like me, an English schoolgirl. It wasn't fashionable to be

A fitting

fashionable then, not if you were a child. I wanted to wear the style of clothes worn by my contemporaries, what my mother derisorily called 'the nanny look' — short ankle socks; shoes with two bars across; a fitted coat piped and trimmed with velvet, with pleats at the back; a bonnet hat, half tweed, half velvet; Aertex shirts and grey divided shorts for sports; and smocked dresses with puffed sleeves for parties.

I did not want, as I was forced to wear, a navy coat made by my mother, long white socks, black pumps and a dark blue tam-o'-shanter with a pom-pom on top. What my mother was after was not just a fashionable look for children — which she characterized as bright, plain knitwear, sleeveless cotton dresses, pleated or gathered skirts, brown strollers, coloured sandals, well-made fitted coats with raglan sleeves, and plain, man-style dressing-gowns in strong colours. She also wanted daughters to wear the sort of clothes that their mothers were wearing — and in particular for me to wear what she was wearing.

'One thing that mothers and daughters can share is the general principle of good dressing,' she said.

The last thing I wanted was to look like my mother or for my mother to look like me. It made life so confusing. Oddly, it was my own mother who, in a book, once quoted an American fashion expert, Miss Estelle Hamburger: 'If a mother buys mother-and-daughter look-alike dresses to surprise Daddy, she may be escaping to her own childhood or making a rival of her daughter so that she can destroy her.' There was certainly a competitive element between my mother and me, for my father's affection.

More important was the question of identity. Even then, I felt emotionally blackmailed into looking like her, when I longed to be so different. I did not want to look like my mother — and yet, with hindsight, I imagine that 'becoming' her held a revolting kind of attraction. I would then not only be loved by her — or at least my looks would be loved by her — but I would have her with me always and she could never ignore me or leave me.

Clothes became a constant source of friction between us. My mother rarely hugged me or cuddled me; indeed, the only time she looked at me or touched me was when she was pinning clothes on me. Then she would stare, feel me, ask me to turn round so that she could see me from the back, pinch the material around me into darts, hands all over me, tweaking, picking and pulling me. She seemed to pay no attention to me, just my clothes.

I might stand on a chair in front of a mirror with my arms high in the air, while my mother inserted a gusset in the fabric under my arms, marked where the buttonholes should be, or tugged a dress down to see how it would 'sit'. Sometimes I would stand on the floor while my mother knelt in front of me, her full red mouth full of pins, hands crawling all over my body, pinning, pinning, pinning.

'Oh, do stand still, darling.' 'Can you lift your arm?' 'Well, of course you get pins in you if you don't stop wriggling!' 'I won't be much longer.' 'Oh, *don't* bend your knees! Stand straight!' Then she would get up and stare at me again, assessing me as if I were an object, a model or fashion-plate, not her own daughter. I had the same feeling as I now have when being examined by a doctor. Everything would be compounded by the fact that the clothes she was constructing on me, and which I knew

I had, eventually, to wear in public, nearly always made me feel like a complete idiot.

She made me a little two-piece which, although my heart melts when I look at pictures of myself in it now, I disliked intensely at the time. I can still feel its scratchiness even today. It's true that being made to wear particular clothes is not like being beaten or ignored, but always being made to look how my mother wanted me to look was a constant source of anxiety.

This hatred of being stared at resulted in my father only being able to paint one picture of me, when I was about seven. The portrait shows a rather solemn little girl in the hated tam-o'-shanter hat. 'Darling, it makes you look so French!' my mother said. I can remember the feeling of her pulling and pushing the hat with its tight, shiny ridged band, until it was slightly at an angle, then putting her finger under my chin, and crouching down to look at my face straight on; my father's stare was similar as he painted me in his studio, holding out his pencil and measuring every line of my face. 'Don't talk, Pinny . . . just a few minutes more, it won't be long now.'

There was only one occasion when my mother and I argued about clothes and I got the upper hand. She wanted me to model a dress she'd designed. I said that I would do it on one condition – that she buy me a pair of grey divided shorts from Harrods. She agreed. I carried out my side of the bargain, and she carried out hers, even though it must have been almost unbearable for her to see her own daughter in such a hideous garment. I loved those divided shorts. I wore them again and again.

That was my only success.

Once, I had been asked to a fancy-dress party by Rose Dugdale, the terrorist's-moll-in-the-making. I didn't want to go, but my mother, eager to make me a dress, accepted for me. She copied one of the Infanta's dresses from Velasquez's *Las Meninas*, making a grey skirt wired in a semi-circle around my waist, tying a ribbon in my hair, and pinning a pearl brooch to my collar. I can see now how sweet I looked, but I certainly didn't enjoy the party. Most of the children were dressed up as recognizable figures – an Indian, Henry VIII, a milkmaid, a Dutch girl. An Infanta by a painter called – 'What was it? Villosquish? Who?' – prompted puzzled and suspicious whispers.

Dressed as an Infanta, I'm last on the left, second row. Rose Dugdale is in the front, the fifth along.

Another time, my mother set her heart on buying me some pink pumps with a strap across. They were extremely chic, but I didn't want to wear them. We had a terrible row, and my mother must have stormed off or, worse, become tearful and hurt that I refused to allow her to buy them, leaving me in tears myself. I ran to my father and threw myself into his arms. I desperately needed support to stand up to my mother.

'I don't want to have those shoes! I hate them!' I said.

'Oh come along,' he said, in a conciliatory way, taking his red spotted handkerchief out of his pocket to dry my tears before lighting himself up a soothing Woodbine. 'It's not worth getting upset about. It's only a pair of shoes, Pin. I'll come with you and we'll buy them together. You needn't ever wear them. It's just not worth the trouble not getting them.'

We went out and bought them.

He didn't understand that agreeing to buy those shoes felt like selling my soul. Buying and wearing them meant that I became less my mother's daughter and more my mother's little mannequin, less myself and more my mother. I wanted to look different, to be able to say to my mother: 'Look, look, for heavens sake! This is me! Not some clothes-rack!' But whenever she looked at me, she would just say: 'Oh, darling, you must let me cut your fringe.' 'Oh, sweetie, the back of your neck! It's filthy!' As I rarely opposed her directly, I realize now that it was then that I started a campaign of resentment towards her, a deliberate policy of appearing to love her, but deep down feeling nothing for her at all. I would do my duty by her. I would try to help her. I would never let her down or let her know how I felt. My excessive concern for her and my kindness towards her, in later years, were survival techniques to cover up the indifference, born of unhappiness and anger, that I felt underneath.

The ironic result of all this was that as my mother started to dislike me if I wore certain clothes, so I started to dislike her if *she* wore certain clothes. There was a hat and a yellow and brown hairy suit – I called it her 'hedgehog suit' – that I found particularly unattractive, and I would refuse to kiss her if she was wearing it. I would beg her not to wear various things, hoping, I suppose, that were she to put on a full floral skirt, a print blouse and an apron, she would then turn into the cake-baking, lemonade-brewing, picnic-making mother I wanted.

Anne Scott-James, then the fashion editress of the *Sunday Express*, suggested that she write a feature on my mother and me wearing clothes designed by my mother. One Saturday morning – I was about eight – we took the 49 bus to Kensington Gardens to have our photographs taken. The sky was grey and I felt embarrassed changing my clothes behind the trunk of a large plane tree. Everyone walking about was staring. Worse, I hated being pushed around by the photographer.

'Big smile, Victoria!' he shouted. 'Lovely, Janey, super . . . Cheer up Veronica, it'll never happen, think of ice-cream, yummy yummy . . . ! *Don't move!*'

As I stood in the cold, trying to smile, I thought, inside myself: 'You disgusting little creep! Ice-cream! Who do you think I am! I like Marmite and vinegar and sucking lemons and raw garlic! I hate

Another fitting

ice-cream!' Few people knew how vengeful were my inner thoughts.

My mother also approached the editress of *Vogue*, who in turn asked Clare Rendlesham, the 'Young Idea' editor, to come to see her. Between them, they managed to get the man in charge of the children's ranges at Horrocks to agree to a small pilot collection of my mother's work. I was photographed in these clothes in Clare's house in South Kensington, with Nicolette Harrison — who later become Mrs Georgie Fame and eventually jumped off the Clifton Suspension Bridge to her death.

Dressed like
DODOS!

One mother slams out hard at those Olde Worlde Junior Fashions

I'VE been talking to someone with pretty strong views on clothes for daughters. And Janey Ironside is qualified to have strong views. She is herself a professional designer and dressmaker, is married to stage designer and painter Christopher Ironside, and is the mother of a pretty 10-year-old daughter, Virginia.

Mrs. Ironside has been shopping for her daughter's summer clothes. RESULT: She's making nearly all of them herself.

— by —
Anne Scott-James

"The clothes they make for children are simply antediluvian," she says. "The designs seem to have stuck fast 20, 30, even 50 years ago —at any period except our own.

"I don't want to see my child in velveteen dresses with puff sleeves and lace collars (Victorian look), . . . in deep pudding-basin hats (Twenties look), . . . or in coats with military padded shoulders (pre-war look).

"Why can't children's clothes be contemporary? I don't mean grown-up, sophisticated clothes. But I do mean that they should bear a close relation to what their mothers are wearing."

This got a big response from me.

Having endured the sight all winter of my own daughter in a poke bonnet, if you please,

which is about all you can get to go with toddlers' winter coats. I long for some new thinking in little girls' clothes. (Little boys come off much better. It's a man's country.)

☆ ★ ☆

"Tell me the sort of clothes you like for your daughter," I said, "and let's have comments on whether you can get them or not."

"I LIKE (she said) coats with raglan sleeves like my own. (Hard to find and mostly in the expensive ranges.) . . . Bright, plain jerseys and

cardigans (plenty of these), but also never-looking fisherman-knit sweaters like mine (they just aren't made. I have to knit them.)

I LIKE cotton dresses which look contemporary. I like them sleeveless—most children have such pretty shoulders —with the sort of necklines I wear myself. (Very scarce. I make them all at home.)

☆ ★ ☆

I LIKE skirts pleated, gathered, or flared on to waistbands—my daughter hates those bodice tops. Skirts must have pockets, be in bright colours and good prints or plaids. (Possible to find but easier to make because children's fabrics and paper patterns are so much better designed than ready - made garments.)

I LIKE, for shoes, brown strollers, coloured sandals, coloured Grecian house shoes. (All have to be hunted for and

Mrs. Ironside gives Virginia's clothes some of the new fashion details she likes herself. NEW for a Sunday dress: the tartan fabric, three-quarter sleeves.

PICTURES BY HANS WILD

NEW for a cotton dress: the sleeveless line, the horseshoe neck, the flowers tucked into the belt.

NEW for a party dress: the permanently pleated skirt, worn over a waist petticoat like mother's.

Janey and me photographed in Kensington Gardens

Lady Rendlesham was a talented but ruthless fashion dragon and was known, behind her back at *Vogue*, as the Monkey's Paw – not only because she looked like a shrivelled little monkey, but because of the sinister Saki short story (anyone who wished anything while touching the Monkey's Paw would find some horrible thing happening to them). My worst experience was when Lady Rendlesham took me and some other child to the Brighton Pavilion, to be photographed for *Vogue* building a card-house in the Chinese Room. The photographer was the famous Norman Parkinson, who, with his cheeky smile and little embroidered cap, was amiable enough, but Lady Rendlesham was in a filthy mood. She shouted at me in the Brighton train because I had forgotten to bring a vest or a pair of suspenders and I felt terrified and furious. At Brighton Pavilion, the card-house kept falling down, Norman Parkinson kept calling me 'love' and 'darling', which in those days was extremely strange, and I longed to be home with Christopher. When I got back, I rushed into his arms, crying.

I was photographed with my mother in Neville Street for *House Beautiful*. I am smiling and my mother is, as usual, pinning my clothes. I was photographed by the Round Pond, grinning endlessly, until I felt faint. My mother suggested I sit down for a while, but then continue with the photo shoot. I was photographed and photographed, until I was a teenager.

'I don't want to!' I'd say.

'Oh darling, please, just for me!' was the usual wail, and I went along with it.

But however much backing my mother had from the press, the buyers in the shops weren't interested in her designs. My mother had scarlet and black labels made up, saying 'Janey Ironside London'

At Brighton Pavilion, I try to look as if I'm enjoying myself making a card-house that kept falling down.

on them, and took some of her children's clothes' designs to Daniel
Neal to see if they might be interested, but the buyer took one look
and sneered.

'Impossible!' she said. 'I wouldn't touch one of them!'

'Why? French children are dressed in clothes like these!' replied
my mother, with an edge in her voice.

'But that's in France!' replied the buyer, brusquely – a reply that
at the time I would have thought very sensible and agreed with
wholeheartedly.

My father tolerated my mother's business. He liked Janey being at
home, and was well aware of how hard she worked – often until
four in the morning. His only mild complaint was that when he
walked into what he thought was his own drawing-room, he would
be shooed out because there was Lady Bloggs with nothing on, being
fitted.

Like every other man of his era, he wouldn't dream of washing-
up or cooking or shopping, so as well as running her business, my
mother had to do all the housework. To be fair, my father was also
working extremely hard. Four days a week he was teaching life
drawing at the College, and on top of this, in 1952, he was collab-
orating, at home, with his brother Robin, designing the costumes
and sets for the Covent Garden production of Delibes' *Sylvia*, with
Margot Fonteyn and Michael Soames dancing the major roles. (The
brothers had already collaborated in 1947, on the designs and
costumes for the opera *Der Rosenkavalier* at Covent Garden.)

Now Neville Street became even more cluttered. As well as the clothes and bales of material, there were scale models of the proscenium of Covent Garden, with scale figures to match, bits of scenery and drawings balanced on every spare surface.

Robin's contribution to the designs (and his drawback) was that his ideas were not inhibited by any consideration or knowledge of how they could be realized in three-dimensional terms, and his lavishly impractical notions often maddened my father, who had to execute them and ensure that they would work. It was all very well Robin being self-taught and claiming this was the only thing to be, but he relied hugely on Christopher to get himself out of structural scrapes.

After inviting himself to lunch (his refrain went: 'May I make the time-honoured request to share your modest?'), he would come round. I recall him standing over my father, who sat on the sofa with a sketchbook and pencil. Perhaps he wanted to be shown how to draw a hand. Christopher would start, patiently and laboriously, while Robin got more and more impatient and edgy.

'Yes, yes,' he'd say, looking over his shoulder at the drawing, 'I know about *that* bit' — as Christopher began, painstakingly, at the wrist. 'It's the little finger I can't get.'

'But you can't do the little finger until you've got the wrist right,' Christopher would reply with equal irritation as he continued drawing. 'Now, you see, it goes like this, curving *here* . . .'

Downstairs, the driver of Robin's taxi, his only luxury, would ring the bell for the fourth time. 'Oh, yes, I know . . . all right, all right,' Robin would say to Christopher, irritably. 'But hurry up!'

'I can't hurry up,' Christopher would say, firmly. 'It goes like *this*.'

'Yes, yes, yes . . .'

As there was a mutual, but unspoken taboo against quarrelling, Christopher would modify Robin's work with impunity and Robin had no hesitation in altering Christopher's. Sometimes a design would go back and forth between them, each trying to supply what the other couldn't manage. What made Robin particularly difficult to work with was his perfectionism. He found it almost impossible to meet a deadline. He even consulted a doctor about the problem, but he could suggest no cure. Once, when they were already hours late for an appointment to deliver some work to the scene-painters, Christopher became enraged when, on the taxi-journey there, Robin was still painting a small bit of forest that showed through an open window on the set. On arrival at the studios, Robin continued to sit in the back of the cab, painting away with a large drawing-board on his knee. Christopher hopped about on the pavement, counting his money as the clock on the taxi kept clicking up the fare.

'For God's sake, stop! No one in the audience can possibly even see the bits you're now painting!' he protested. Eventually my father ended the scene by emptying the jar of paint water into the gutter.

Sylvia was Frederick Ashton's second ballet, and it was enormously well received by the critics. One wrote that the sets and costumes were 'greeted with prolonged applause by an audience well accustomed to the bare swept boards of modern ballet'. Margot Fonteyn set a Covent Garden record, with thirty curtain calls on the first night; at this performance, which I was allowed to attend as a treat, I was amazed to see both my father and uncle appear on stage to be kissed by Fonteyn, who gave them each a flower from her bouquet.

The next commission was the interior of a small glass facsimile

Harold White

Robin and Christopher in his studio, designing *Sylvia*. Notice the
primitive fire escape peeping out behind the curtains.

of Paxton's great pavilion of 1851 at the Crystal Palace, for the
Festival of Britain. The gnome-like — and increasingly successful
— Hugh Casson secured this job for Christopher and Robin, and it
was also through him that my father designed the fireplace of the
Royal Yacht, *Britannia*.

Although the minuscule Hugh could be a charming and delightful companion, he had too fond an eye for the ladies. I used to go to children's parties given by his daughters, and Hugh would dress up as a monkey or a fortune teller, which delighted everyone but me. I shrank into a corner with terror and started to cry. At the end of the party, Hugh gave the children tiny water-colours. My father once said that Hugh's real talent was for 'sleeping with other men's wives, stamping on other people's faces on his way up the professional ladder, taking credit where it wasn't due, oiling up to royalty – and dashing off the most divine water-colours'.

Perhaps my father was so scathing about Hugh Casson because he was aware that my mother and Hugh often flirted together at parties. That was one of the problems with going out with my mother; she would get rather tipsy and start making eyes at men – who, since she was extremely attractive, were very happy for her to continue. It was certainly partly because of her behaviour that I felt so anxious when my parents went out for the evening – I must have sensed Christopher's trepidation as he stepped out of the door. When they came in later, I would often hear the door of my parents' bedroom click shut and a whispered argument begin.

During the day, they would appear normal enough, each busy in their own work. But at mealtimes there were often cold, foggy silences, when I would sit at the dining-room table, staring at a still life of anemones, painted by my father, which hung on the opposite wall. I swung my legs as I picked at my food. Sometimes, to break the silence, my parents talked in halting French after one or other had uttered that frustrating phrase '*Pas devant les enfants*'.

Once, over lunch, they spoke about drinking.

'Have you ever been drunk?' I interrupted, looking at my mother. She gave a wincing kind of smile.

'I'm afraid so,' she replied, as she cleared the plates away. My father looked extremely uneasy, coughed, and stared at the table.

'What was it like?' I asked.

'I'll tell you when you're older,' she said, smirking. I felt like a child who, on innocently wandering into a lion's cage, is hastily hustled out by the keeper and hears the door behind clang shut.

One of the reasons the atmosphere at home was so tense was because it wasn't just customers in search of dresses who swarmed to our house. I became increasingly aware of the presence of men 'just popping in', and of my father's icy and disapproving looks when he returned from work to find some male – perhaps an apparently innocent character like my mother's cousin, Jonathon – having early drinks with my mother in the sitting-room. It was quite clear to my father – and to me – that there was something going on, even if we were not quite certain what.

Her visitors included our immediate neighbour, a glamorous ex-naval man called Mickey Hodges. Hugh Burden, the actor, lived down the street, and would often meet my mother for tea, and Bill Bergne, the ex-husband of my parents' great friend, Diana Holman Hunt, dropped by rather too often.

There was one trendy young Lord who took my mother out one afternoon, and although I only caught a glimpse of his head through the banisters as he came up the stairs, I still remember my feeling of disgust at the sight of his dark curly hair and the dashing spotted

scarf tied around his neck. There was something dangerously attractive about him that made me realize that he was less of a jolly old
chum who happened to be passing by and more of a predator. And
why did he want only to see my mother and not my father?

These men were always very nice to me, but I never trusted their
friendliness. I could almost read the bubbles over their heads: 'When
will this miserable little pest bugger off to her room?'

At last, at thirty-three years old and with the help of the New
Look, my mother was beginning to realize that even if fashion buyers
were wary of her ideas, she could have a devastating effect on men.

six

SUNGLASSES *Originally sunglasses were worn as protection from the glare of the sun. They were first made of tinted glass in 1885 (before this they were 'goggles' of mica). They became a fashion accessory in the 1930s and 1940s, popularised by Hollywood stars who often wore dark glasses, it is said, both to hide from their fans and to hide their crowsfeet when out in public. They are sold everywhere from Woolworths to Bond Street.*

Janey Ironside, *A Fashion Alphabet*

'How *ghastly*!' was my mother's general reaction to most things that occurred or, indeed, to anything that was about to happen. When I was older and told my mother I was going, say, to the theatre or to the opera, she would screw up her face in anguish and say 'Oh, poor you! How *ghastly*!'

Once, I went with her to buy some buttons in a shop behind Oxford Street. I was seven or eight. I remember looking out of the front window on the top deck of a bus, my mother beside me. We were laughing together hysterically, so much so that she could hardly ask the conductor for the ticket. Outside in the street, I slipped my hand into hers. I had to skip along in order to keep up. She was still smiling. I pulled her hand to my face, kissing the back of it, feeling the slight bumpiness of her wedding ring. She squeezed my hand back and then, releasing it, ruffled my hair.

'Darling,' she said. 'I'm so lucky I had you and not some *ghastly* child.'

One of the many things that my mother found ghastly about married life was family holidays. They epitomized everything that she had found so claustrophobic about her own upbringing and which she feared might entrap her in her present domestic circumstances.

As the eldest child, my mother had felt stifled on the big holidays she had been forced to go on when she was young, sometimes with fifteen cousins, aunts and uncles, in one big country house. At seventeen, she wrote in her diary: 'I know I should enjoy this holiday, but I can't. Mummy and Daddy irritate me so much. I've discovered that the one time I really can't bear Mummy is when she cleans her teeth. She rattles the water about in her mouth and puffs her cheeks out and gurgles and bubbles in the most horrid way. I can't bear Daddy at meal times, he talks with his mouth full, and asks for more before he has finished what he has got, and nearly *always* manages to get a crumb on his chin. I know we're meant to be enjoying ourselves, but I feel horribly lonely. I get sick of everyone here and I can't get away from them, I can go for walks by myself but I always have to come back. I get a desperate feeling of being caged in, closed in by my beastly family. I want to go away, miles away, for some time and then I would appreciate it again, because it's all my own fault. I'm a beastly, selfish, boring fool, but I can't help it.'

She was delighted to go on holiday, with me and my father, to Northumberland to stay with Diana Holman Hunt, whose second husband, David Cuthbert, had inherited a superb Victorian-Gothic, Dobson-designed castle, set in an enormous park full of peacocks, overlooking the Tyne river. I had my own room furnished with sofas, chairs and a great double bed, the sheets and blankets of which were turned down each evening by the unseen hands of servants who lived behind a green baize door. I also had my own bathroom, with a huge bath, worn brass taps and a gigantic threadbare bath towel. In the mornings we came down to breakfast to find, under silver domed covers, kidneys, scrambled eggs, kippers, welsh rarebit and crispy bacon. I had never seen such luxury. Even my father enjoyed himself.

Robin Darwin was also a frequent guest at Diana's castle, to my parents' great pleasure. Once he boasted that he could make a mayonnaise so thick that it would stay in the bowl even if he turned it upside-down.

'I bet you wouldn't risk holding it over your head, Robin,' said Diana, mischievously.

'I most certainly would!' boomed Robin, and took up the challenge at once.

Everyone was delighted when, after a great deal of beating of eggs and olive oil, the great man entered the dining-room with his creation and ceremoniously held it upside-down over his head. Suddenly his hair, glasses, moustache and suit were submerged under a great gloop of cascading mayonnaise. He had not taken account of the fact that when the cook had transferred the mayonnaise from the ceramic bowl to one made of silver, it lost its prehensile grip on the sides.

'My *dear*, it was too, too *weakening*!' tittered Diana when she recounted the story later.

But it was because of her childhood memories that my mother

disliked so much our annual seaside holidays to Littlehampton, where my father had been taken as a child with his mother and nanny, and a place which meant, for me, paddling, sandcastles, donkey rides across the common — the very same donkey rides my father had been on as a child — playing clock golf, or riding on the miniature railway to the nearby town of Rustington.

My grandmother Phyl would pay for us all to stay in the Beach Hotel, a grand seaside pile with a garden that opened straight on to the beach. My mother's verdict was that it was 'an unspeakably awful place with a dinner band'.

I loved this dinner band — the Sidney Barker Trio. I was particularly entranced by Sidney himself, a man with Brilliantined hair and a tiny moustache, who played a small upright piano. As we entered the dining-room, my grandmother, with a slightly regal nod of the head, would announce 'Good evening' to all the other guests. After we had eaten the starter — usually a melon boat skewered with a twirled piece of orange or a grapefruit decorated with a glacé cherry — and before we had been served slices of grey beef, heated by hot Bisto gravy and surrounded by peaked and browned whips of mashed potato, I would be persuaded by my grandmother to go up to the little rostrum and ask Mr Barker to play 'The Skaters' Waltz', 'The Blue Danube' or 'Greensleeves', the only three tunes I knew. He always responded kindly and I would listen, swinging my legs, as I waited for the sweet trolley to come round.

After dinner, there might be a trip to Butlins, then a funfair within walking distance of the hotel, or we might saunter down to the front to look at the lights garlanded up on the lampposts and listen to the swish of the night sea roaring up against the pebbly beach.

In the mornings at the beach, Christopher and I jumped the waves and splashed each other. My grandmother waited patiently for us with bags of plums and eating gooseberries. She would hold out our towels as we stumbled back. 'My goodness, you were clever!' she would say, rubbing me down briskly. 'I thought I saw you *swimming*!'

If my mother had come with us on the holiday – she usually only stayed a couple of nights before fleeing back to London – she rarely made an appearance on the beach. On the occasions when she did, she was so frightened of her skin becoming piebald with the sun as a result of her vitiligo that, however hot it was, she sat on the shore, somewhat sinister among the bathers, under her umbrella, wrapped in a scarf, hat, trousers and long socks. The rest of the time she would spend in the hotel with rather bad grace, picking at her food and, in the afternoons, curled up in the faded chintz covers of a hotel sofa, her nose wrinkling at the cabbagey smell, while she immersed herself in *A la recherche du temps perdu*.

Family holidays with her own parents were duties that even my mother could not wriggle out of. What she found so frustrating about these visits were, first, that there was so little to drink – my grandfather kept his bottle of sherry under lock and key; secondly, that it was so uncomfortable and cold; thirdly, that staying with them was so boring; and, fourthly, that everything about their house was so ugly.

In order to be close to my uncle Anthony, who lived on a fruit farm, my grandfather, when he had returned from Germany and retired in 1950, had bought a 'perfectly *ghastly*' house in Ross-on-Wye.

West Bank was a detached Edwardian villa made of sandstone,

Janey on the Littlehampton beach, wrapped up in long sleeves, scarf, trousers, and with a protective umbrella against the sun's rays

with a huge garden. It was vast — and what my father called 'staggeringly perishing'. Swathed in jerseys, waistcoats and mittens, stout boots and hairy socks, my grandfather would come into a room, in which I might be sitting huddled over an Enid Blyton, march over to the window, fling it open, and then walk out immediately.

He had three interests: chess, crossword puzzles and apples. In the evening, over a glass filled with a frugal couple of centimetres of sherry — my mother disappeared now and again 'for a walk', nipping out to a pub or an off-licence to buy an emergency bottle of something — he sat in a wing chair, puffing and tamping his pipe. After listening to the news and the weather on the Home Service, and shouting to my grandmother – 'It's going to be wet tomorrow, Vio!' – he would say to me: 'Now, are you going to help me with *The Times* crossword?'

As an impatient child, I only saw him as a rather boring but kindly old gentleman. It never occurred to me that later I would bitterly regret not asking him about his Indian experiences, because when he was young he would think nothing of riding into the hills of the North-West Frontier, armed only with a few outriders and the knowledge of twenty-three Indian dialects, and then facing a whole crowd of murderous Pathans with daggers in their mouths. He could diffuse a dangerous situation with fair, kind words, no doubt shot through, although the Pathans did not know it, with the thoughts of Aristotle and Seneca.

The only times my mother perked up on these holidays were when we climbed into the car and went for what I called, with a groan, 'beauty drives'. We would drive miles and miles to the Golden Valley to see Abbey Dore, or to Tintern Abbey, get out, walk about, have tea, and come home.

While we walked round these, to me, tedious ruins – who wants to see bumpy bits of mown grass with four lines of broken brick around them, with the word 'Refectory' written on a post stuck in the middle? – my mother would do her best to engage my interest.

'Oh, darling, can't you just imagine the monks coming down those stairs to have their breakfast? I can almost hear the abbey bells ringing . . .'

Try as I might, I couldn't imagine any beastly monks; it was then my turn to find everything 'ghastly' and my dismal calls of 'When are we going home?' started when we had barely parked the car.

The family holidays that my mother never even considered going on – they were '*so* ghastly' – were our jaunts to Scotland to stay with my headmistress great-aunts, Rene and Nellie. I adored these trips.

My father and I would set off from Neville Street in our second-hand Standard Vanguard, with its damp, leathery smell, and I would sit with his daily box of fifty Woodbines on my lap, ready to light one up for him every quarter of an hour or so as we made our laborious way up the A1. We stayed the night in a salesmen's hotel in York, which smelled of carrots and beer, sometimes enjoying a little escapade – like visiting a wrestling match, or a cartoon cinema – and then drove on to Aviemore, now a flash ski resort but then a grey, grisly, granite town, indistinguishable from all the other grey, grisly, granite towns in Invernesshire.

Every summer, my great-aunts rented the same freezing house in Aviemore, called Balavoulin. The floors were covered with linoleum designed to look like carpet, with painted fringes around the edges; there was a worn bit in the place where I got out of bed. After a compulsory drive in Rene's brown Ford in the pouring rain to see a loch, we returned to a supper of rectangular sausages from a tin, and would all sit in the living-room, bitter with cold and lit only by a single bulb hanging from a flex in the centre of the ceiling. Rene might put the finishing touches to a watercolour (always with brown, green and purple mountains), but usually she just sat in a hard, upright, Mackintosh-style chair, waiting till about 9.30 when we all went to bed.

I can well understand why my mother refused to come. These trips were not smart or amusing and they were devastatingly uncomfortable. I loved them because I loved the wild scenery, the chilly rays of Scottish affection that emanated from my great-aunts, and I adored being with my father alone. We were more like brother and sister than father and daughter, raising our eyebrows to each other when no one was looking, sitting on his bed in giggles over some appalling piece of meanness about the number of baps we were allowed. Safe in my father's affectionate protection, I didn't need my mother. I was quite pleased she had stayed behind.

I was eight when my mother suggested that she and I go to France for a holiday on our own. I was, at first, very excited. It would not only be my first time abroad, but I was flattered that my mother wanted time alone with me. The idea was that we would go on the ferry to Normandy and stay in a village by the sea, Varengeville-sur-mer. I imagined that we might have a happy seasidey time, just the two of us, eating ice-cream, building goblin museums in the sand, like I did with my grandmother when she took us to Littlehampton. Maybe my mother might for once agree to swim.

But as the day of our departure approached, I felt instinctively wary and fearful. I wanted to know why Christopher wasn't coming. He was 'busy' — working on the design for the huge coat of arms for the centrepiece of Whitehall's Coronation decorations, a rococo explosion of finely moulded silver and gilt aluminium. Or perhaps he just didn't want to go to France. I was also anxious because I had never been anywhere with my mother on my own, except to her parents, and I think I caught a whiff of the excitement that filled her when she talked of our trip. Her eyes were bright and a little bit cunning.

She tried to make the expedition sound fun, by telling me that the church near the hotel featured stained-glass windows by Georges Braque, and she explained that Impressionist painters like Monet had painted at Varengeville, as well as Corot, Boudin and Matisse. Writers such as Victor Hugo, Dumas, Gide, Beckett and Guy de Maupassant and the musician Offenbach had set up home there, she said. In the village itself was a house designed by Sir Edward Lutyens. I would love it. But I didn't like the sound of any of these strange men, Impressionists or not — whatever they were. My mother booked the tickets and checked her wardrobe — and mine — rather too assid- uously. And I became more nervous at the absence of the familiar and now reassuring phrase: 'How *ghastly*!' My mother appeared to be looking forward to our holiday. Something must be wrong.

On the ferry to Dieppe, we had lunch at a communal table, where I ate my first banana. Everyone watched me as I peeled it and sank my teeth into it, like Eve tasting the forbidden fruit. Disgusting! I spat it out. The whole venture was starting to become alarming. Boats, Impressionists, foreign languages, Lutyens, lunch with strangers, bananas — whatever next?

We took a bus from Dieppe to Varengeville and found our hotel, an Edwardian chalet-style villa perched on a cliff-top. We shared a little room and, after we had unpacked, we went for a walk before supper. Within five minutes, any hope of my having an enjoyable time was ruined. Looking over the cliff-top, we saw, on the sand below, the body of a huge white horse, already beginning to swell and covered with flies. It had apparently leaped, crazed, over the cliff to its death, a few days before. I couldn't stop imagining it just at the moment before it plunged to its death, mad with terror.

For me, this horse was a premonition. When I looked down at the beach, it was no longer a place where I wanted to play — I imagined every grain of sand soaked in the poor beast's fear-filled blood. This, I knew, would never have happened in Littlehampton, where I imagined kindly deck-chair attendants would have organized for the body to be removed for a quiet burial before anyone could see it. I wanted to be as far from the beach as possible, as far from the hotel, as far from Varengeville and even France itself, to be relieved of the noise of the terrified horse's galloping hooves which thundered in my brain.

With this tragic image firmly fixed in my head, and wanting to get home as quickly as I could to Neville Street and Christopher, I held on tightly to my mother's hand as we walked back to the hotel and into the dining-room for dinner. We had not even started our first course before I was aware that my mother's attention was elsewhere. A young man had entered to eat on his own. He was dark, extremely attractive, and he couldn't take his eyes off our table.

The following day, we were sitting on the beach (our backs to the horse, of course) when he approached us, holding a Rolex camera. I remember, even at eight years old, feeling faintly flattered. But it was not me he was really interested in.

'May I take some photographs of your daughter?' he asked my mother, in French. 'She is a very pretty little girl. And so well-dressed.'

Pierre 'had a perfect young man's body; tall, perfectly proportioned, wide shoulders, slender waist and long legs. He was extremely attractive and I felt that dreaded lurch of the heart which normally spells trouble,' my mother wrote in a journal. After he had crouched down on the rocks with his camera, squinted through the lens at me and snapped his camera a few times, my mother and he started to talk. She told him that she was in the fashion business and designed and made my clothes herself. He said he was a student awaiting conscription, and that he was to be joined by his parents before they went on to the South of France. He asked what she enjoyed doing on holiday. She replied that she liked sightseeing, and buildings and the countryside, all of which would be impossible on this trip. But he said: 'Not at all. If you will allow me, I will take you to see an interesting little church, at least. When could you go?'

The following day, my mother left me with a little French girl and her family while she and Pierre went off to the church. 'Pierre was in shorts and Roman sandals and I was in jeans,' she wrote. 'He was quiet, though pleasant. His eyelashes were long, his expression was gentle. I congratulated myself on finding such an agreeable companion, in spite of the difference in our ages, which must be well over ten years. It was no good pretending not to realise that we were attracted to one another. The little Norman church was charming. A choral rehearsal was in progress so we sat on a pew at the back and waited until it was time to go back.'

While my mother was enjoying this deliciously thrilling escapade, I was distraught. I had been abandoned on the beach with a group of foreign people with whom I could not communicate and the little girl spent the day putting crabs into an empty bucket. I could not bear to imagine their agony, clawing desperately at one another in their attempts to find water and escape from the baking sun. The moment I saw my mother, I burst into tears and begged her never to leave me again.

She didn't — but she still saw Pierre every night after I had gone to bed. To my great relief, I discovered that this poisonous blight on our holiday would be leaving the day before we were due to return to London. But our final day together was not spent on the beach, as I'd hoped. Janey dragged me off to see yet another Norman church. A service was taking place, and everyone in the congregation was dressed in black. Inside the church, lying in a grotto of white flowers, lay a sad, small coffin.

It contained the body of a little girl of eight who had been drowned at sea. Once again, I was in tears.

Janey and me on the boat at Dieppe, on the way home
from Varengeville

I had no idea what went on between Pierre and my mother, but on the boat my mother said: 'By the way, darling, there's no need to say anything about Pierre to Christopher. He wouldn't understand.'

I managed to keep this secret until some photographs of me and Janey on the beach at Varengeville arrived for my mother.

'Who took these?' asked my father, warily. It was then that the word 'Pierre' popped out of my mouth.

'And who is Pierre?' asked my father, grimly.

For days afterwards the atmosphere in the house was sour with suspicion and resentment, choked with unspoken accusations of betrayal. Once, my mother came into the sitting-room and said 'Hello'. My father remained impassive behind his copy of the *Evening Standard*. She said: 'I said "hello",' but there was no answer. She looked at me imploringly, then left the room.

'Oh, Christopher,' I begged. 'Do say hello to mummy!'

He put the *Standard* down and I saw not my father but a stranger. His face was cold and unhappy. Seeing my alarm, he tried a smile.

'Don't worry, Pin,' he said. 'It's nothing. Go upstairs and get into your dressing-gown.' I got up slowly, dragging my feet. 'Go on,' he said. 'Don't worry. Everything's fine.'

I went upstairs to my room as quietly as possible lest my footsteps conceal any reassuring sound of reconciliation. My ears were prickling with listening. All I heard was the sound of my father's steps to the kitchen, the slam of a door and my father's faint voice: 'Janey . . . Virginia . . . upset . . .'

My mother rattled some saucepans and said: 'It really was nothing, Christopher . . . Don't go on about it. Supper will be ready in a minute.'

Some composure had been achieved by the time I was called down again. At table, when my father asked for the salt, it was passed to him; when my mother said that she was sorry the lamb chops were burned, my father said they tasted fine. Apart from that, nothing was said. The meal was over in minutes.

While my mother washed up, my father suggested he and I play a game of L'Attaque and I got out my little stool and arranged the pieces. When he went to the kitchen to make the coffee, my mother came up and sat behind me in the red armchair and put out her hand to stroke my head and said: 'Oh, Pinny Bean, I'm sorry . . .' But I didn't want to forgive her. I hated her, I hated her, I hated her. I wished she would go away and leave Christopher and me in peace.

I had learned for the first time about betrayal. I realized what was behind these terrible and endless silences and these indigestible stony-faced meals. I realized that my parents' marriage was desperately unhappy.

One day that year, after the holiday, I remember looking in a mirror and seeing my serious little face, framed by my dark bobbed hair, and saying to myself: 'I am eight, and I am grown up.'

seven

PARIS   *Perhaps this is the moment to discuss that endless question 'Why does Paris lead Fashion?' Why has Paris got this magic power of producing or appropriating the best fashion designers in the world? The main reason I am sure is that the French are as a nation highly sensitive to fashion atmosphere — they are quick to sense a change or an idea and to express it in terms immediately acceptable to the world, whether in painting, in dresses, or in their surroundings (apart from their own homes which for some unknown reason are usually hideous).*

Janey Ironside, *Fashion as a Career*

O ne Sunday, Robin Darwin asked us all to lunch. He lived in a beautiful little eighteenth-century pavilion on the banks of the Thames in Isleworth, in the grounds of Syon House, courtesy of his friend, the Duke of Northumberland. The park had been designed by Capability Brown but was now a romantic expanse of unkempt, raggy lawns, great avenues covered with weeds and rampaging roses, punctuated by broken glasshouses. His home was originally designed by Robert Adam as a boathouse but had been converted into a proper house, all on one floor.

As we got into the car to set off, my father groaned and lit up a Woodbine. Then he pulled out the choke and started the engine. My mother, I noticed, was not saying 'How *ghastly*!' but was sparkly and flirtatious. She was looking particularly glamorous, with her big red lipsticked mouth; she wore tapered black trousers and a scarf tied jauntily around her neck.

When we arrived, Robin welcomed us into his circular drawing-room. It had a high, domed ceiling decorated with classical motifs and it overlooked the river and the grass and trees on the opposite bank. My father and mother drank Martini while I had orange juice. Robin Darwin's Italian housekeeper had cooked a delicious meal — the unusual sweet, alcoholic whiffs of Marsala or boiling vermouth and cream always evoked Robin's house, used as I was, at mealtimes, to the smell of boiled potatoes or boiled carrots.

After lunch, which was accompanied by a great deal of wine, I asked if I could get down and then slipped from the table to play with the housekeeper's four-year-old illegitimate daughter. (A child without a father was a real curiosity in those days, and we all wondered whether Robin Darwin himself hadn't played some role in her existence.)

When, later, I joined the adults for a walk through the crumbling and overgrown grounds of the park, my father seemed rather depressed; my mother and Robin Darwin were deep in bantering conversation, she, giggling and funny, while Robin looked big and immensely confident. Back at the pavilion, I spent a few moments on my own, standing under the weeping willow on the embankment, smelling the damp river and thinking, until, at about five o'clock, we drove home.

There was a queer silence in the car. Without the presence of Robin, we all felt small and ordinary. Then my father said: 'We-ell, if you're sure it's what you want to do . . .'

'What *do* you want to do?' I asked.

My mother turned to me in the back, her breath smelling of white wine.

'Robin's offered me the job of being Professor of the Fashion School!' she said. Her eyes were bright. 'What do you think? You're older now than last time . . . I'd be home in the holidays . . .'

'*Professor!*' I replied, astonished. 'But what about Madge?'

My father laughed. 'Robin said — and I quote — "We disagreed. She threatened to resign and I accepted her resignation." Typical!'

My mother turned back to me, like a conspirator. 'Oh, darling, do you think I *could*?' she asked. 'It just seems so incredibly *daunting* . . . but . . .'

I saw so little of my mother as it was, and I knew — as my father did — that she would take this job whether we liked it or not, so I couldn't have cared less what she did. If it would make her happier, then fine. The result was that in 1956, the same year that Bill Haley released 'Rock Around the Clock', my mother became Professor of Fashion at the Royal College of Art at a salary of £1,800 a year, considerably more than my father could earn in two.

My only comment in my diary was: 'Had quite a good music lesson. Did some prep. Got new bottle of ink. Latin exam tomorrow — eeek! Heard about mummy being made professor at RCA — now it's official. Cold began to go. Felt dead tired and had splitting headache (Ugh!).'

I still had constant headaches.

*

On the day her appointment was announced, my mother bought every newspaper she could find, spreading them all out on the dining-room table, turning the pages and scouring the columns for a mention. In each one was a piece about her new job, with pictures and interviews.

For a married woman with a child and only a little experience of teaching to become a Professor of Fashion was an extraordinary achievement. The whole idea of a female 'professor' was considered so outlandish as to be almost ludicrous in those days, and prompted a great deal of tittering among Janey's friends. True, Madge Garland was a woman and had run the Fashion School, but she wasn't married, was much older than my mother and was rumoured to be a lesbian. (When she had married Sir Leigh Ashton of the V&A, a homosexual, it all was, according to one of her students, 'a dreadful affair'.) This wasn't the same thing at all. My mother's appointment was revolutionary.

In the *Daily Mail*, Iris Ashley, the woman's editress, wrote a piece about her, Muriel Forbes devoted an entire page to her in *The Times*, and Winefride Jackson, the fashion editress, discussed the whole phenomenon in the *Daily Telegraph*.

'It's been a wonderful time in the world of dressmaking,' my mother was quoted as saying to one journalist, 'but I shan't be altogether sorry to leave it behind. Dealing with people all the time, even such charming customers, is very wearing. And then I'm so looking forward to my new post. I love working with the very young who are still enthusiastic and excited about what they're doing. I have the greatest admiration for art students – they're so full of life and spirits and I'm always lost in wonder as to how they manage, for the most part on

SHE'S A PROFESSOR—
OF FASHION

By ELSIE M. SMITH

And she's a housewife, mother and business woman, too.

MEET the new Professor of Fashion Design whose work can have an important influence on clothes of the future.

"Professor" sounds altogether too formidable a title for a slender young woman with a gamine-like face—eyes large and dark, mouth generous, dark hair cropped short.

But 38-year-old Mrs. Janey Ironside is well qualified to take up this responsible post at London's Royal College of Art although she follows in the illustrious footsteps of one of our leading fashion experts, Mrs. Madge Garland, who retires this year.

For one thing, she does not go entirely as a "new girl." She was Mrs. Garland's assistant at the College a few years ago. She has also had many years' experience of running her own fashion business and now has a title-studded clientele.

CAMOUFLAGE

"I started designing and making my own dresses when I was about 17," she told me. "I became so interested that when I had to think about a career I decided it must be something to do with fashion."

She took a course in tailoring, dressmaking and designing (not at the Royal College, which had not then a fashion section) before getting her first job as a designer with a small wholesale fashion house.

Then came the war and in a wave of patriotism, she deserted fashion for a factory. This took her to Leamington where she had to inspect brakes for any faults in construction. "A bit monotonous" she laughed, "and I never discovered what sort of transport the brakes were for."

At about that time she met and married Christopher Ironside, a young artist whose talents were being used on war-

'A RECENT portrait of Mrs. Ironside by her husband, Christopher.

time camouflage, and in 1944 their daughter was born.

Mrs. Ironside is typical of the modern woman who manages successfully to lead a "double life." She lives with her husband and daughter in a tall, narrow, Kensington house which also contains a studio for her husband, a fitting room for her clients and a room for her ten work-girls.

During the day she attends to the needs of her 150 to 200 regular customers, and the hustling Americans who dash in with lengths of English tweed to be made up in a week. At night she dons an apron and cooks the evening meal for husband and daughter.

At the Royal College she will have 25 in her care, 25 carefully selected students who take a three-year course, ranging from the designing of a garment, the making of the paper pattern, to the actual cutting out and making up.

"But," says Mrs. Ironside, "the aim is to produce good designers, for which, at present, there are more jobs than students to fill them."

GRECIAN GOWNS

Her present concern, however, are the dresses for the wedding of Princess de Chimay's daughter, Louise, in London on July 12, which will be one of the most fashionable of the season.

The bridal gown is a lovely full-skirted affair in creamy brocade embroidered with gold roses, but the bridesmaids' dresses are an expression of Mrs. Ironside's originality in design. Instead of the picture dresses of most London society weddings, she has created Grecian-style gowns in draped white silk jersey.

Classic styles are indeed those she favours. And before we parted she gave me this tip for the woman who strives for smartness: "Choose plain styles of good design, good colours, good material and good fit. With these a woman cannot fail to be smart." ▪

One of the announcements of Janey's new post.

about tuppence a year, to put up such a wonderful appearance —
somehow they always manage to have the latest thing in accessories!

'Of course they're not all geniuses. There are always the plod-
ders, the idlers, the just plain dim. But in every bunch there's invariably a shining talented one that you know will reach the top some
day. And it's wonderful to feel that you can help those talents unfold,
guide them to the right path, and then later on watch that promise
fulfil itself in the great world outside.'

When a journalist from the *Daily Mirror* asked her what her aim
was, she boldly replied that she wanted 'to promote an internation-
ally accepted new English look'.

'How do you mean?' he asked.

'Well, French, Italian and American clothes all have an individual
good look,' she said. 'But the general view of the English look at
the moment is of rather dowdy tweeds and Cashmere twin-sets worn
by horse-faced women.'

'And you want to change that?' he asked.

'Yes'.

'Hmm,' he replied. 'Well, thank you anyway.'

When, later, the 'English' look swept America and Europe, he
must rather have wished he'd printed her prescient words.

It was now my mother, not Madge, who sat behind the huge desk
in the daunting office on the first floor of Ennismore Gardens. And
it was not my mother who quaked when she set foot there, it was
her own staff and students who were on the quaking end of things.
Even I felt rather over-awed when I came to see her.

Janey sitting in her office, with the fuchsia wallpaper clambering behind her

The first thing my mother wanted to do was to redecorate Madge's office, to make it look chic and fashionable rather than like the salon of some old French dowager. Unfortunately, Robin Darwin insisted on choosing the new wallpaper — a riotous fuchsia paper clambering all over the walls, which my mother abhorred because it made her feel as if the fuchsias were clambering all over her. She dumped Madge's old, pink velveteen curtains and replaced them with glazed white chintz which hung from cool brass rings on a white painted pole.

My mother had always dressed fashionably, but now it was essential that she should look immaculate at all times. As far as her face went, she decided to trade on the drawbacks of her vitiligo and, rather than try to bring colour to her skin, she continued to keep out of the sun and cultivated a dead-white appearance. Her ashen face was interrupted by an enormous gash of red lipstick and surrounded by gamine, spikily cropped hair, dyed jet-black. It was small wonder that Mary Quant's husband described her as having a 'vampire look'.

Her aim was for a black, red and white face – a 'rather negative beauty look' as she described it. But however amazingly chic she undoubtedly looked – the papers compared her to Audrey Hepburn or Leslie Caron – to me, my mother seemed like someone out of the Addams family, a kind of unnatural ghoul.

She chose her College clothes with care. Her much-admired fashion innovation in the early days was a V-necked, hand-knitted, cable-stitch jersey made to dress length. She also bought a man's long V-necked cashmere sweater from Marks and Spencer and had it dyed black; she wore it with a black skirt and rows of pearls. Ridiculously simple as it sounds, this was then a new idea. She ironed her clothes regularly and maintained her cardigans' perfect shapes by keeping them under the carpet during the night. Sometimes – particularly when she had a hangover – she would wear dark glasses, which added to her remote and immaculate image, making her resemble an Italian film star. Although she occasionally wore dark grey, dark brown and scarlet, she nearly always dressed in black. ('I feel happiest, most myself, in black,' she said once.)

One fashion journalist asked her how women should dress. 'As Dior said, a woman should always use red, white or black if she wants to be attractive to men,' she said, smiling and staring rather pointedly at the journalist's brown two-piece.

Every morning, she left for the office with her eyes glued to the ground. This was partly because she had a horror of meeting anyone's eyes and partly because she couldn't bear to see how utterly drab everyone looked. She deplored the fact that although there were cheap clothes for everyone in the shops, no one had the imagination to wear them properly.

'They *will* wear what I call "desperates" rather than "separates" and I can hear them thinking: "Oh well, I don't think they look too bad together" – but they *do*,' she used to moan.

In my mother's first month at the Fashion School, a Fashion Advisory Committee was assembled to help her cope. It consisted of a glossy fashion magazine editor, the editor of a textile trade magazine and a couturier, but, to my mother's dismay, no one from the mass-production end of the business. Her main aim was to train designers to meet the demands of the wholesale and mass-production industries and she needed advice on how to set about it.

Realizing this ambition was one of my mother's major contributions to the world of fashion during her time as Professor of Fashion. She asked Hans Schneider, head of the fashion department at Marks and Spencer, to talk about mass production to the students; she enlisted the support of the Wallis brothers of Wallis shops, and she badgered them all to take students to work in their businesses during the holidays. She virtually invented the concept of work-placement schemes.

She also assembled an excellent team. A bright ex-student, Joanne Brogden, became her assistant, and she found a splendid secretary, Mrs Herbert-Smith, a kindly and efficient sergeant-majorly giant of a woman who would have been perfectly at ease in the ATS. Roger

Brines taught tailoring, Irene Elfer taught mass-production methods of garment construction, Miss Frankl taught toile-cutting for couture, Bernard Nevill, who designed for Liberty, set the students projects and Peter Shepherd taught hat-design.

When Janey arrived, there were seventy applicants for twenty-five places a year, the vast majority of whom had been trained at another art school already. It was essential that she made the right choices, and the reason she was so successful was because she had an almost psychic gift of being able to tune into whatever was 'in the air' at the moment, and had an uncannily accurate idea of what would be 'in the air' in the future.

She regarded fashion as more of an atmosphere than anything else, and she knew that to be successful you must not only be attuned to that atmosphere, but have the extra-sensory perception that means that you actually *know*, rather than guess, what is to happen next. This didn't mean being able to foretell mundane things like whether skirts would be long or short or whether waists would be in next season, but, rather, having a feeling for colour, for texture, for outline, and a general certainty about what was contemporary in everything from office buildings to hats.

A student's design didn't have to be elaborate for her to be drawn to it. If my mother could see some kind of spark of originality or energy in the scruffiest portfolio, she insisted on interviewing the student who had sent it in. She picked rough diamonds with talent, not girls from finishing schools. People from the North in those days were considered beyond the pale and were never given a chance, but my mother welcomed the likes of Anthony Price, a farmer's boy from Yorkshire, and Ossie Clark from Salford and gave them an opportunity to use the College as a showcase. Then she persuaded leaders of the fashion industry to hire them.

In the late fifties, she wrote: 'Class has always influenced fashion in Britain and the working-class influence has been strong. They have a wider outlook, are inventive and are not hidebound by convention. Indeed, one of the best results of the social revolution in Britain since the Second World War has been the release of many young designers to the world. By a system of local and government grants, young people are enabled to go to art schools and colleges and to have freedom to experiment. Before the war, most of the people who are now well-known designers would probably have been maids in other people's houses, miners or working in shops, and would never have had a chance to show what they could do. But now they have this chance. People have frequently asked me, especially foreigners, what my secret is, producing all these bright people. The answer is there is no secret. It's the social revolution. There are no class barriers in design.'

After she had managed to wangle special qualification exemptions for highly talented young people in whom she detected a spark of brilliance, she took on all kinds of unlikely students, from Norman Bain, a librarian from Glasgow who had had no art-school training at all, to Hylan Booker, a black US airman who couldn't draw properly and whose sketches had nothing to do with fashion, but whose sculptural scrawlings and very personality made her say: 'Let's give him a chance.'

Janey did away with all the white glovery of Madge, didn't ask her students questions like 'Have you ever been to Ascot?' and told them to forget about Jane Austen and, instead, read Jack Kerouac

– but only if they wished. She impressed them from the very start of her reign when she was interviewed on *Woman's Hour* and chose, as her favourite record, Duke Ellington's 'Sleepy River'.

Most of her students worshipped Janey, and their adoration gave her confidence. No longer did she have to bite her tongue and be polite all the time, as she did when she was a little dressmaker or Madge's assistant. At last she could say what she really thought. She developed a regal presence that some students found daunting. The late Bill Gibb, one of her students, said that she first stalked round you, with this 'incredible aura'. Then, if she decided you passed some test in her head, you were OK. She only had to say 'We-ell' and the students would know at once that whatever they'd designed hadn't come off. She had an alarmingly cool gaze. When she said 'Very nice', it could mean 'Very nice' or it could just as calmly mean 'Not very nice'. All depended on the nuance in her voice.

She also possessed a disconcerting frankness. When Ossie Clark, who was doing a part-time course in the Silver and Jewellery Department, proudly showed her a brooch that he had designed, she stared at it rather coldly and said: 'Yes, very charming. But it does remind me of a dental plate.' And when Hylan presented a design for a wedding dress, she pursed her lips and said: 'Hylan, that's the most beautiful wedding dress for someone getting married at fifty for the first time.'

Fashion was not taken seriously in Britain in the late fifties. Men – and many women – sneered at women who were fashionable and called them stupid sheep. There was a widely held view that designers got together in Paris, dreamed up some new piece of nonsense in a dark cellar and then inflicted it on a foolish public who

would follow their ideas slavishly, however ludicrous they were –
leaving the designers to howl with conspiratorial laughter and rub
their hands as the money rolled in. My mother always pointed out
that those who sneered were themselves slaves to fashion – or,
rather, to an *outworn* fashion. Those middle-aged men who criticized
young men in tight jeans had themselves been censured for wearing
Oxford bags by their fathers, whose own legs were encased in
Edwardian stove-pipes. When men said that women's fashions were
impractical, she drew their attention to distinguished generals in the
eighteenth century who conducted campaigns and led charges
corseted and wearing make-up, like Wolfe's soldiers who scaled the
Heights of Abraham in tight white breeches, tight scarlet jackets and
bearskins. And people who complained about the 'decadent' look of
lipstickless young girls wearing black stockings forgot that only
twenty years back black stockings and no make-up had been the hall-
marks of the innocent English schoolgirl.

Until she started as Professor at the Fashion School, my father
and I never quite realized that, for my mother, good design meant
much, much more than just good design. Good design and fashion
for Janey were moral imperatives. Good design was more important to her than my father, me or her entire family. It was her reason
for living.

She came home, cooked the supper, read the paper, kissed me
goodnight and laid out my clothes, but each night she had only one
thing on her mind: to get back to the College and her talented
students.

Thorstein Veblen once said that the need for dress was
'eminently a higher or spiritual need' – and my mother needed

the spiritual food of fashion to keep her going. She once wrote: 'Fashion in clothing is one of the great living arts of civilisation; self-decoration is a fundamental human urge. Fashion is contemporary life and history on a personal scale. Its language is not only interesting but important.'

When my mother joined the Royal College, I used to take the bus from school to Knightsbridge twice a week. I walked up by the Brompton Oratory, through the graveyard and along to her office in Ennismore Gardens.

The T-shaped drawing-room had been turned into an enormous work-room filled with students who were cutting, measuring and sewing. Dressmakers' dummies stood in corners, wearing half-pinned suits, and there was the crisp smell of freshly cut material, mixed with the dusty whiff of French chalk. The rhythmic treadles of sewing-machines purred away, a background to the deep crunch-crunch sound of fabric being chopped on cutting tables with pinking scissors. Various students said hello to me, but I rarely talked to them, being both sulky and shy.

I would slouch into the office with my music case and kiss Janey hello. Nearly always, she would appraise me, a look of despair coming over her face. 'Darling . . . !' she would say, her eyes becoming all vulnerable and squishy. 'Your neck! You *must* wash it!' Or it would be: 'Your knees!' Or: 'We must get rid of that cardigan! I hadn't noticed, but it's all out of shape at the back, and the buttons . . . !'

In the school holidays, which were longer than the College

holidays, I often had lunch in the Royal College of Art's Senior Common Room, a huge private dining-and drawing-room for college staff and 'extraordinary members' like Francis Bacon and E. M. Forster. The Common Room came to play an important part in the life of the College. Housed in two large rooms – one an old ballroom – on the ground floor of 21 Cromwell Road, full of marbled and gilt columns and two fine eighteenth-century fireplaces, it was very dear to Robin Darwin's heart. It was run on gentlemen's club lines: the wearing of ties was obligatory, no draught beer was allowed (too vulgar), and all drinks were served by Robin Darwin's manservant, a Jeeves-like character known as Mr George.

There were many more staff than in the pre-Robin Darwin days and since he was a tremendous gourmet who took regular gastronomic trips to France and knew everything there was to know about wine, the lunches were more than respectable.

I stood with my mother, drinking orange squash, while everyone else sat about with Scotch or gin and tonic; then all the painting staff assembled in the dining-room. Ron Carter had designed (and the College had made) all the dining-room furniture, and on the long so-called 'painters' table' were placed the set of salt, pepper and mustard pots in the form of silver chessmen designed by Philip Popham, also made at the RCA.

My mother and I usually tried to sit near the window. We were rarely joined by anyone else. Only painters and their guests could sit at the painters' table – Robin Darwin made sure of that. Painters were the aristocrats. Robin believed that the fine arts gave birth to the applied arts, so although Mary Fedden was allowed at the painters' table (the only woman), her husband, the distinguished

Robin Darwin eating in the Royal College of Art Common Room's
dining room

lithographer and painter, Julian Trevelyan, could only sit at the painters' table by invitation, since he taught at the Printing School. But I saw Francis Bacon there, and Ruskin Spear, with his huge beard, and Robert Buhler, Carel Weight and Rodrigo Moynihan, head of the Painting School. Every day, they would all proceed to get enormously drunk – or so it seemed to me.

The mood was bohemian, the room reeked of cigars and wine. Everyone was having affairs, and the cry was for self-fulfilment. 'I am an artist, I must be true to my desires, while the rest of the world is trapped in loveless marriages' was pretty much the painters' credo.

I always tried to get a seat with my back to them, because I didn't like them looking at me and leering.

After lunch, the painters staggered into the drawing-room, with its navy blue ceiling peppered with gold stars, and there we sat drinking coffee out of tiny white cups – again, all College-designed – and watched the painters sleeping off their lunch in the huge sofas and leather armchairs. John Minton might walk by, or Edward Ardizzone, the illustrator – and they might stop and have a brief chat with my mother. I found it all rather intimidating.

At twelve, I was old enough now to put my foot down when it came to appearing in my mother's dress shows. I certainly had no desire to have anything to do with her first show, about which she became extremely anxious. She so wanted it to be different.

At the time, dress shows were very conservative and followed a formal pattern. First of all, there were the day clothes, dresses and light suits, then tailored suits and coats, then beach and leisure clothes, afternoon dresses and cocktail dresses. Evening wear was followed by a wedding dress as a finale. My mother had to stick to this routine up to a point, but she courageously veered from tradition at her début show by sending out an invitation that had, rather than the usual formal lettering on a white background, a chic Japanese theme to it.

She got her old work-girls to make her a dress of black and white spotted organza, and after weeks of preparations it all went ahead. Robin Darwin was at his most genial, sitting through the entire event, applauding. When a journalist asked him if he thought it had been successful, he replied 'Yes'. (When the same journalist asked him if he thought *he* had been successful, he replied: 'Magnificently successful. Who could deny it?')

All my grandmother said as she climbed into a taxi in her hat and astrakhan coat − she'd been asked to an afternoon dress-rehearsal − was: 'Well, Janey's certainly very clever, but do you think *anyone* will wear those clothes?'

Afterwards, we all went to have supper in a penthouse in Gloucester Road owned by a great supporter of my mother, Hans Juda, who ran *Ambassador* magazine. It wasn't a happy occasion. My father seemed slightly uncomfortable about the fuss, and my mother drank too much. For quite a few days afterwards, she suffered from a post-adrenalin depressive hangover, even though the show had received rave reviews in all the papers. Still, she had got over her first hurdle. She had proved she was up to the job.

It was after this show that my mother embarked on a routine which she maintained until she left − giving the students a 'thank-you' champagne party afterwards. I was dragooned to hand round drinks and crisps and nuts, gritting my teeth as everyone said 'Oh, you can tell she's Janey's daughter!' 'You must be taken for sisters!' 'Aren't you lucky to have such an efficient little helper!' Luckily, no one could read the furious words inside the bubbles above my head.

As the daughter of the Professor of Fashion at the Royal College of Art, it was even more important to my mother than ever that I was immaculately dressed. I continued to be sent to school in uncomfortably fashionable clothes, while everyone else looked perfectly normal. My worst humiliation came when the first 'sack' dress appeared in 1957, a look that caused as much controversy as the miniskirt in the 1960s.

The 'sack' look was originally introduced by the Spanish designer, Balenciaga, but it was Dior who took it over and publicized it. The general effect was of a fairly loose but straight garment tapering to below the knees.

It was a Saturday, and we were having an afternoon concert at the school, in which I was due to play in a chamber trio, having been persuaded by Christopher to continue my music lessons. That morning, the headlines in all the papers were along the lines of 'What ridiculous clothes will Paris designers think of next!', showing cartoons of the 'sack' as a grotesquely ballooning affair.

To my horror, my mother immediately insisted on running a 'sack' dress up for me to appear in at the concert.

'I can't possibly wear it!' I pleaded. 'Everyone will laugh at me!'

'Don't be silly, it's terribly smart!' said my mother.

'But Rene will have hysterics! And what will my friends say? They'll laugh at me. I really don't want to wear it.'

I arrived at school with the hated dress covered by a coat. Even the rigid, stone-faced Rene could not resist commenting when she saw what I was wearing. 'Is this really what your mother wanted you to appear in?' she asked. When I said it was, she looked extremely disapproving. My friends, who wore full petticoated skirts and little jerkins, or plain summer dresses, all giggled at me behind my back. When I hobbled on to the stage, the parents clapped and laughed, turning to compliment my mother who had, for once, turned up at a school event. I felt a complete fool.

My mother was working so hard that our family life was almost non-existent. I buried myself in getting top marks at school, and Christopher buried himself in his own work. He was teaching life drawing at the Royal College of Art and, on Wednesdays, at Maidstone School of Art, where Quentin Crisp posed as a model. Quentin would occasionally come for supper, and I sat staring at him, alarmed by his extraordinary appearance, his bouffant lavender hair, his make-up and his camp manner. I was particularly astonished when he declared: 'Love has genuinely turned out to be a mistake. If I were asked what the main causes of the downfall of the world were, I would certainly list love as one of them.' (After listening to so many marvellous stories and *bon mots* in the train going down to Maidstone, my father encouraged Quentin to write his first book, *The Naked Civil Servant*, which transformed him from a nude male art-school model to a sultan of style.)

My uncle Robin was also causing a great deal of anxiety. He was trying all kinds of drugs, especially ones that induced hallucinations, and came round to tell us about his experiments. Although my father laughed at the time, I knew he was worried underneath.

Once, under the influence of mescaline, Robin became captivated with a cabbage that lay on his kitchen table. Obsessed with the vegetable's dazzling shape and colours, he had drawn a meticulous picture of it at four in the morning, before he went to sleep. When he woke up, he found he had executed an exquisite drawing – of a cabbage.

On another mescaline trip, he took a taxi to the Embankment, got out and stared at the water, mesmerized by its radiance, until the taxi driver, certain that my uncle was on the verge of suicide, came out of his cab and said: 'It's not worth it, guv. 'Op in the cab and I'll take you 'ome for nuffink.'

Robin didn't look after himself. He rarely ate, he stayed up till dawn, with the aid of all kinds of pills, and then slept all day. He was chronically short of money. His only extravagances were taxis and the occasional meal out. When my father protested that he should learn to cook, Robin replied that if he didn't go out some days, he would stay at home working in his dressing-gown and 'go funny'. He was so overdrawn that whenever he got a cheque he would assign it to Christopher and get him to give him the cash.

His rich friends tried their best to help. John Rothenstein even persuaded him to become a member of the Athenaeum, but Robin's idea of black tie was to wear a double-breasted grey flannel jacket over my father's dyed black, black jeans and black espadrilles. With a white shirt and a black bow tie he looked acceptable by artificial

Christopher's
drawing of Robin, who
wanted to know how
to draw someone
praying for money

light – or so he claimed. Unfortunately, the Athenaeum did not agree.

Robin's situation was worrying enough; the fact that my mother had less and less time for her family was even more so. My mother was increasingly out on a limb; I was growing up fast and my suspicions that my mother was a woman with feet of clay when it came to parenting were being confirmed. She, too, seemed to have realized this.

I was surprised to read in her autobiography: 'For about ten years after I had a child I led a double-life – grown-up on the surface but all too soon I began to realise that the game was up. My daughter's eyes were penetratingly understanding and said clearly: "Well, you're no grown-up."' Nor was she: at ten, I was starting to realize that I had been brought up by a charming, sweet, talented but totally self-centred and wayward child.

She tried to juggle work and family life in her own way. When the atmosphere at home became unbearable, and perhaps feeling a tiny bit guilty that she was so little at home with us, my mother suggested that Christopher and I accompany her to Paris to see the collections. While she went off to see Balenciaga, Givenchy and Dior, my father and I binged on sightseeing.

We visited Napoleon's tomb, we went to Versailles, we climbed up the Arc de Triomphe and we visited the Musée Grevin. This was a waxwork museum, which featured the *Palais des Miroirs*, a wonderful Victorian piece of fantasy still in existence in which, by means of grinding cogs, ropes, old machinery and pillared mirrored columns, a room was transformed from a sultan's palace to a Roman amphitheatre, to the heart of a Rousseau-like jungle or Egyptian temple, all accompanied by crackling music appropriate to the particular scene.

Together, we walked and talked, we sat and drank cups of coffee on the Champs-Elysées in the sun, we sauntered by the Seine. I remember our trip almost as a honeymoon – but the honeymoon belonged to me and my father, not to my parents, who were increasingly cold with each other.

At home, my mother again struck the wrong note in her attempts to keep up an impression of a happy family. Perhaps imagining that a strong social life would cover up some of the gaping cracks in her and Christopher's relationship, she slaved over the new Elizabeth David cookbooks and produced exotic French dishes for dinner parties. No longer did she serve lamb chops, boiled potatoes and carrots; instead, my mother cooked with extraordinary new ingredients – wine, herbs and garlic. Smoked mackerel, then a rare delicacy, bought from the first supermarket in South Kensington to open on Sundays, might be served as a starter, followed by pork chops in cider with apples, accompanied by potatoes *Lyonnaises* and then a pudding of home-made chocolate mousse.

But 'Oh Gawd!' my father would say at the prospect of guests. He seemed to dread these events increasingly, because my mother insisted on inviting the dangerous men with philandering reputations who kept appearing in their social circle – men like Freddie Ayer, the Grote Professor of Philosophy of Mind and Logic at the University of London. (Freddie once claimed to have had 150 women – quite a lot for those days – and said that to get one, 'All you have to do is to pay her the smallest attention since, in this country, no one else does.') My father, being intellectually at least Freddie's equal and having the confidence to conduct long philosophical sparring matches with him over dinner, must also have rather resented the way that every woman responded simperingly to Ayer's flirting.

Coming down for drinks before supper and meeting Freddie, I sensed danger in this man who, with his big nose, moist red mouth, sparkling eyes and quick way of talking, was highly attractive. My mother was so taken with Freddie that she even tried to wade through his great work, *Language, Truth and Logic*, but soon gave up.

Another man my father hated having in the house was Arthur Koestler, then famous for his books on the Spanish Civil War, whom he thought a pretentious phoney. The fact that he had a terrible reputation with women didn't help. I can hear my father saying: 'A *frightful* man!' Naturally, I agreed with him, and when I saw Arthur's big head and pock-marked skin, I couldn't imagine how anyone could bear to kiss him.

Then there was The Temperance Seven, a Victorian-style traditional jazz band made up of Royal College students. It was its leader, Cephas Howard, whom I saw as the menace here, since I knew my mother admired him enormously. (Poor man. He was probably oblivious to my mother's secret yearnings.)

She once came back from the College with a 'present' for me. It was a record-player and a Temperance Seven LP.

'I don't want it,' I said. 'There's nothing wrong with our old wind-up.' My heart beat with anxiety as she unwrapped the machine and started fixing a plug into the wire. The anxiety turned to fury. 'I don't want to *listen* to it! I don't *like* it! I never *asked* for it!'

My angry tears cut no ice. As I had known all along, the record-player was for her, not for me, and she had only bought the record, not to give me pleasure, but to enable her to moon over the music, listen to Cephas's solo in 'Yes Sir, That's my Baby' and swoon over the photograph of Cephas on the front, a tubby little man in a striped blazer, playing the trumpet.

The song that dominated my early teenage years, however, was a calypso called 'Island in the Sun' sung by Harry Belafonte. My mother played this record over and over again. She sat on the edge of the sofa, as near to the record-player as possible, her chin resting leadenly in one hand, a glass of gin and tonic in the other, her eyes watering with sentimentality, and with a stupid, lustful smile on her face. Occasionally she opened her mouth and licked her lips with her tongue, and I would turn away, disgusted. She wasn't completely drunk but something almost worse – perhaps tipsy, squiffy or woozy. She was both there and not there, all at the same time.

I hated this record, though I never understood exactly why. It was partly because my father was clearly angry when it came on – I found out later that it had been given to her by one of her many admirers. But even before I had discovered this, the moment I heard the opening notes of the steel drum, I felt tense and upset.

The other piece of alarming newfangledness that my mother insisted on bringing into the house was a black-and-white television.

When I was small, the only television I had ever watched was in my friend-over-the-road Sally's house, where we watched black-and-white children's programmes like *Hopalong Cassidy*. But I was vehemently against the idea of our having television at home. I realized that this fourth party would invade our lives and enable my parents to say even less to each other than they did already, and that my mother would pay me even less attention. I begged her to change her mind, but the television arrived and stayed.

It is bad enough to be trapped in a loveless marriage; to be the powerless teenage product of one is almost worse. I was now thirteen. The whispered arguments became more and more frequent, and my father was exhausted. He had been working hard on designs for *A Midsummer Night's Dream* with his brother, and the day after the show opened, drained by so much work and stress, he contracted shingles, then an excruciatingly painful disease with no drugs to relieve it.

This would have been bad enough, but it meant that he was unable to come to the Royal College of Art Summer Ball, an event which my mother longed to attend and had been looking forward to for weeks. The theme being the French Revolution, my mother had spent hours making a special dress for herself, with a white cross-over top and a long black-and-white-striped skirt.

Had my mother been a woman he could have trusted, I have no doubt that my father wouldn't have minded in the least her going on her own. As it was, there was a tense and bitter discussion behind doors. They emerged with white faces and narrowed lips. My mother simply said that she was going and that was that. She insisted that I take a photograph of her in her fancy dress, on the stairs, before she left for the party. After she had gone, my father sat on the sofa, in terrible pain, looking more depressed than I'd ever seen him. Later, he struggled to cook some potatoes and lamb chops which we ate together, while watching *Highway Patrol*.

Janey in her French
Revolution fancy dress,
before she left on her own
for the party

It didn't seem to matter to my mother what we thought. If she wanted to do something, she just did it. She no longer even hesitated. She longed to go to America, and badgered Robin Darwin to release the funds to allow her the trip. Eventually Robin relented, and found the money for her to spend a week in New York.

My father was totally opposed, and so was I. We both knew that there were other reasons for my mother's yearning to go to America, that she would meet men there who would be attracted to her — she had already been enchanted by Charles Eames, designer of the famous Eames chair, whom she'd met when he came over from the States to be made an honorary Fellow of the College.

After supper one night, when she broached the American idea again to my father, he said once more that he didn't want her to go. I heard her going to our red bathroom. Terrible retching noises emerged.

'What happened, mummy?' I asked, when she came out.

'I asked Christopher what he thought about my going to America and he said he didn't want me to go, but I said I was going, and as a result I've just been sick,' she said.

'Oh, dear,' I said, not quite knowing what I was expected to say.

While she was away, Christopher and I tried not to think about what she was getting up to. When she returned, she brought with her masses of presents, but, like the record-player, the Temperance Seven LP, the Harry Belafonte record and the television, everything seemed to carry a hidden menace. I especially resented the three 'amusing' kaleidoscopes that Charles Eames had given her to distribute among her family and friends.

Life at home, never easy, was rapidly becoming intolerable. The atmosphere was icy, my father was miserable, and our evenings were like deserts of silence, broken only by spasmodic flashes of irritation that sparked between my mother and me. She would come home from work, make supper, have a few drinks and then, when we were all in the sitting-room and my father was reading, she would gaze at me, her face suffused with squiffy adoration.

'Stop looking at me!'

'But, darling, you're sho . . . beeootiful . . . !' she would slur. 'I can look, can't I?'

I wasn't aware at the time that she was drunk. But there was something about the sight of her two big moist eyes staring at me, her full, almost seductive mouth, her dead white skin and her jet-black hair, perhaps a bit awry, which, when I recall it, fills me with terror and revulsion. On the one hand, I felt she was trying to suck every drop of youth, femininity and life out of me; on the other, I felt her oppressive gaze pushing in on me, suffocating me.

'*Stop it!*' I would snap.

She would give a horrible drunken giggle and say: 'But whaaay, darling?'

Or she'd copy me, drawling: '*Stop* it!'

'Stop saying "Stop it"!' I shouted. There was a seductiveness in her gaze, a sexual undertone that I could almost smell, though I could never quite put my finger on what it was.

'But whaaay? *You're* saying "Stop it"!' And she'd laugh, still staring, with those awful eyes. 'Can't I just *look* at my beoootiful dau-er?'

*

One morning, I woke up to find that she wasn't there.

'Where's mummy?' I asked Christopher, who had come into my room to draw my curtains. He looked washed-out and unshaven, in his dressing-gown. He sat down on the end of my bed. 'She didn't come back after the party last night,' he said.

'But why?'

He smoothed down his hair, which was sticking up like a schoolboy's.

'She got a bit drunk, sweetie, and I came back on my own, and she hasn't come back. She's all right. She rang me. She's staying at Diana's.'

'Why didn't she come back?'

'I think she felt she wouldn't be welcome,' said my father, rather sheepishly.

'Why?'

'You know Janey. I'm afraid when we go out, she gets drunk, and then she flirts with men, and the usual happened last night, and I said that either she came home with me or she needn't come home at all.'

'So has she gone for ever?'

'Well, I don't know, but it rather looks like it,' said my father. 'You'd better get dressed for school. I'll make some breakfast.'

That afternoon, when I returned home, my grandmother was waiting for me in the hall, with a finger melodramatically to her lips. She beckoned to me to come into her sitting-room.

'Oh, my toosie,' she said, holding my hand and looking at me with the most sympathetic face. 'This is all so sad! Mummy's upstairs, and she's packing, but when she's gone, I want you to come down and we'll have a cup of tea. It's just such a very difficult situation. Poor, poor Christopher.'

I went up to the drawing-room and found my mother in her dressing-gown, sitting – vulnerable, make-upless and pathetic – on the arm of a chair. She was crying.

'Oh, daarling,' she said, looking at me pitifully. 'You don't think I'm *awful*, do you? Will you be all right on your own with Christopher? You don't *mind*, do you?'

I could hardly bear to put my arms round her to kiss and console her, but I did my best.

'No, Mummy,' I said. 'It's much better like this. Don't worry. I'll be fine. You weren't happy. None of us were happy. It's for the best. Don't worry.'

I was longing for her to take her clinging arms off me, to get away, to hear her bang the door with her suitcases and go off for ever.

That night, my father, emotionally drained, returned from work. I rushed into his arms in floods of tears. He comforted me, and poured out a glass of port for himself. On a whim, he said: 'I think you need one, too', and poured me out a glass. For the first, but not the last time in my life, I got terribly drunk.

eight

CAREER   *One of the main disadvantages for a woman with a successful career is in the conflict it causes in her own mind. To start with, it takes up so much time. Most women love their husband, their children and their homes and have this inbred feeling that they should come first and so will torture themselves with worry and/or exhaust themselves trying to live two full-time lives.*

Particularly difficult is when a man and woman have started a life together on the conventional terms of man equals bread-winner and woman equals home-maker; and the woman, by some horrid trick of fate, turns out to be the ambitious and talented one and finds that she is better at winning the bread than the man. The man has no intention of stepping down into the position of housekeeper and slipper-warmer and, another of life's little ironies, all the atavistic instincts of the woman might well make her turn round and despise him if he did.

Janey Ironside, *Fashion as a Career*

The marriage had failed for two reasons. One was because of my mother's career. The other problem was sex. Janey often complained to a close relative later in life that she could never find sexual satisfaction, and instead of coming to terms with the fact that lots of people feel the same way and it's no big deal, she was hell-bent on finding it. I am told that she took to leaving little notes around the house, much to my father's astonishment, on which were written ideas that she thought would perk up their lives in bed.

Nothing worked, so an appointment had been made to see a psychiatrist together, after which they were interviewed separately. My mother was given a 'truth drug', probably a shot of Valium. At the end of the session, the psychiatrist took Christopher on one side, put his hand on his shoulder and said: 'You have to come to terms with the fact that in your wife you have an attractive, beautiful, talented woman, who loves you 60 per cent.' My father said: 'But that's not enough!' The psychiatrist replied: 'It wouldn't be enough for me, either.'

Even after my mother had left home, the scent of her frustrated sexuality must have lingered on around Neville Street, curling around the white pillars of our porch, turning men on as they passed. Not long after her departure, one of my mother's admirers, Bill Bergne, rang the bell one afternoon. My father went downstairs, opened the door and, rather angrily, told him that Janey had left.

'Oh, well,' said Bill, grinning. 'Perhaps *Virginia* would like to come with me to look at the pictures at the Victoria and Albert Museum.'

Aged about thirty-eight, Bill was ancient in my eyes, with tight curly greying hair, a little nose, and bright Puckish eyes. Why my father allowed me to go, I don't know – I was only fourteen and Bill had been one of the men who had flirted with my mother – but perhaps it was because Bill was an old friend, and he could hardly refuse. I was startled, flattered and rather thrilled. After we had walked up the marble staircase at the V&A to the exhibition hall at the top, we stood looking at the Constables. Then Bill took my arm

(I can still feel the grip on it now) and whispered: 'Do you know why Constable was such a wonderful painter?'

'No,' I said, puzzled.

'I'll tell you,' said Bill, in a low and important voice. 'It's because he could do *skies* so brilliantly!'

Later, over a supper of boiled potatoes, grilled tomatoes and pork chop, I said to my father, my face a contortion of amusement and contempt: 'Do you know what Bill said when we were at the V&A?'

'No,' he replied anxiously, fiddling with his fork.

'He said that the reason Constable was so great was because he could "do skies"!'

'*What*!' my father replied, with a guffaw of contemptuous laughter. '"*Do skies*"*!* He knows absolutely *nothing* about painting whatsoever!'

And we both laughed in relief to discover that this charming and dashing pursuer of women was, in fact, rather a chump when it came to important matters like why Constable was a good artist. With this one facile remark, Bill had stolen the power from all of my mother's admirers. My father and I would often mutter to each other, 'You know why Constable's a great painter, don't you?' and giggle.

When they had been together, I never heard my parents rowing openly and I don't think that they ever lost their tempers even behind closed doors. They had their whispered irritable conversations, but neither my mother nor my father were people to let fly at each other. I, too, am almost incapable of having a shouting match and on the two occasions I may have raised my voice in my life, I have been acutely aware that much of the performance was acting. Like my parents, I can despise people, and keep up long and icy coldnesses, but I have only perhaps once in my life let myself go with red-hot rage – probably because I feel such contempt for those who have hurt me that the idea of making myself vulnerable by losing self-control is anathema.

It was because of this aspect of their natures that, after the split, my parents found it quite easy to carry on what they described as a 'civilized relationship' for my sake. For a year, my mother returned at weekends to cook lunch and supper, to try to give the impression that we were still a happy family. Since we had *never* been a happy family, this was a ludicrous exercise. The weekends we spent together were farcical, and yet they were designed entirely with my welfare in mind. My mother bitterly regretted leaving and did everything possible to persuade Christopher to allow her to return – until the day she died, she complained that she should never have left him, that he was the only man she had ever truly loved. Christopher, who had been driven to the end of his tether when they were living together, could not risk putting himself through such torment again.

Only quite recently did I learn that the reason my father had stayed in the marriage for so long was because he felt it would be too irresponsible to leave me with Janey. In those days, there was virtually no possibility of a father getting custody of his child, and were Janey to return, she certainly would not make the mistake of walking out of the marriage again. At least now he had the house and me.

The night she left home, my mother had gone to stay with Diana Holman Hunt, who lived in a tiny flat in Draycott Place in Chelsea. Diana's second husband had died. At the time, she had just written a best-seller, *My Grandmothers and I*, for which my father had designed the jacket. Once, when I rang my mother, Diana picked up the phone and confided that she thought Janey had been a '*frightful ape*' in leaving Christopher. There was hardly any room for two women in 'the cupboard', as Diana called her flat – and since Diana never stopped talking, my mother was rather relieved to move, a few months later, into a flat in Cromwell Place – back near South Kensington tube station. She was delighted to learn that John Millais had once lived in the same house and, more recently, the painters Robert Buhler and Francis Bacon.

The flat was ideally placed. It was three doors down from the Senior Common Room, and pretty much equidistant between Neville Street and the Fashion School. My mother decorated it beautifully, with white walls, the usual white chintz curtains, and cheap old-fashioned lacquered bamboo furniture, spotted long before the prices reached their current heights. Bernard Nevill had given her an enormous leather Gladstone sofa from a now defunct old gentleman's club, the Bath Club.

Meanwhile, at school, during the week after the break-up, my great-aunt had sent me out of the classroom while she addressed my form-mates on my remarkable situation (separation being completely out of the ordinary in those days), urging my friends to be sympathetic if I was upset.

But I was far from upset. I didn't miss my mother at all. Apart from the weekends when my mother came round, I was totally happy, alone with Christopher, having him all to myself. We were like an old married couple, relieved to be rid of a worryingly feckless teenage daughter.

We had a routine. At six-thirty, my father would have a drink while reading the *New Scientist*, and then he'd come up to my bedroom and play and sing 'Hong Kong Blues' by Hoagy Carmichael on the piano. He composed his own blues tunes, too. We often played duets by Telemann together on the recorder, Christopher being a great one for going on jaunts to Boosey and Hawkes and Chappell's to find new composers to suit us. Sometimes he'd play the recorder and I'd play the piano. He found a book of rounds in a junkshop and for a while we had a round jag, singing endlessly a mournful song about a caged thrush, called 'Thou Poor Bird'.

After an early supper, Christopher would set up the L'Attaque board. L'Attaque was still our favourite game, and he had painted by hand all the black and white pieces to make them look more interesting. He gave the Spy an especially evil expression. Or, as we both adored Raymond Burr, we might watch him in *Ironside*. Or we would look forward to Thursday and *Highway Patrol*. Now my mother was gone, television was no longer a threat, but a shared, enjoyable experience.

Sometimes we argued and debated. I said I didn't — or did — believe in hanging, and my father argued tenaciously that it was — or wasn't — a good idea. His knowledge and rational powers were exceptional, and witnessing one of my arguments demolished by my father was to watch an expert at work. He discussed the topic from a social point of view, from a cultural point of view, from an ethical point of view, from an historical point of view, from a personal point of view and then explained how wrong it was to consider it from an anecdotal point of view. At the end of the discussion, a neat conclusion was reached, without any stray threads of it unaccounted for, even if, as occasionally happened, the conclusion was that as both sides were pretty convincing it didn't really matter which one were to take. I came to consider my father always to be right, and certainly the majority of my views today are heavily influenced by his.

We were always doing things together. If he had a picture accepted for the Royal Academy of Arts Summer Exhibition, we would go together to Varnishing Day (when the painters had a last chance to touch up their work), and complain together how badly hung the exhibition was. Once, we went to the Ideal Home Exhibition and bought a French polishing kit called Furniglas. We rubbed away for evening after evening, and eventually the table, which I still have, came up a treat. 'You two *are* clever,' said my grandmother when she came up for a rare supper. But 'Never again' said Christopher as he shook his aching wrist. Sometimes we went to art galleries together. If my father ever came across some absurd piece of modern art, he stood in front of it and bowed. 'Indeed,' he would intone. Sometimes he commented, in a dignified way: 'Well, if you say so.'

When he was rung up by the Arthur Murray School of Dancing and informed that he was the lucky recipient of a free dancing class, he went straight off and demanded a rock-and-roll lesson – the steps of which he promptly taught me when he returned that evening. We rolled up the carpet and danced like maniacs.

'What were you two up to last night?' asked my grandmother when I saw her in the hall the next day. 'I thought a herd of elephants had moved in.'

One of Christopher's real interests, apart from evolution – he was always telling me about *Australopithecus* and Piltdown Man –

was statistics. He was constantly explaining to me how they always lied. He would sit on the sofa, with a Woodbine. 'If there is one card which is red on both sides and one which is white on both sides,' he began, 'and there is one which is red on one side and white on the other . . . No. Start again. There are three cards. Two are red on one side and white on the other and one is red on both . . . no. No.' He would light up another Woodbine, and work his lips in and out. Then, five minutes later, he would say: 'I've got it. No. *Now* I've got it. There are three boxes. In one box there are two drawers, one with one gold coin, one with silver. In the next box . . .'

But what we shared most of all was humour. We both adored P. G. Wodehouse, and Christopher had been brought up to believe it was a social duty to entertain — a duty he carried through to his private life.

One of our favourite pastimes was laughing at other people, and doing imitations of them. 'Other people' were beyond our pale and together we laughed and sneered at them. Never did Christopher return from an evening nor I from some event at school without tales to tell about how frightfully silly someone else had been, and to regale each other with their fatuous and clichéd remarks.

'Christopher, there was a ghastly woman who kept saying: "Oh, you know that really London is just a collection of villages",' I might say.

Or he would say, putting on an earnest upper-class voice and thrusting his face into mine. '"Oh, my dear, I think one *loves* gardening as one gets older because one feels more *in tune* with the seasons."'

If I felt like outdoing him, I might have leaned forward and replied: '"And isn't it extraordinary how if you're looking for something you never find it? But the minute you stop, it turns up on your doorstep?"'

Our humour was cruel and black. Sometimes he would tell me stories about his childhood and his unspeakable relations, stories told amid gales of laughter. There was his cousin, an entertaining but 'dreadful' man, who was caught with a Scotsman under the cliffs of Dover and 'went to jug for nine months'. Eventually he committed suicide, probably because he was being blackmailed or 'beaten up by queers'. Another relation, who was very keen on running boys' clubs, suffered the same fate – he jumped off a roof either because he discovered he was homosexual and couldn't stand it or because he suddenly lost his religious faith. Great-Aunt Ella was mad and married a man called Major Loaming who was even madder – but at least his madness could be explained because he had been in Ladysmith before it was relieved and had survived on eels fried in bicycle-oil and had eaten bread made of face-powder instead of flour. All this we found hysterically funny.

The outside world was our enemy and Christopher and I were in cahoots against it.

Good-looking and entertaining, Christopher, separated from my mother, was now 'spare', and he was besieged by women who wanted him as an extra man or to have affairs with or, worse, to marry. Occasionally he would come back from a dinner party looking quite dishevelled, saying: 'This frightful woman, her husband was upstairs, and she simply sprang on me on the sofa! So embarrassing!'

Christopher by Christopher – as the debonair boulevardier
and the frowsty person at breakfast

'What did you do, Christopher?' I'd ask.

'Oh, tried to make myself as small as possible, slid out from underneath her, brushed myself down and said that although I liked her
as a friend . . . you know, blah, blah, fishcakes. Apparently she and
her husband spend their lives chasing other people. What a crew!'

Sexual gallivanting still wasn't my father's style. And when he heard of married couples having affairs, he would shake his head. Infidelity was not for him. 'I'm afraid I just can't stand it,' he said.

There was only one time when I was worried. He had taken a woman to dinner, and obviously had a good time. She started to pursue him, and he did not seem as reluctant as usual to dismiss her. When he told me he was going out with her again one evening I felt a sinking feeling in the pit of my stomach. I suddenly burst into tears.

'What on earth is the matter?' he said.

'I just can't bear the idea that you might fall in love with someone and go off with them,' I choked between my tears.

'Highly unlikely,' said my father, rather coolly. 'You really mustn't worry about that. But I don't want to upset you in any way, Pin. If you'd like, I won't go out at all. I'll stay in. I don't want you upset.'

I was in agonies. I felt, as he probably knew perfectly well, that asking him not to go out at all would be completely unreasonable. I was forced into making the only answer that I could. 'No, no, I wouldn't want that. It's fine. Don't worry. I'm just upset. It all suddenly came over me. I'll get over it.'

'Are you absolutely sure?' asked my father. 'I promise if ever you want me to stay in, I'll just put off any date I have. You only have to say.'

Naturally enough, I never did.

When I was about fifteen, I was with Christopher at a party. He was on one side of the room and I was on the other, wearing a full skirt made by my mother out of a chintz print of black and grey roses. My father approached with his wine glass in his hand, but when he came nearer, he started, and then laughed. 'Good heavens, I had no idea!' he said. 'I was just looking round the room and the only attractive woman I saw was this person standing by the wall and it turned out to be you!'

I had reminded him of Janey.

Some time after the split, my father was asked by Robin Darwin to dine with him in his pavilion. They had supper together, discussed the Royal College — Robin depended on my father enormously for advice — and then, over coffee and brandy, Robin asked: 'Do you ever think of getting back together with Janey?'

My father later gave me a blow-by-blow account of what followed. He had sipped his coffee and shaken his head. 'I don't think I could bear it,' he said. 'I've thought about it a lot and I know she wants us to get together again, but although I'm pretty certain she was never actually unfaithful, I just couldn't cope with all that flirting she used to do — you know how drunk she'd get at parties, don't you? — and just seeing her being so seductive with other men — no, it would be impossible to go through that again.'

There was a silence. Robin got up and poured himself another brandy. He stood in front of the fire, towering above Christopher. There was a long silence. Then he burst out: 'Flirting! Flirting! You think it was just *flirting*?'

Christopher frowned. 'Well, I'm sure it wasn't anything more. She would never have . . .'

'Oh, come on, Christopher, come on. You *must* have known! None of us knew how you could have *stood* it!'

'Stood what?' asked my father.

'Janey having all those affairs!'

'Affairs? Don't be ridiculous!'

'You can't mean you didn't know!'

'Know what?'

'My dear man, you must be mad,' said Robin. 'She had *everyone* – Robert, John, Hugh Casson, Martyn, Bernard, Bill, Freddie, Arthur . . . then there was Richard, and that photographer, and Charles, and – what's the name of Diana's ex-husband, man with curly hair, always chasing women, you know . . . Bill . . . Good God, it's more a question of whom she *didn't* have rather than whom she *did*! Come on, Christopher, you *must* have known!'

My father looked up at Robin in horror and astonishment. He simply could not believe what he was hearing. 'It's impossible. Flirting, yes . . . but affairs, never!'

'My dear man, it was the talk of the College. She's had absolutely *everyone*!'

'You can't prove it!' said Christopher, rather desperately.

'Christopher, listen to me: *everyone*'s had her. Look – even *I*'ve had her!'

Christopher was devastated. I cannot imagine how he didn't know, but he was probably living in what today is called 'denial'. He didn't want to know. He must have realized at some level that if he found out, he couldn't continue to live at home, and he had to live at home to look after me. He came back to Neville Street concealing his tears as he looked in to kiss me goodnight. The betrayal, the shame, the humiliation he felt meant that there was no way that Janey could ever return. Even he could not maintain the pretence of a 'civilized separation' any longer. My mother stopped coming over to cook; she stopped coming over at all.

When I visited her on my own, my mother's flat always seemed to be full of men, men I referred to jokingly as her 'rum chums'. There was the troll-like, bowler-hatted cartoonist Osbert Lancaster, his moustachioed face covered with acne-scars. ('I could *never* understand her

POCKET CARTOON
by OSBERT LANCASTER

"*Considering what most of one's friends can do with their imaginations unstretched, Cecil's New Year advice seems to me simply playing with fire.*"

Maudie Littlehampton talking to Janey
in Osbert Lancaster's cartoon

affair with him,' said one gay man who taught at the Fashion School, when I talked to him later. 'She didn't *fancy* him. She didn't really like him. The thought of them *coupling*! *Ugh!* Particularly as she always had a great *lust* for younger men. Oh, *yes*. By the way,' he added, with a twinkle – and by now I sort of knew what was coming – 'you do know that your mother was the only woman I ever did "*it*" with, don't you?')

There was an advertising executive, and an art director, and a lord. There was Derek Hart, a famous television presenter who used to knock around with Princess Margaret. And there was a very good-looking photographer who lived downstairs. Rather to my mother's alarm, he suddenly declared that he wanted to take some photographs of me, 'before it all goes', as he put it. I was just fifteen.

If her flat was full of men, my mother always seemed to be full of alcohol. Although I had a key, I would press the buzzer to let her know I was on my way, and before she picked up the receiver in her flat I could tell whether she was drunk or not. The way the receiver was lifted off the hook, the pause before her voice came . . . I could almost smell the drink before the first words: 'He-e-llaw, da-a-rling, come upstaaairs.'

One Sunday, I rang the bell and a man's voice answered. He didn't press the buzzer to let me in and the sound from my mother's flat upstairs was funny through the plastic slats on the Ansaphone – the murmur of voices, an unfamiliar crackling. I let myself in, made my way up the stone staircase and walked into the flat. A man I recognized, a liberal studies teacher at the Royal College, wandered past me in the passage, a glass in his hand. He nodded hello, as if he lived there. He had a predatory look. In the sitting-room, another man sat on the sofa. And standing by the mantelpiece, reflected in a beautiful gilt-edged mirror that my mother had bought for ten shillings in Leamington Spa, was yet another man with greying hair and a balding head. The man on the sofa got up. My memory is of three pairs of corduroy trousers of different colours, brown, black and moss-green. One of the men wore glasses and had a spiky nose.

No one said very much, and I didn't know what to make of this unlikely scene. They all seemed perfectly polite, but they all had a kind of funny grin in their eyes, and I felt they were prowling, waiting.

'Where's Mummy?' I asked. One of the men nodded towards the bedroom. I went in.

My mother was sitting in a dressing-gown on the edge of her bed, applying lipstick rather smudgily to her mouth. She had put her glass down to do so. 'Why, hello, daaarling!' she said. Her voice was slurred, her eyes were fuzzy and swimming with some kind of drunken gunge, and her mouth was falling all over the place. As I leaned to kiss her — something I never enjoyed; I hated to feel the closeness of my mother's skin against my lips — I could smell the mixture of wine and old saliva, hanging around her mouth.

'Who are these apes?' I asked. We always referred to anyone we didn't know as apes. Cocktails parties were full of apes. People standing at a bus-stop would be apes. It was quite an affectionate term.

My mother smiled slowly, put out her hand and pulled me close to her. 'Which one shall I sleep with?' she asked me, confidingly, a wicked smile playing round her face. 'Which one? Tell me!'

I withdrew, taking her glass from the table. 'Oh, Mummy,' I said.

'I think you've had enough to drink. Why don't you go to bed?' I hauled her up and pulled back the bedclothes. She slipped in between the sheets, chuckling.

I went back into the sitting-room where the three men were still walking about, silently, expectantly.

'I don't think my mother's very well,' I announced coldly, in a voice that didn't sound as if it were mine, 'I think you should all go.'

Reluctantly, and sniggering, they pulled on their coats and left.

I went back in to my mother.

'So, who's it going to be?' she asked, seductively, clutching the sheets up to her chin.

'None of them, Mummy,' I said. 'They've gone.'

'Gone! Where have they gone?' My mother pushed away the bedclothes and tried to stumble out of bed.

'I told them to leave,' I said. 'You're not well, Mummy.'

Then she fixed me with a stare of black and poisonous fury.

'I hate you!' she hissed, her rheumy eyes suddenly flashing with loathing. 'I hate you! I hate you! I hate you!'

There had never been any question of my going to university. There had never been any question of any pupils from Miss Ironside's School going to university. University was something that never crossed anyone's minds in our family. My father had never been to university; my mother had never been to university. There was not even talk of my taking A-levels. Rene had wanted to retire when I was fourteen, but she kept the school open another year especially so that I could take my O-levels – in a tiny class of only four other girls – and after getting top marks, that was it.

And so, after my fifteenth birthday, it was decided that I should be sent to a finishing school in Paris, Mademoiselle Anita's.

First of all, however, there was a party. My social life was much the same as any young person's in London in the early sixties. On Sunday afternoons, I used to go to Cy Laurie's New Orleans Jazz Club in Great Windmill Street in Soho to skip-jive with an attractive but elderly – he must have been about twenty-six – art student called Steve Hill, who was studying graphics at the London School of Printing. At weekends, I might go to the odd rock 'n' roll party. I had my first kiss from Reginald Bosanquet, the louche ITN newscaster – he must have been at least thirty-five – and my first date with Ian Ogilvy, later to play the Saint in the television series.

I knew the sort of birthday party I wanted: a bottle party. I got together some records – including Frank Sinatra's LP, *Songs for Swinging Lovers*, an essential ingredient – hauled out the old Dynatron record-player that my mother had left behind, at last a useful piece of equipment, bought a few bottles of Hirondelle wine, made sandwiches and spread the word. My father very decently left for the evening and didn't come back till midnight. When he returned, dressed in a devastatingly attractive white suit, my friends (or friends of friends who didn't recognize him) shouted: 'You can't come in without a bottle!'

'I happen to live here,' said my father grandly, making his dignified way upstairs.

A little later, a gatecrasher 'did the coats', as it was known, stealing cash and chequebooks, which got everyone into the papers under the headline: 'Father blames "the Chelsea Vortex"'. Not my father, but the father of the girl who had been caught red-handed.

After this exciting entry into London life, the last place I wanted to be was Paris. I was particularly nervous because before I left I had discovered a half-finished letter on my father's desk in the sitting-room, which he was writing to a married woman friend. It was lying there for anyone to see. I saw it — and I read it. 'So sorry to have burst out with all that stuff about Jean and Carshalton Beeches . . .' I didn't have to read any further. I felt I had been punched in the face.

Who was Jean? Where was Carshalton Beeches? What was happening?

When my father returned, I admitted I'd read the letter and asked, anxiously, what was going on. I not only felt guilty; I also felt terrified. A few moments after my confession, my father sat down, looking extremely concerned, and lit a Woodbine.

'I've been trying to find a time to tell you,' he said. 'At Maidstone' — the College of Art, where he was teaching — 'I met this girl called Jean Marsden. She is very nice, very young, and I like her very much. She lives at the moment in Carshalton Beeches. The reason I wrote the letter was that I had got rather emotional about her when I was with Diana at dinner, and I was writing to apologize for going on about her so much. I should have told you, but I kept waiting for a good time, and I'm sorry you've found out like this.'

The shock had almost winded me, my body felt bruised with his betrayal, my brain felt as if it was leaking blood into my skull. And there was a pain in my heart as if it had been wrenched out and thrown on to a fire. I could hardly stand up.

'Whatever happens, you'll always be number one in my life,' he said. 'I promise you that.'

But deep down I knew that I was losing the only parent I had left — and the only person I loved in the whole world.

I set off for Paris full of foreboding. I hated Mademoiselle Anita's and the French family I was billeted upon, who lived in a flat near the Gare de Lyons. When I arrived, I was put into a room little bigger than a broom cupboard. There were two extremely unpleasant girls, with whom I didn't get on, and their younger brother, a wretched creature who stole money from my room. After accusing the maid, and then me, his parents finally caught him in the act and punished him by thrusting his head under a tap until he couldn't breathe and I had to beg for his release.

It was around this time that I started to become truly unhappy, prey to the depression that has dogged me all my life. I was desperately homesick, but the home I was sick for had vanished. Home was no longer just me and Christopher at Neville Street. Another woman had entered the equation.

I started to thrash around desperately for some kind of security, and the only way I felt I could find it was by finding a boyfriend of my own, someone to love me. I developed a painful crush on a boy called Martin Wilkinson, also in Paris. He was tall, good-looking and so cool that he hardly ever spoke. My complete obsession with him was probably a way of blocking out the pain I felt about my father's new love.

Both my parents visited me in Paris, and my mother tried to find me a better room, but by then I was used to it and just longing to get home. When I returned from Paris, after three months, my depression had become so obvious that I made the first of a series of visits to doctors.

One such visit was to a gynaecologist recommended by my father. Very responsibly, Christopher had suddenly insisted that I get myself fitted out with proper contraception. I was pleased in one way, but also amazed, particularly as I was then a virgin. Most parents in the early sixties were extremely strict, and if their daughters went out in the evening they had to be back at a certain time or face terrible scenes. My father, on the other hand, seemed almost to encourage a rackety life-style, a life-style that was becoming increasingly like my mother's. He explained to me later that he was at sea. He had no idea of how to bring up a teenage girl, particularly in a time of such social upheaval, and a doctor friend had recommended that to prescribe me a diaphragm was the surest way of keeping me out of trouble. I myself couldn't understand what was going on. Since he had been so disapproving of my mother, why was he appearing to encourage sexual freedom when it came to me? I couldn't help feeling that this was another form of rejection, that I was being treated rather like a cat sent to the vet to be neutered. I felt he didn't care enough about me to put his foot down or to offer me guidelines on how I should live my life.

After Paris, I was sent to a secretarial college in Oxford, but was so unhappy that I returned home after ten days with, oddly, a stammer. And then, since there was nothing else for me to do, I enrolled at Chelsea Art School. It was very easy in those days. You didn't need a portfolio; you wandered in and signed on. Unfortunately, art schools had just decided that teaching people to draw was old hat. The plaster casts and *ecorchés* figures were chucked out of the cast rooms, and life drawing was despised. My father despaired when I told him that all I'd been asked to do during the day was to throw matches in the air and mark where they fell on a piece of paper. I became more and more bored and miserable. I pined for Martin. Eventually, just after my sixteenth birthday, I met him at a party and stayed the night with him. Although I hardly saw him again, my pitiful, and rather embarrassing obsession lasted for the next four or so years. To fill in the time while I waited to hear from him, I started on a career of promiscuity that brought me nothing but anguish. In twelve books of diaries dating from my time in Paris, there is barely one word about any kind of ordinary daily life; only thousands and thousands of words describing one-night stand after one-night stand, the agony of waiting for a telephone call from Martin, pages of utter self-loathing, describing the bleakest of inner landscapes. Sometimes I just took the train to Oxford, where Martin was now a student, and hung around, walking about, my brain humming with longing, anxiety and loneliness, having tea at the Randolph Hotel on my own, sauntering down St Giles', hoping to bump into him – which I never did. Then I took the train back in the dark.

Jean had moved discreetly into the house, staying, for form's sake, in my grandmother's spare room downstairs. Once again, I was sharing my father with someone else – someone he clearly adored. But however kindly Christopher and Jean behaved towards me, nothing could erase the truth. They were a couple in love and, although it was never spelled out, they would have been much happier if I hadn't been around.

Even when Robin Darwin had confessed — or, rather, boasted — that he'd had an affair with Janey, Christopher wouldn't blame him. It was Janey who was at fault. He and Robin remained friends, with Robin continuing to visit for drinks and to ask Christopher for advice about how to run the RCA.

One evening, Robin asked Christopher and Jean to the pavilion for supper, plied them both with wine and was at his most attentive and charming. Before they left, he went out into the garden by moonlight and gallantly gathered a huge armful of roses for Jean to take home.

Next morning, however, the phone rang and it was Robin.

'Christopher, you have to tell me,' he said. 'Are you going to divorce Janey and marry Jean?'

'That's the general idea,' said Christopher.

'Well, you must remember that the Council won't stand for divorced couples being on the staff together. Now, we have one of two options. We can sack you, or we can sack Janey.'

Christopher was so astonished by this further betrayal that he put the phone down. Within twenty minutes, Robin was ringing the bell, moustache bristling.

'My dear Christopher, for heaven's sake,' he said on the doorstep. 'We can't have all this. Of course I'll sack Janey if you want, but I was thinking that it would be so difficult for *you* if she were unemployed — alimony and all that. If you resign, I'll find you the headship of an art school somewhere. I assure you that you'll be all right.'

Fashion design school chief seeks divorce

One of several articles about Janey's divorce. Notice the glass in her hand.

Although Christopher had ample grounds to divorce my mother (there was no 'no blame' divorce in those days), Robin Darwin was dead against it. My mother's success was an enormous asset to him. If the number of affairs she had had were to come out, it would have done the College a great deal of damage and the Board would eventually have been forced to sack her. It was essential that Janey divorce Christopher, on the grounds of his adultery, even though the situation was grossly unfair.

But Robin, as we discovered later, had more than a professional motive behind his insistence. He found Janey irresistibly attractive and was thinking, once she was a free woman, of asking her to be his wife.

Christopher refused to discuss the situation any more with Robin, but before long he was sacked by Bernard Meadows, the then head of the Sculpture School. Robin Darwin swore that it was nothing to do with him, that it was Meadows's decision entirely. Bernard Meadows admitted, truthfully, that he had been forced into kicking him out by Robin.

Soon after, my mother divorced Christopher, and they both said that they were 'glad I was old enough not to mind'.

But I did mind. 'I mind about Jean, too,' I wrote in my diary. 'I like her, I want Christopher to be happy, but I DON'T WANT. I dreamt I hit them both the other day. I felt so depressed and sad and hurt, I had a Dubonnet to take it away, I put the gramophone on loud, I cried and I cried and I cried and I SMOKED MY FIRST CIGARETTE!'

Naturally, I did not dream of expressing my feelings to anyone except my diary, and bottled them up under a jokey, and mildly sulky exterior, because I was becoming more and more confused and depressed underneath.

On 9 December 1961, when I was seventeen, my father and Jean got married.

Christopher and Jean at
their wedding reception,
very much in love

nine

CARNABY STREET *A back street off Regent Street, London, where small menswear shops began to show for the first time in the 1960s clothes for young men which were the masculine counterpart of young women's clothes, displaying bright colours, new shapes and constantly changing fashions. Carnaby Street has lent itself to a state of mind connected with youth, fashion, and the 1966 image of 'swinging London'. There are boutiques called 'Carnaby Street' in almost every corner of the world.*
Janey Ironside, *A Fashion Alphabet*

My mother's new flat was in Stanhope Gardens, only a few minutes from the nursing home in Cromwell Road where I was born and in the same South Kensington square in which she had rented a room in her early days in London. It was on the second floor of yet another stuccoed, pillared Victorian house.

Short of money and short of possessions — nothing had yet been moved out of Neville Street — she made a feature out of sparseness. Having gone through the Victorian knickery-knackery stage, she already had a sense of the advent of minimalism.

The flat was carpeted in flat, grey haircord and on the windows hung the usual white glazed chintz curtains. The furniture was nearly all cheap Edwardian japonais bamboo, except for Bernard Nevill's

Chesterfield sofa and elegant Victorian brass oil lamps. My mother had taken what she thought was an old carpet to be repaired, but finding that, despite the fact that her family had been stamping on it and grinding cigarettes out on it for years, it was in fact a valuable tapestry, she hung it above the fireplace. On the floor in front of the

Eric Wilkins

Janey in her immaculate flat in Stanhope Gardens. I still possess the mirror, the chair, the desk and the picture. Notice the glass on the floor again.

fire was a grey Chinese wolfskin. It was all cool, polished, immaculate.

When I visited, I now found a beautiful, dark young man, John Wright, an interior design student from Yorkshire, who was at the Royal College, in residence. His shy and quiet presence was a great relief for me. His knowledge and interest in taste and design more than matched my mother's, and although he was much younger than her, they seemed to suit each other well. John brought with him a gothic hand-painted cupboard, designed by an assistant of William Burgess, which dominated one wall. (After one of their rare arguments, it seemed that John might move out, taking with him his Burgess cupboard. 'Such a pity that one can replace *people* but one can't replace *things*,' said my mother, looking wistfully at it.)

My mother was happy. She led a reasonably peaceful and domestic life, working non-stop during the week and at the weekends reading Trollope, cooking meals for John and having me to lunch on Sunday. She even managed to stop drinking. In the afternoons, John went out to window-shop in Kensington Church Street or go to an exhibition, while my mother sat with her legs curled up under her on the leather sofa, a glass of slimline tonic in her hand, and we talked, exchanged gossip and giggled like old friends. I couldn't even imagine her as my mother. Over tea and buttered crumpets, we might watch the children's serial on television on Sunday afternoons or she helped me cut out the pattern for a nightdress, now an enjoyable instead of a hateful task.

The Fashion School had moved, too, with the rest of the Royal College, to the new building next to the Albert Hall, a grey brick-and-concrete structure, designed by Robert Goodden, H. T.

Peter Laurie

This was taken outside Janey's office in the new RCA building, overlooking the Albert Hall. I'm wearing boots only available at the theatrical costumiers, Annello and Davide.

Cadbury Brown and Hugh Casson. My mother's affair with Robin Darwin was long over, and though she had felt alarmed by his proposal of marriage, just after she had left Christopher, worrying that if she were to reject him he would turn against her, he had come to terms with the situation, or so it seemed. She told me how happy and relieved she felt as she looked out of the window of her new office, which faced on to the Albert Memorial and Kensington Gardens. At last the Fashion School was part of the Royal College proper, and not some outcast department flung into the wilderness.

Her staff and students adored her and spoke of her generosity and her high standards, and how she gave her students her all. Some said that she was like a second mother to them, advising, steering, encouraging and even revealing a ruthless side when it came to protecting them or furthering their interests.

It was not just her 'youthfulness, generosity and integrity', as one student put it, that inspired real respect; she was also admired as a woman in a man's world, because she had to work twice as hard as a man for any kind of recognition. She was always fighting for her students, getting major figures in the fashion industry to give talks, persuading them to shell out bursaries, and networking in a largely unsympathetic industry.

Others found her – although admirable – cold and unapproachable and, because she was so revolutionary, frightening, challenging and scary to meet.

'She was the last person I'd have gone to with an emotional problem,' said one student. 'She never appeared to show any emotion at all except, on very rare occasions when she felt threatened, when she would start shaking.'

For long after the war, fashion was still an exclusively female domain. My mother wanted to change this. Men's fashions were beginning to develop radically, and my mother longed to start a menswear department at the Fashion School. In 1964, Hepworth, a multiple men's tailors, was looking for ideas for how to celebrate their centenary, and their consultant designer, Hardy Amies, suggested that the Fashion School should receive £20,000 to fund a new course at the College. The first five male students were chosen. Dougie Hayward, who designed the Beatles' clothes, taught part-time, as did Gordon Deighton, of Trend at Simpsons.

Nowadays, a Fashion School which did not design clothes for men would seem ridiculous, but my mother had to struggle to overcome Robin Darwin's disapproval.

'Fashion for men!' he said, as he brushed the crumbs from his moustache down his soup-stained Etonian tie. 'Idiotic!'

No matter that new men's boutiques like John Michael and John Stephen were starting to proliferate, and Carnaby Street was beginning to swing: the people who ran the Royal College considered it to be above such things as men's fashion, which was inextricably linked to homosexuality, then still illegal. To make matters worse, the RCA was full of male painters and sculptors with messy hair and corduroy trousers, bursting with testosterone, and they didn't like the introduction of image-conscious, often gay, men.

My mother had to put up with a great deal of scoffing. When she announced, on radio, that she thought Mick Jagger was the best-dressed man in Britain, stuffy professors at the Royal College could hardly believe their ears and their lips wrinkled with disapproval. They felt that her views reflected badly on the dignity of the institution.

She's the most feminine of all professional women; she's the only Professor of Haute Couture in Europe; but Mrs. Janey Ironside admits:

MEN ARE THE BEST AT FASHION DESIGN

"**THE** Professor will be here soon," said the secretary.

The Professor entered the room—a neat, petite figure.

Above elegant ... she wore a sm... tightly cut black ... a string of whi... beads at the th...

Under her co... hat she wore ... hair - do of ... tresses.

No, no. No ... It was the ... right. Profess... Ironside.

● Her sub... design at ...

making and designing clothes.

She was running her own successful business for private clients before being ... assistant to the

The Grimonds ask Janey Ironside to help solve the

The woman who changed fashion

A firm fist in velvet glove

From LYNNE BELL in London

Janey Ironside is small, and she has a ...

... way as you can other subjects. But I felt it was more than unfair to exclude the Fashion De- be."

... up with mat... can do anythi... thing one war...

Janey, Queen of fashion

executive black.

She also has devastatingly frank ideas on fashion — which British University off... know...

Press supported ... did ...

Fashion gets an exciting kick

PROFESSOR JANEY LEADS HER DESIGNING STUDENTS TO GAIETY

...side will resign as professor in July, and

...tion, and wt... seeing is p... never had th...

'Do you mean men will be wearing *handbags?*' people still asked her, amusedly, at parties. My mother would have laboriously to explain her opinions about men's fashion.

All the best fashion designers of the time seemed to have had their roots in the Fashion School at the Royal College of Art — Sally Tuffin and Marion Foale, the shoe designer Moya Bowler, Graham Smith, the hat designer, Janice Wainwright and James Wedge, who started the very successful shop, Countdown, on the King's Road.

Another star graduate was the designer Anthony Price. He created the much-copied spiral-cut skirt, which was universally worn during the seventies, and later he was credited with the styling of Roxy Music's Bryan Ferry, for whom he had designed record covers, stage sets and clothes.

And then there was the late Bill Gibb, who was described as fashion's Hockney. He was so successful that he didn't even finish the course, and in 1970 he was chosen by *Vogue* as Designer of the Year. He created his own label in 1975 and his phenomenal success was marked by a Bill Gibb retrospective at the Royal Albert Hall two years later.

But my mother's shiniest star was Ossie Clark.

Ossie had run away with the publicity at one dress show with a sweeping evening coat, the collar of which was edged with battery-operated lightbulbs. Later, there would be paper dresses, with epaulettes made of little aeroplanes. He was a real fashion adventurer, hugely gifted in his cutting and tailoring skills, and renowned for his Diamond Python coat bought by Britt Ekland. Similar coats were made for Twiggy, Marianne Faithfull and Sharon Tate. The craze for snakeskin that pervaded the late sixties and seventies began

Annette Green

Ossie Clark's show at the Chelsea Town Hall. Janey, with John beside her, sits on the left.

in 1966 when Ossie Clark visited a supplier of handbag leathers situated in a Dickensian cavern under the Thames. Here he found the skin of a twenty-six-foot-long boa constrictor, which he bought for thirty shillings a foot and made into his first snakeskin suit.

My mother was becoming such a success that she was credited as being one of the people who created the great British fashion boom of the sixties, responsible for King's Road boutiques, Carnaby Street and, indeed, the whole 'English look'. My mother was now a fashion icon, as well known in her own way as Mary Quant. She was regularly quizzed by journalists about what the next trend would be, and newspapers ran huge double-page spreads devoted to the latest designs coming out of the Fashion School at the Royal College of Art. 'It was extraordinary how self-assured I was becoming,' wrote my mother, 'perhaps because I believed so passionately in what I was doing.'

At one point, she was even knocked by the Glenda Slagg of the day, Jean Rook, who wrote in the *Daily Express* after one particularly innovative show: 'Why did Janey Ironside, probably the brightest fashion brain in Britain, let these kids run riot? They say "they're sick of Courrèges, they're sick of mini-skirts, they're sick of everything but colour and movement." They're sick all right!'

Meanwhile, Barbara Griggs wrote in the *Evening Standard*: 'Isn't it about time the fashion world put up a statue to Janey Ironside, or struck a medal or SOMETHING?'

If they had had any sense, the heads of department at the Royal College should have relished the publicity got by the Fashion School. Instead, they felt tremendously threatened and jealous. Why weren't *their* departments getting all the publicity? Why was this *woman* hogging the limelight? Why was *fashion*, of all trivial, ephemeral things, always in the spotlight? So they were filled with gleeful *Schadenfreude* when my mother engaged in her first big clash with Robin Darwin.

Robin longed for university status, and in order to achieve this he had to make the College, an institution sparkling with new design ideas, seem dignified and academic as well. He decided that the standard of the students' education should be compulsorily improved.

From now on, it was decided, it would be impossible for students

to enter the College unless they had some kind of educational qualification, and once enrolled, they would be compelled to attend a
General Studies course. They were supposed to spend part of their
time reading literature, learning philosophy and so on.

Iris Murdoch lectured on Sartre, Kierkegaard, and J. S. Mill; Isaiah
Berlin talked about Marx; Julian Huxley discussed Charles Darwin;
T. H. Huxley and George Steiner argued about de Sade, and
Raymond Chandler told the students about his writing for the *Black
Mask* magazine. To qualify for their diploma, all students had to
write a 12,000-word dissertation in General Studies.

My mother was one of the few people at the College to take a
stand against the General Studies course. She was absolutely furious.
What was so special about literacy?

Over Sunday lunch, she fumed about the situation.

'I bet Iris Murdoch didn't have to pass a fashion-design test before
taking her degree in theology or whatever it was!' she raged, as she
opened a tin of peaches.

'She certainly would have failed if she'd tried,' I said.

'She writes such fey, pretentious books anyway, about people
called Hugo and Jolyon. Have you tried *The Bell*?'

'No.'

'Don't,' said my mother. Then she added: 'And her *hair*!'

Why should my mother's students have to mug up on subjects
that were totally irrelevant to their chosen careers? Artists and
designers didn't need to know about the origins of man, or who
Kant was, or what century Molière lived in. If they wanted to
know, they could find out for themselves, and they probably
would. But to force all this irrelevant information down their

throats not only demeaned them, but demeaned their chosen art and craft.

Janey also argued that if the 'must-have-passed-a-certain-number-of-O-or-A-levels' rule had been in place a few years earlier, star fashion students like Ossie Clark and Sally Tuffin could never have got in. It was all a load of tosh.

But while at home John and I were passionately on her side, at the Royal College her criticism was not appreciated.

Much to my mother's fury and despair when the finals came that year, not only did two of her students not get diplomas because they failed the General Studies course, but, worse still, when David Hockney, star pupil of the Painting School, failed too, he was given an escape route. Since the College would have looked idiotic had they not recognized his talents in some way, the Board devised a gold medal to give him instead. Hockney had backed my mother to the hilt about the stupidity of General Studies and had never attended a single General Studies lesson in his life. He drew attention to the lunacy of the whole affair by receiving the award in a gold lamé suit, with his hair bleached bright yellow.

No gold medals were struck for my mother's two unfortunate fashion students.

While Christopher and Jean were downstairs, basking in all the pleasures brought by a new-found relationship, I lurked in my two upstairs rooms like a malevolent insect, a lone sniper, writing a book.

There is usually an element of unhappiness in every writer, so that must have been one reason why I had started the novel. It was also an acceptable way of leaking out a lot of misery and rage without hurting anyone directly, so I thought, or, more important, risking confrontation, a skill that I have never been able to master very successfully, preferring the oily, devious and placatory method of solving problems.

When I went out in the evenings, I said very little – I was still very shy – but when I got up from restaurant tables and popped to the lavatory, I got out my notebook and wrote down all the idiotic things that people had said.

I was not short of material, since I was knocking around with men much older than myself, many of whom worked in that easily mockable profession, advertising. They took me to places like the Colony Room in Soho, where a repulsive old lesbian called Muriel Belcher sat on a tall chair and shouted 'Hello, cunty!' to people like Francis Bacon and John Minton. Behind their backs, typing up in my room, I sneered at the pretentiousness of the teachers at art school and wrote an ungenerous but funny account of a weekend with my grandparents.

The style of the book consisted of descriptions of how I behaved on the surface ('"How nice to see you!" I said, warmly, giving him a big kiss') and what I was feeling underneath ('"You total creep," I thought to myself as I surreptitiously wiped the saliva his mouth had left on my cheek, when he wasn't looking').

In a way, this was a reflection of how I was acting every day of my life. I had a fairly amiable, quiet social front, apparently pleasant and amusing, but underneath I was seething with resentment.

I returned each night from another social engagement and siphoned off all my bile into the book, typing away on a rackety old portable until after midnight, a forbidden Woodbine in my mouth.

Chelsea Art School was in a state of near-collapse. Students were uncontrolled, even the teachers often failed to arrive and, when I left, after a year, no one even noticed. I became more interested in the idea of a life in journalism and although I'd failed to stay the shorthand and typing course at Oxford, I discovered a new secretarial technique called Speedwriting. This was an American style of shorthand that could be learned in three months, and the Underground trains were plastered with advertisements which read: 'Gt a gd jb + mo pa.'

On the strength of my new skills, I gt a jb, as we said in Speedwriting, for six months at the Fabian Society. I worked for Shirley Williams, who spoke so fast I have no idea how I managed to get down everything she said. The Fabians had old-fashioned offices in Victoria and every week I was given £9 in a brown paper packet. In cold weather, even with the gas fires on, I sometimes wore my gloves to type. Turning down a surprising offer to edit their magazine (I knew absolutely nothing about left-wing politics and cared even less), I left.

In an effort to get on to a more mainstream publication, I joined the copywriting department at *Vogue*, where the frightful Lady Rendlesham, who had tormented me when I was young, was fashion editress. The job had been found for me by my great old school-friend Georgina Howell, who had won a *Vogue* Writer of the Year award. I typed and made the tea, while Georgina and the rest of the department frantically dreamed up headlines and captions for the fashion photographs. 'How to make trends and influence people';

'Hand in glove'; 'Don't skirt the issue'; and, a particular favourite, featuring Italian shoes: 'How to be stood up by an Italian heel'.

I was drifting ever closer to journalism. One evening, I wrote a short, funny and cruel monologue delivered by a fictitious bore of the kind who had often taken me out to dinner. I sent it to *About Town* magazine and Michael Parkinson, then the features editor, accepted it at once.

I was amazed. I had no idea that getting into print was so easy. Even more extraordinary, after the *About Town* article had come out, I got a letter from a company called Secker & Warburg asking if I had ever thought of writing a book.

I had no idea who on earth Secker and Warburg were, but luckily, the same day that I received the letter, my uncle Robin was downstairs having lunch with Phyl, my grandmother. As I came into the dark basement dining-room, I found Robin with his head in his hands and my grandmother standing, puzzled, saying: 'Did you say you were suffering from cosmic gloom, darling? What *do* you mean?'

Lifting his head, my uncle Robin explained to me that Secker & Warburg were publishers and I understood. Charlotte Bingham, who was then no more than twenty, had just had a big hit with a book called *Coronet Among the Weeds* about life on the deb scene, and every other publisher was looking for a follow-up.

The publishers at Secker & Warburg must have been unable to believe their luck when they got a letter back from me saying: 'I enclose the manuscript of a book I have just written, so do give me a criticism of it.' I was unable to believe my own luck when, almost by return of post, a contract arrived. Secker and Warburg wanted to publish my book, under the title *Chelsea Bird*.

The book was extremely frank about my private life, and actually contained a bed scene, something of a scandal in the days when even the innocent *Lady Chatterley's Lover* had been taken to court for indecency. (My own bed scene consisted of the paragraph: 'I screwed myself up and shut my eyes as tight as I could. I felt I wasn't going to enjoy this, so I nerved myself to the ordeal. I hoped he wasn't going to be a two-hour character.')

I was worried about what my father would say when the book was published, but to me at the time he seemed so preoccupied with Jean that I felt he didn't have much time for me any more and wouldn't pay much attention. The truth was that it may well have been Jean who felt neglected in this *ménage à trois*, but being a selfish teenager I was unable to consider her point of view. Certainly when my father said to me: 'Don't worry if you want to stay out all night. Just ring me so I know you're all right and I'll see you at breakfast,' I didn't accept the words as those of a kind, liberal father rather out of his depth, but as a hurtful and neglectful brush-off.

My portrait for the jacket of the book was taken by Jeffrey Bernard, who walked me down to Chelsea embankment in complete silence, bummed a cigarette off me, threw it away in disgust when he saw it was a Benson and Hedges, on the grounds that it was too posh and, after snapping me, left without saying goodbye. I felt extremely small.

Publication day came at last. Tongue-tied, I was taken out to lunch in Dean Street by Fred Warburg, the publisher, and later that evening I was invited to a drinks party at his flat in Regent's Park. Lonely, prickly, guarded and contemptuous, I wrote to my mother, who was on holiday, about the ghastly people there – Penelope Mortimer ('awfully old and ragged'), Malcolm Muggeridge ('hideous!'), Elizabeth Smart ('frightful and drunk') — and the white wine ('the most revolting I have ever tasted. It was the sort that when you leant forward to sip it your eyes started watering because of the vinegary fumes that rose upwards.').

During the following days, we waited for the reviews.

What appeared to fascinate the media about *Chelsea Bird* was that it was about this brand-new, affluent, emancipated species known as 'Young People'. I was one of them, and I was spilling the beans.

'The cast of characters in her brief chronicle is quite orthodox: dumb model girls, fashionable criminals, young TV executives, useless art students, various updated versions of the chinless wonders with their eyes glued to the glossies for the latest trend signal. The unusual thing is not the girlish narrator's conclusion that her chums are weeds; it is her demonstration of the full extent of their weediness,' wrote the reviewer in the *Daily Telegraph*.

I was photographed in almost every glossy magazine and every paper — in my miniskirt, on top of ladders, walking down the King's Road in high boots, in black fish-net stockings, crossed-legged in studios. Now that I was being photographed for myself and not as some clone of my mother, I didn't mind it at all. For a few months, I was getting almost as much publicity as my mother herself.

But the publicity meant nothing to me and the publication of *Chelsea Bird* had absolutely no effect on my low opinion of myself. I felt I had simply been lucky, that anyone could write a book if they tried. I despised myself for being so unpleasant about people in the book, and was convinced the whole affair was a fluke. I experienced no feelings of pride or excitement; I became more depressed and

Photograph: S. Djukanovic

Art Disease

"CHELSEA BIRD" will be the name of her novel, which Secker and Warburg are to publish in the spring. Her own name is Virginia Ironside. She is 19. She comes from a very painterly family. Her father, Christopher, and uncle, Robin, are both artists. Her mother, Janey Ironside, is Professor of Fashion at the Royal College of Art. The principal target of her book is that traditional institution the Art School.

"All those debs," she says in sorrow, "going to Art Schools because they think it smart . . . Young men with ski-trousers and without talent . . . And, inside these places, the daily alternation of boredom and despair.

"The central male figure in my book is dreadful typical . . . Buys 'Private Eye' and 'Queen' the dot . . . it's boringly 'with-it' to the point of cliché . . . right, appalling, things . . . Like: 'I h . . . girls I do not fan It is too b . . .

Anoth . . . this: 'It ment and . . . tive. O . . .

BOOKS by Arthur P

MEET VIRGINIA IRONSIDE, aged 19, whose mother, Janey, is Professor of Fashion at the Royal College of Art. Secker and Warburg publish her first novel this spring . . . title: Chelsea Bird.

Principal target of her book: Art Schools. Virginia spent a year at one herself. "It was awful," she says. "I haven't enough words to say how crummy it was.

"All those debs going to Art Schools because they think it smart. Young men with ski-trousers and without talent. And, inside these places, the daily alternation of boredom and despair."

The Chelsea Bird, I'm glad to report, is neither boring nor desperate.

Layabouts

MISS VIRGINIA IRON-SIDE, 19-year-old daughter of Christopher Ironside, the painter, has written a book on life in Chelsea.

"It's about the King's Road layabouts and con-men and advertising people." she tells me.

Miss Ironside decided to write the book after a year at art school, which he hated.

Of art school she says: "It was awful. They tried to teach us abstract art. I

MISS VIRGINIA IRONSIDE
A book on Chelsea.

haven't got enough words to say how crummy it was."

The central character of her book is "an endless sneerer." Who? "Me" "But I am n . . . sneerer. It w . . . was so angry a . . . school," she sa . . .

"I have beer . . . very sad book. . . . mean it to be. . . .

And what this year's birds are choosing:

OUR Chelsea Birds gave their whole-hearted approval to the pale-honey-and-ginger convertibles pictured above.

They liked them on two counts.

One: Simplicity didn't mean dull and dowdy.

Two: Their obvious gu-anywhere quality made them clothes you'd wear to shreds.

SNAPPY

For Anna-bel, the two-colour waist-coat and skirt effect of the dr . . .

Annabel and Virginia
They liked simplicity.

People

GIRL ON THE FIRST STEP TO SUCCESS

THE ladder symbolises success. Publishers Secker and Warburg think 19-year-old Virginia Ironside has found it

They are publishing her first book—Chelsea Bird—which they say - shows up the utter disillusionment of youth today.

She is the daughter of artist Christopher Ironside and Professor of Fashion Design at the Royal College of Art, Janey Ironside.

And what does Mademoiselle think of it herself?

"It seems pretty rotten to me," she says. "Disillusionment! It is supposed to be funny. I don't want anyone to take me seriously. They will though.

AUTHORESS VIRGINIA IRONSIDE, PICTURED YESTERDAY BY FRANK APTHORP distant from myself. I had no idea what I was going to do in my life and realized, the more I came into contact with my contemporaries, that I felt different from all other people in a fundamental way. Everyone feels odd when they are in their early twenties, but I felt as if my actual genetic make-up was different, as if I had been born without an essential chromosome, that I came from a distant and extremely cruel planet. I could never look forward to anything, as other people seemed to do, I felt unreal, as if a pane of glass lay between me and the rest of the world. I found it impossible to feel love, except occasionally a kind of deep pity and sympathy with people who were in desperate emotional straits.

However, more on automatic pilot than with a sense of adventure, with the money I got from *Chelsea Bird* — the enormous sum of £400 — I went to America by myself, knowing absolutely no one. I thought that that was the sort of thing a normal person of my age would do if they had been in my position.

I stayed at the Pickwick Arms in New York, the cheapest hotel there, and walked up and down Park Avenue feeling very silly and very blank. I bumped into Rose Dugdale and she took me to see *Phèdre* with her brother. I went to visit Robin Grove-White, an Oxford undergraduate I had met on a Spanish holiday at sixteen, who was working at the comedy theatre, Second City, in Chicago. We had an odd on–off relationship which seemed to last years — we would go out together, I would drop him, and then, realizing I had made a terrible mistake because he was bright, kind and funny, would go to enormous lengths to get him back again. Then the cycle would be repeated.

Finally, I went down to New Orleans. I took a bus trip round the plantation houses — I was the only person on the bus — and I went on my own to a blues club. Later, I went to a Creole restaurant alone and ate gumbo on a barstool, staring at myself reflected in a mirrored wall. I had no idea what I was doing there at all.

My uncle Robin still came round to Neville Street occasionally, but he was burning himself out with non-stop creative activity. He still took too many drugs — uppers and downers as well as mescaline and Dr Collis Browne — he stayed up till all hours, slept less and less and ate irregular meals. While he grew progressively thinner, his eyes had a nervous, glittering look and he suffered from acute indigestion.

I remember the grey colour of my father's face when a hospital rang to tell him that Robin had been admitted the night before with a heart attack. He was shocked and then, when it was clear that his brother was doing fine, enormously irritated. It seemed natural that Robin had got himself into another major scrape. My father didn't say 'Typical Robin!' but it was written on his face.

My father visited him and reported that everything was going well. We had begun to wonder how Robin would cope when he came out, and whether the crisis would force him to alter his way of life in any way, when news came that he had died from a massive heart attack. My father was devastated. (It turned out that a well-meaning visitor had been to see Robin in hospital and given him a bottle of Dr Collis Browne.)

It was I who had to ring up my grandmother, who was staying in the country, and break the news to her. She never really recovered from this blow, the death of her favourite son.

After Robin died, Christopher got a letter from Angus Wilson, describing him as one of the most 'stimulating, loyal and valuably critical friends I can ever hope to know . . . a natural 19th century dandy – not the false kind that is so common to meet now'.

At the end of the letter, Angus dropped a bombshell: he revealed that in the last years of his life, Robin had formed a relationship with a young man. Angus asked Christopher to get in touch with him, because he 'must be feeling so lost'.

The existence of Robin's lover was a complete shock to my father. Although he knew of Robin's sexuality, it had always been a taboo subject. It was illegal and, wisely, never discussed, even behind closed doors. The boy had been a waiter at Wheelers, and Robin had looked after him like a son. They had been making plans to live together just before Robin died. Before the funeral, he came round once to the house but after that we never saw him again.

As my father leaned more and more on Jean for support, and as Jean, being a normal and affectionate young woman, naturally wanted to start a family, I felt increasingly like a gooseberry. To make room for the baby girl who eventually arrived, I had to move out of one of the rooms I had been given at the top of the house, my father having long relinquished his studio. Although I was out all the time and rarely used the room next to my bedroom, I perceived this as a drive to squeeze me out of my father's new life. I tried to blot out my feelings and numbed my emotions. In my diary I wrote: 'I now have a half-sister. It has fair hair and a big nose. It is very odd or is it? I don't feel much enthusiasm or non enthusiasm. Mummy was very bitter about it all, so horrible and vindictive and I hated her and felt for her and it was terrible.'

Night after night, the baby screamed and screamed. Night after night, my father and Jean were up with it, burping it, patting it, comforting it, singing lullabies to it, both besotted. Jean was a scrupulous, loving and devoted mother, now rarely to be seen except in a confusion of spotless aprons, steam, thermometers, powdered milk, sterilizing equipment and Napisan. Days were spent boiling nappies, drying nappies, fluffing up towels, making tiny beds, worrying about the existence of lead paint on cots, waving rattles, taking the baby for walks in the pram, giving it baths, feeding it every five minutes and powdering its little bottom. Everywhere smelt of Johnson's baby oil and milk.

It was an atmosphere which struck no kind of familiar chord in me at all. So *this* was what being a mother must be like. This, too, was what being loved by a mother must be like. It seemed utterly mysterious to me.

All I experienced was the feeling of increasing redundancy, of having no place in this alien and, for them, extremely happy family.

Soon after the birth of their second daughter, Christopher and Jean found a new house which, I was quick to observe, did not have room for me. My grandmother found a hot little box-like flat in a block in Earl's Court, and before I knew what was happening, the whole family was off, in a whirl of feeding bottles, baby alarms, carrycots and nappies, and I was left alone in Neville Street with no heat and no water, until I found a flat for myself.

Suddenly I found myself in an almost identical situation to my mother a few years before.

The flat I moved into was only a few doors away from Diana's 'cupboard' in Draycott Place, where my mother had stayed immediately after she left home. At the time she had written: 'My personal life at this time was one familiar to many women who suddenly find themselves on their own after years of marriage – unbearable loneliness mingled with too much social life.'

I felt exactly the same.

ten

MINI *Mini-dresses and mini-skirts introduced in the 1960s are self-explanatory, i.e. very short, worn up to 8 or 9 inches above the knee. Universal wear for British teenagers and adopted elsewhere, they have been accorded the usual share of condemnation and appreciation.*

Janey Ironside, *A Fashion Alphabet*

It often doesn't take much for an alcoholic to start drinking again, particularly if, like my mother, they haven't really acknowledged the fact that they are alcoholic. The General Studies affair had undermined my mother's confidence and her 'pegs were never very high', as she once wrote. Her nanny in India may have had some part to play in it all, since she was always threatening hell-fire when my mother was small. When they shared a room, the nanny said that if my mother peeped through the umbrella she put up in the bedroom to divide it, the mark of Cain would appear on her forehead.

'Although no outward mark appeared, she succeeded in making me feel thoroughly guilty, a trait which has pursued me into adult life and caused me and others a great deal of unhappiness,' wrote my mother, later.

After about eighteen teetotal months, my mother must have thought: 'Oh, well, just the one can't hurt.' 'Just the one' always turns into 'Just the two' and 'Just the two' turns into 'Well, as long as I don't drink at lunch-time', which turns into 'I'll drink what I like when I want as long as it isn't spirits . . .' As one who is wedded to alcohol myself, I know the pattern all too well.

I watched her progression back into her old drinking patterns with terror. Every time she telephoned, I listened, my ears pricked like a dog's, for any tiny sign of a slur. When I kissed her hello, I sniffed her breath. When she went out of the room, I tasted her Slimline tonic to see if it was spiked. I made mental notes when I looked at the bottles of drink in the kitchen — could John really have drunk all that whisky by himself since I was last there?

'Oh, don't worry, darling,' my mother said, when I questioned her. 'I seem to have got it under control now. You can't live without drink — well, I can't anyway.'

John tried to reassure me that things were all right, but Ossie Clark recorded in his diaries that my mother was 'wearing black, always in dark glasses, clutching her bag having plucked up Dutch courage with gin to stealthily teeter in to College . . .'

She had been offered the job of editing the fashion page at the *Observer*, on top of that of fashion professor, and blithely took it on, thinking it would be possible to do both at once, despite Robin Darwin's angry warnings against it. The staff at the *Observer* were delighted to sign up such a star, but were horrified when she started to reel in late, 'slightly high', and ask to be shown the pictures to accompany her copy. When she saw them, her comment might have been a rather slurred and scathing 'I can't say much about *those*' before staggering out again. Often she didn't turn up at all, and soon it became obvious that she wasn't up to it.

Though sorry about my mother's tribulations at the *Observer* and the College, I became less sympathetic when she suggested that, since John was working too hard to take time off, I accompany her on a trip to Glyndebourne. She had been invited to put on a show at the opera house in aid of the NSPCC. Princess Margaret and Snowdon were to attend. Osbert Lancaster, who designed the sets, would be doing the commentary; dinner afterwards would be at Firle, a great eighteenth-century house.

'It's the last thing I want to do,' I said. 'I couldn't bear it.'

'But you'd meet Lord Snowdon and Princess Margaret and I'm sure it would be fun . . .' said my mother in a wheedling voice.

'Why should I want to meet Lord Snowdon or Princess Margaret? Anyway, Glyndebourne's ghastly!'

'I know, that's why I want you to come. Oh, *please*! Darling! Just for me!'

In the end, I went with her, most ungraciously. As I heaved her suitcase on to the netted rack above our second-class train seats, I knew that the only reason I couldn't hear the tell-tale clink of a bottle was because she had wrapped it up in her nightdress. Sitting alongside us, on a third seat, was what looked like a ghostly third party — a white crêpe dress with long sleeves set with silver studs, echoed in the collar like a man's denim jacket, specially designed for her by Ossie Clark.

We arrived at Glynde House. Our hostess, some grand widow,

was clearly repulsed by my mother's entrance as she staggered across her great hall. To make matters worse, the evening was organized by a woman whose taste and imagination was not really up to my mother's when it came to staging a smart dress show. Her idea of 'groovy' was to hire a ghastly pop group from Oxford, made up of upper-class twits who were used to playing at débutantes' balls. She could not begin to understand my mother's original and radical ideas, and Janey ended up raging at her. In the end, my mother took refuge in the whisky she had brought with her, and I had to pick her up when she fell down in the mud in her Ossie dress on the way to the grand dinner. She sat next to Snowdon. I sat at a nearby table twisting my hands nervously, apologizing to everyone about my mother's condition. I was probably the only person who realized, or certainly minded so acutely, how drunk my mother actually was.

There seemed to be two Janeys. One was the giggling, girlish and amusing woman, highly intelligent, well read and sophisticated. The other was a drunken, slurring bag-lady, with emotions ranging from aggressive to amorous to self-pityingly sentimental. I never knew which one I was going to meet for lunch on Sundays, and began to dread my mother's telephone calls and invitations.

John and I tried to put pressure on her to consult doctors to see if they could help with the problem, but in those days no one knew anything about alcoholism. She was willing to come with me if I made an appointment, but nothing ever came of any treatment recommended. She tried Antabuse, a drug that you take which makes you sick if you drink, but it didn't seem to work. One doctor told me privately: 'There is no hope for her. She will just continue drinking until she dies.' 'Your mother's an alcoholic and there's

nothing I can do for her,' said another. 'She'll never stop being one.'
I found an addiction counsellor, but she hated him. 'Horrible little
man,' she said. 'He had a mangy beard and one of those jerseys you
put in the washing-machine. Ugh.' I emptied all her bottles down
the sink, but she only bought more.

John was clearly worried — he loved and admired Janey enormously — but there was very little he could do. He was working all
day and although I'm sure that sometimes he must have felt like moving
out, he realized that she was vulnerable and that she needed him.

In those days addiction was a concept that very few people understood. I certainly didn't. I could not comprehend why my mother
couldn't stop drinking. I felt she was doing it deliberately to annoy
me; I was convinced that her drinking was evidence that she cared
so little about me that she wouldn't even try to stop. Only now, as
I notice myself very occasionally reaching for the white wine at
eleven in the morning ('nearly lunch-time') do I understand how
great is the grip that alcohol can have on a person's life.

Alcoholics Anonymous was not then the groovy venue it is today,
bursting with rock stars and interior designers. The only people who
attended in the sixties were Irish drunks and down-and-outs who
had reached rock-bottom. There was no way my mother would go
to one of their meetings.

London was, by then, officially swinging. The Beatles were high in
the charts, Young People dominated the news, the fashion craze was
booming and pop was increasingly important. The group that was
top of the pops each week was featured on the front page of the

tabloids. Belatedly spotting what was going on, the editor of the
Daily Mail, realizing that he needed someone young on its pages,
had yelled: 'Get me a "pop column" or whatever it's called! Get me
a young person to write it! Get it now!' I was interviewed by the
Mail, wearing the mini-est of miniskirts, long black high-heeled
boots and fish-net stockings. Mouthing a few words like 'fab',
'groovy', 'square', 'Tamla Motown', 'cover version' and 'backing
group', I managed to persuade the astonished features editor, who
had never heard such language before, to hire me on the spot.

Every week it was my job to listen to piles of 45 rpm records –
I soon learned to pick the hits after listening for only a few seconds
– and every week I interviewed a group. During my time at the
Mail, I interviewed the Beatles, the Rolling Stones, Jimi Hendrix,
James Brown, Janis Joplin, Ravi Shankar and Marc Bolan. My father
said later: 'I didn't know what a glamorous job it was until one day
when I answered the phone and it was Paul McCartney asking for
her.'

Paul McCartney may have rung once, but I was never part of the
sixties in-crowd. The nearest I got to the stars was interviewing
them, or getting drunk and sleeping with their PRs.

The sixties have been built up in people's memories as the most
exciting time to be young in the twentieth century. It may have been
for some people – particularly men – but I was never anything
but acutely unhappy. Although I tried nearly every single drug going,
from pot to heroin to coke (I never dared try LSD as I was certain
I would risk madness), none of them suited me as well as alcohol.
Then the class revolution terrified me because I was often mocked
for my South Kensington accent. And the advent of the Pill meant

I found it almost impossible to say 'No' to any man – you couldn't argue that you might get pregnant, and feminism and the 'No Means No' campaign had not yet been dreamed up.

My pathetic lack of security and inability to stand up for myself, and my desperation for affection, had resulted in my having had sex with at least fifty men before I had even left Neville Street. But now I was living on my own, my father was preoccupied with his new family and my mother had taken to drink, I went completely off the rails. It wasn't long before I was well over the 100 mark and still counting. I was desperate for men to put their arms around me and kiss me – and I could get that if I agreed to sex. I never enjoyed the actual act of sex particularly, but got some kind of buzz from the closeness and lack of control of the men when we were actually in bed together. I drank too much, I had two boyfriends at the same time, I even once had sex with three different people within twenty-four hours. One young lawyer enticed me into bed with the romantic words: 'Oh come on, I've paid for dinner, it'll only take a couple of minutes.'

I also suffered from a phobic anxiety about catching VD, as sexually transmitted disease was then known. 'Could it have been Tony?' I wrote in my diary. 'He had slept with a tart the day before, so that is a possibility. Then Mark came on Monday. Tony B was Wednesday. A possibility. Nick was the following Tuesday. Burning pains started a week after Derek. He could easily have slept with a scrubber, but would he have risked it being married? Then Chris last night . . .'

I used to visit my father in tears and beg for advice or some ideas to relieve my constant depression, but however kind and sensible he was, his new house was 'ghastly, all strange and different', as I wrote in my diary. My father dispensed sensible advice, but I knew that the moment I closed the front door behind me, he would be back at his drawing board, getting out his rubber and pencil, completely pre-occupied with whatever particular design he was working on at the time – he had started to design medals and coinages for developing countries. My doctor prescribed tranquillizers, but nothing seemed to help. I was becoming more and more unhappy. I'd already had the first of three abortions (having discovered that I did have some sexual infection, I was panic-stricken that I might be infertile and there was only one way to prove I wasn't) and there was never a moment when I wasn't anxiously worrying about my mother's drinking.

In my diary I wrote: 'I realize that I am different, and not different in the way that everyone thinks they're different. I'm so cold and hard, really, apart from odd flashes which are sheer stupidity and very unpleasant. I have never had this terrible deadly feeling before. Morbid – no, not really, just evil. This morning I was crying all the way to work and in the underground, tired and mis. It's one thing to cry at night, but another to cry in the morning and so miserable. I'm just so sick of all this, so MISERABLY MISER-ABLY MISERABLY SICK OF LIVING. I WANT TO CRY SO MUCH I CAN'T BEAR IT ALL.'

Although it seems obvious to me now what 'it all' was, I didn't understand at the time why I felt so suicidally depressed.

Robin Darwin's intense dislike of my mother must have grown slowly. I suspect that it started after she had refused to marry him.

He felt angry and hurt at being rejected. The fact that he had learned that she was living with John Wright, a beautiful, talented young man, must have felt like a snub to her old lover. His hatred may have intensified because she was drinking. Whatever it was, having been happily ensconced in the new College building, and no longer feeling like an outcast, my mother was suddenly ordered to move out to make way for the expansion of the new Stained Glass School.

The Fashion School had to return to 23 Cromwell Road.

It was an extraordinary decision, because the Fashion School was by far the best-known school in the entire College. If anyone said, abroad, that they were studying at the Royal College of Art in London, it was immediately assumed that they were fashion students. And because fashion was becoming such an asset to British industry, and because the Royal College of Art was at the centre of the fashion revolution, people began to assume that the Fashion School *was* the Royal College of Art.

But perhaps that was what it was all about. Robin Darwin and the professors at the College were becoming steadily more jealous.

The jealousy was also inspired by a male chauvinist attitude, deeply ingrained in people who didn't realize that fashion was a multi-million-pound industry. My mother felt, rightly: What did Robin Darwin know about fashion, himself a watercolourist who liked nice lunches, who thought of fashion as wafting off to Paris and 'buying a gown'?

'And those professors resented her not just because she was a strong woman, but also because she was an attractive woman,' said her secretary, Mrs Herbert-Smith.

My mother was even accused by the Council of allowing her students to become swollen-headed due to the amount of publicity they received.

'But as publicity brought all sorts of assets with it in those early days, it was a risk I had to take,' she said.

Within a matter of a couple of months of the school's move, my mother's drinking became completely out of control. It started to affect her work, which it had never done before. 'Sometimes she could hardly stagger in to the College,' said Mrs Herbert-Smith. 'It was very difficult. Some days I had to lock her in her office. Once, she was supposed to be giving a talk to the London College of Fashion and I got all the students to come on the stage and answer on her behalf. She just wasn't in a fit state to give a talk. She could hardly stand.

'She accepted that I knew she brought in drink in the mornings and had it in her desk. For a time, she was drunk every day. She told me she had learned to like the taste of alcohol in India, when she was twelve.'

Despite her behaviour, she still retained her students' total admiration.

'Janey was far from normal,' said Anthony Price. 'And that was partly why we respected her so much. She was a Disney-esque character, a mixture of Cruella De Vil and the wicked stepmother in *Snow White*. She was a completely archetypical figure. We were in the world of looks, and how she looked was more important than anything. She didn't have to say much because she was queen supreme.

'We knew that she drank but we thought it was great. It was like having a fabulous head who took Ecstasy at work; everything she did was OK as long as she wore her long black boots, she had that ashen white face, and those big red, almost Grace Jones, lips.

'You went up to see her in her office, which was guarded at the door by Mrs Herbert-Smith, and inside, Janey would be sitting behind her desk with a black polo neck and a black suit, with her head sort of balanced on it and she was sort of gazing, and it was wonderful. She was like a greenhouse and we were exotic plants and she was just smiling and drinking and sprinkling a bit of water on us.'

The more my mother drank, the more she lied. She even claimed to have stopped drinking altogether. As she staggered about the flat, she said that she was 'ill' or 'had flu' but swore that she hadn't touched a drop.

Despite my depression, I always managed to remain the sensible adult in charge when it came to my mother. I was now having to look after her, to tick her off, to encourage her through her various College crises. But the situation was becoming too much for me. I tried to cope, and asked Christopher for advice, but even that great fount of all wisdom could give me no guidance. The pressure was becoming intolerable, so when she became too ill to go in to the College, John agreed that I should ask her brother, Anthony, to come up from his farm in the country to talk to her.

He arrived on a grey Sunday afternoon. My mother lay in her bed, yellow with jaundice. Her grinning face peeped over the sheets. 'No-o, I haven't had *any*thing to drink,' she said, in a bleary way. 'No-oooo . . . I promise . . . Would I lliiiie to you? No, tell, tell tell me wha you boooth doinn', bin doin' . . .'

Anthony and I looked at each other across the bed in despair.

After a while, she staggered up to go to the bathroom. She lurched out of the room, holding on to the furniture. Her legs, sticking out from under her nightdress, were covered in bruises.

'She *must* be drinking, Ant!' I said, desperately.

'Well, she *says* she isn't,' said Anthony, helplessly.

As I shifted my position on the bed, I felt something hard underneath me. I patted the blankets. Hysterically, we pulled back the bedclothes. There was a half-empty bottle of gin. There were two others in the bed, and we started a frantic search of the room. In her cupboard, behind a row of black dresses and skirts, were more bottles of vodka, and more behind the curtains and under the bed. The room seemed to be packed with bottles. When we confronted her on her way back from the bathroom, she admitted she had been drinking, and when the doctor came the following day, she agreed to go to the Priory to be dried out.

The Priory in those days was not like the smart hospital it is today. There were no proper treatment programmes for alcoholics. Although it had once been a beautiful gothic mansion, built on the same lines as Strawberry Hill, it was now run-down and overgrown, like a Victorian asylum.

When I had a breakdown in the nineties, my son drove me, in my car, to the Priory for a month's stay. It was depression rather than drink that had brought me there, but the irony of the situation was not lost on either of us.

More recently I visited the Priory to see a psychiatrist myself, and as I climbed the familiar stairs, I had one of those Proustian flashbacks that happen a couple of times in a lifetime. For a brief second, I was transported back to that moment when I visited my mother at the hospital; and the overwhelmingly intense pity and pain I felt for myself – completely unfelt at the time – was almost unbearable. I burst into instant, paralysing sobs and then slowly felt myself climbing back into what felt like an old donkey costume, putting on the face, pulling myself together, shutting the doors to the old experience, throwing away the key.

At the Priory, a doctor stood at the end of my mother's bed as she put down her suitcase and prepared to undress, and said: 'So you're that woman who tries to get everyone to look like stupid monkeys!' My mother was put into a drugged sleep for a week, the only treatment for drying out in those days. After a few days, I went to visit her.

There being no one at reception, I wandered down long, empty, linoleum-covered corridors, peering into rooms full of addicts and mad people, who looked straight out of a Brueghel painting, searching for my mother.

Finally I found a grey-painted room, with what appeared to be a bundle of dung-coloured blankets heaped on top of an iron bed. Just before I turned away, I spotted something sticking out of the top, like spiky black grass.

'Mummy?' I said.

The blankets whirled and my mother started up in her iron bed, wild-eyed.

'Who are you?' she screamed. 'Give me mead! Give me mead!'

Most alcoholics find their first few months extremely difficult to cope with after they have been through enforced abstinence, but in those days there was no aftercare. My mother was simply dried out, like a sponge in a heatwave, and dumped back at home, to cope by herself. She went to stay with my grandparents in their gloomy sandstone house in Ross-on-Wye, and I dutifully accompanied her.

'Poor Janet,' was all her mother said, briskly, when I tried to unburden myself to her. 'I'm sure all she needs is a few days in the country with some fresh air and good food. Put the roses back into her cheeks!'

'Virginia and I had rather a depressing weekend with me feeling as normal gloomy and she constantly bursting into tears,' my mother wrote to John from the house in Ross. 'However, I forced her to ask Christopher if she couldn't stay with him for a few days, which she hadn't liked to do because of hurting me. How vile it is of me – and of everyone. And, oh dear, without some alcohol to make me mellow I find my parents get unreasonably on my nerves. I expect I am going through the phase that smokers go through when they give it up, of intense irritability, and yet as I say I have no desire for a drink. I want something to stop me from feeling so glum and irritable! Before, I used to sneak off to the Axe & Cleaver for a drink occasionally, more to get away than anything and to see other people, however awful, but I can't really face that at the moment. I know it's quite easy to give it up; it's the continuing not to drink under stress that is so hard for most people like me. Isn't it awful! If only I didn't suffer permanently from these awful feelings. When I drink I really *can't* help it and hardly ever realise that I am drinking and how much. Please don't abandon me!'

She returned to the Fashion School, frail but sober. Ambitious as ever, she became, over the following few months, even more successful and was awarded the *Harper's Bazaar* award for outstanding achievements in creative design. But whenever the

Fashion School was commissioned to design for some prestigious event — a dress for the Queen for the Order of the British Empire, the British European Airways uniforms — the old jealousy flared up again, grumbling away in the College's corridors.

In 1967, the Royal College of Art was awarded degree status by royal charter, with the power to award its own degrees. Sir Robin Darwin (he had been knighted) became the first Rector and Vice-Provost. Everyone was delighted — until the Academic Advisory Committee recommended that one school, alone among all the others, should not be awarded this special status. This school, the most successful school in the entire college, was the School of Fashion Design.

My mother was devastated. Indeed, there was hardly anyone who wasn't. John and I were not only passionately on my mother's side, horrified by the unfairness of the decision, but I felt my heart turn to stone with the knowledge that such a catastrophe would be too much for my mother to bear without turning back to alcohol for support.

The reasons given for the extraordinary decision were that fashion design was too tied up with industry (never mind that Prince Albert had founded the Royal College of Art for that very purpose), it was too transient and it didn't fulfil the demands set out by the Academic Advisory Committee. Textile design, graphic design, ceramics, jewellery and photography were all considered worthy — but not fashion.

'The trouble was,' said Hugh Casson, when he looked back on the whole fiasco, 'the word "fashion" stuck in academic gullets.' Fashion, after all, only catered for homosexuals and women.

The fashion journalists were outraged at this cruel omission.

Beatrice Miller wrote in *Vogue*: 'One rarely finds an exciting new fashion venture without finding an RCA student there, too. It's a marvellous training ground with the highest standards and a lively atmosphere, a sort of controlled anarchy which means fresh ideas don't get stifled but are channelled into commercial potential. With fashion exports running at over a million pounds a week, this is the moment to stabilise and support the industry in every way possible, and the decision to withhold university status from the Fashion School is harmful to the prestige of the whole industry.'

The students were up in arms, and the NUS took up my mother's cause on her behalf. As one said, 'It's a piece of total academic pomposity to decide that there is less social or academic content in courses dealing with fashion than in jewellery or textiles.'

Clearly, Robin Darwin had it in for my mother. Over the last few years he had relentlessly sidelined the Fashion School. He appeared to be driven by a personal hatred of Janey and there was no way that he could be reasoned with. As a friend, Robin was loyal, helpful, charmingly patronizing and would pull any string to get his chums ahead of the game. But when crossed, he could become a ruthless, bullying tyrant. One of the members of the Council of the RCA was reminded by Darwin's reign at the College of that of the Habsburgs, who ruled by keeping the peasants in 'terror and ignorance'.

'Robin was a nasty man,' said Mrs Herbert-Smith, when I talked to her recently. 'He was a destroyer, and once he got it in for someone there was no hope. It had nothing to do with Janey drinking. They all drank so much. Robin was a bully and a Darwin. He had a lot of rage in him. He destroyed Janey really knowingly.'

Probably because they were so terrified of Robin themselves, few people on the teaching staff supported my mother. There was one particularly unpleasant meeting, at which Robin told her that whatever she said would be struck from the minutes, and Hugh Casson, her one-time friend and lover, conspicuously failed to back her up. Later, she met him in a lift. 'How are you today, dearie?' said the minuscule architect, in an oily way. My mother replied coldly and pointedly: 'I'm suffering from nasty stabbing pains in the back.'

Eventually she had no option but to resign.

'It is clear that the Fashion School is an embarrassment to the college,' she said in a newspaper interview in January 1968. 'They might deny this hotly, but this feeling has built in me until it has affected my health. The stress has been very upsetting. I discovered I was transmitting my depression about the situation to the students and this is wrong. These young people need buoyancy and enthusiasm all around them. They have depressive periods of their own without their tutors or professor adding to it. But still, I can't tell you with what alacrity my resignation was accepted. There was no "Come and see us and we'll talk about it." The acceptance of my resignation was slapped back by return of post. And the attitude has been one of "Thank God she's gone."'

'There is unmitigated gloom here and the students are seriously disturbed,' the College Registrar told the press. 'It was a bolt from the blue. Janey Ironside is nearly irreplaceable.'

'I absolutely refuse to say anything,' said Robin Darwin, when asked for a comment by a newspaper reporter. 'The only reason she gave me for leaving is ill-health.'

The students gave her a leaving party and presents. One was a

College of Art shock as fashion professor resigns 'for the sake of my students'

JANEY IRONSIDE, who influenced a whole generation of designers, has resigned as Professor of Fashion at the Royal College of Art after two years of frustration and three months' sick leave.

Professor Ironside, 49, said yesterday that she resigned from the job she made such a success because she did not believe in the college's policies—and felt that an unhappy professor was no good to bright young students.

She became professor 12 years ago. Her charm, tenacity and talent have been initial driving forces behind the success of fashion names like Tuffin and Foale, Gerald McCann, Roger Nelson.

Most of our top young designers cut their first toile under the guidance of Professor Ironside. The prestige of the School of Fashion has never been higher.

Last night Professor Ironside talked about her reasons for resigning . . .

THE EX-PROFESSOR: JANEY IRONSIDE LAST NIGHT

Why I quit
by Professor Janey

AS TOLD TO LYNDA LEE-POTTER

I'VE been very worried for a long time. I never thought it was a good idea to turn the college into a university. You can't pin academic degrees on creative designers. Creative talent isn't an academic qualification.

But when the college was granted university status last November, students of fashion were the only ones to end their three years with a diploma and not a degree.

I think it was absolutely monstrous that fashion and clothing should have been discriminated against in this way.

Basically, of course, the trouble is that the word fashion just sticks in the gullet of the academicians.

It's not only on personal, frivolous grounds that I object. It affects the students financially. They're finding it increasingly difficult to get grants from local education authorities.

That is why this year I have had to interview fewer than half the normal intake of students I would normally be considering for September '68.

Success

It's just too much. I'm having to follow policies I don't believe in and I'm not

Some of her triumphs . . .

GERALD McCANN

SALLY TUFFIN

MARION FOALE

ROGER NELSON

college. I've had marvellous students. Without them I couldn't have done anything.

And by providing the right teachers, by encouragement, by exposing them to the public, by introducing them to the right contacts, I've played an important part in their success.

In my position I do believe that I've had a very great influence on students and I have a terrific responsibility towards them.

This is one of the reasons why I've resigned. An unhappy professor is no use to bright young people. They want someone who is en-

naturally one doesn't want to give up a good job, but events put me into a ridiculous position. A professor can't be seen to be openly against the authorities.

You have to believe passionately in what you are doing, in the policies that you're following. Because I haven't been doing this I've not been feeling happy and this has made me ill.

My doctor said that I couldn't go on like this and he advised me to resign.

I don't know yet what I'm going to do. It seems awful that I'm going; I still can't quite believe it.

question of "Come and see us and let's talk it over." The acceptance was slapped back by return of post. And the attitude has been one of "Thank God she's gone."

I shall remain at the college until the end of the summer term. I've got a lot of students to launch before I can start thinking about myself.

For the past four years the fashion school hasn't been really welcome in the college. For the past two years I have not been able to take the decisions I have wanted to take.

One of the many articles announcing Janey's resignation

picture by Erte, one of his watercolours based on the Hudson River, which shows a figure wearing a Chrysler-building-style hat, with a huge train held by similar but smaller figures, and black men kneeling and worshipping in front. The other present was a ring with a blue stone ('Oh God,' said my mother to me later. 'It's very sweet of them, but surely they must know by *now* that I *never* wear blue?')

To rub salt into the wound, the Fashion School, under Professor Joanne Brogden, who took over from my mother, was granted degree status only a year later.

eleven

COLLARS AND NECKLINES   *Neck and breasts are the surest evidence of age in humans as teeth are in horses and if older women have any say left about fashion they will not encourage this open age identification. Undoubtedly one woman may look charming and youthful in a Peter Pan collar — another may look as though she were mutton dressed up as lamb; one may look very chic in a polo neck, with its high roll collar fitting close to the neck, and another may look as if she were a kennel-maid manqué.*

Janey Ironside, *A Fashion Alphabet*

Most people are buoyed up by all the attention they get immediately after a disaster and my mother was no exception. She was rung constantly by commiserating colleagues and cheered by reading articles which appeared, condemning the Royal College's acceptance of her resignation. She was kept afloat, consumed with feelings of resentment and indignation and raging against Robin, who she saw as a monstrous traitor.

I, on the other hand, was filled with dread: I knew that she would never be able to cope without her job. Since in the end she had refused to resign on the grounds of ill-health — Robin had been lying when he spoke to the newspapers — she didn't even get a pension. After a few months, the phone stopped ringing and people began to forget. My mother had nothing to do and she was broke. Without the College, she felt she was nothing.

And, now in her fifties, my mother was becoming what she had always dreaded – old.

When she was seventeen, my mother wrote in her diary: 'I have an absolute horror of old age nowadays; every old woman I meet I think: "That's what I'll be like soon." I always feel uncomfortable and unhappy when I hear someone say "What right have old people got to interfere" or "I hate old people." And I hate to hear someone say "Oh, she's ancient!" about someone of 35. When I'm 35 I shan't like being called ancient. Old age is a beastly thing. Why must we get old, why can't we stay young forever, it's so beastly to feel the days slipping past and not being able to stop them.'

At fifty-four, my mother had an eye-lift, followed, a year later, by a face-lift. (I had exactly the same operations at the same ages.) To hide the 'lizardy' look, she started to wear polo-necked jerseys or scarves around her neck. She thickened around the waist; she continued to dye her hair jet black. She may have looked rather inhuman, but she also looked strange and original, something from a surrealist painting.

To make matters worse, my father was enjoying sudden and enormous success. During the last fifteen years or so, he had designed the coinages for Tanzania, Brunei, Qatar and Dubai, as well as memorial medals. Fortunately for him, no sooner had he sent off a series of drawings for approval than the head of state was assassinated or there was a *coup d'état* and he had to start all over again. The work was never-ending. (My father never signed his coins – for three reasons, he said. 'The first is that it would spoil the design.

Janey, vulnerable and depressed

The second is that it is arrogant to sign. The third is that it is even more arrogant not to sign.')

A few years earlier, he had been invited to take part in an open competition for the design of the immensely secret decimal currency – and he had won the competition for the reverses. On the occasions I visited him – usually in tears – he was always sitting hunched over a white plaster cast, scraping into the indents and squinting to see them as raised. Now the coins had hit the streets, amidst a blaze of publicity. While my mother's face had virtually disappeared from the pages of the national press, my father's appeared more and more frequently. And, to my mother's dismay, he and Jean had had a third child, whom he christened, in honour of the decimals, Christian Decimus Ironside.

Janey became seriously depressed and, within a few months, she was drinking again, on and off. When I went round, she would sit on the sofa and say to me: 'Darling, I don't want to live.'

She must have said this fifty, sixty, a hundred times during the following year. In her immaculate and tasteful room, she looked out of place, like the plastic bag full of sweepings and waste paper a maid might leave in a hotel room by accident. 'I just want to die.' Despite the carefully pleated white curtains, the immaculate grey haircord carpet, everything spotlessly clean, the room was like a corpse polished up for the relations to see – and yet the glasses we drank from were smeary.

'I would miss you,' I lied. I leaned over to kiss her cold face to make certain she wouldn't read my thoughts. From the side of her mouth, I touched some of her wet saliva and longed to brush it off my face. The damp spot burned a hole in my cheek.

'Would you?' She put her drink down on the cushion, and I picked it up and put it on a table to stop it spilling.

'Yes,' I said. It sounded a dusty word, meaning nothing. 'I'd miss you and I can't believe this depression will last.' I felt so down myself that every day was like wading through treacle. I didn't know how I could spout such nonsense. When I told people I was depressed, they would tell me it wouldn't last and I didn't believe them, so why was I telling my mother the same rubbish, and why was I hoping that she would believe me?

'What will last?'

'The depression.'

'Oh.'

'We must make a plan so you won't get too depressed again,' I said. The smile cracked around my cheeks; inside myself, I felt as if some desperate ringleader had leaped creakily to the centre of the stage and was exhorting a lot of exhausted acrobats to line up for action for the last time. My limbs ached. I wanted to sob or pass out, but I sat and smiled like some old trouper.

'We must make a plan.'

My mind went blank.

Another time, she said: 'Darling, if ever I get old and gaga, you won't let me suffer, will you? I couldn't bear to be a burden. Particularly to you. And you won't let any doctor just kind of keep me alive, will you? You will promise? You'll see I'm snuffed out like a candle? You won't let me gutter?'

'Of course I won't,' I said. 'I won't let you be in pain. I do promise.' I didn't really care whether she was in pain or not. My feelings about her were blank, as if a wind had blown a great duststorm through my mind and left all the spikes and bumps covered with an endlessly flat, even sand.

My mother leaned forward and patted my hand. 'My darling,' she said, tenderly.

One night, Diana Holman Hunt rang me at ten at night. 'Darling,' she started — and I raised my eyebrows at the girlfriend who had come to dinner, expecting a flow of non-stop 'anecdotage' to follow. 'I have some *very* bad news. It's *Janey*. I knew the moment John went *away* to see his *mother*, Janey would be very *vulnerable*. Now, I was just *sitting* here, having a little *drink* and watching the *television*, when the phone rang and it was *Christopher*. Now apparently Janey was extremely drunk and she had rung up Christopher and *begged* him to come over, and he had put the *phone* down on her. He was just about to go to bed when Jean absolutely *begged* him to ring her back to see if she was all right. Now, understandably he was very *reluctant* to do that, but he telephoned to me and asked if I would ring her up to see if she was compos *mentis*. And when I rang, my dear, she told me that she had taken an overdose of *sleeping* tablets and wanted to *die!*'

'What happened?' I asked. I am afraid that at the back of my mind I was rather hoping she might say that my mother was dead.

'*Well!*' said Diana, taking another long drag on her cigarette. I could hear the inhalation down the end of the telephone. '*Well!* Now, naturally I had to call the police and they went round and they broke down the *door* and they found her in her flat having taken all these *pills* — my dear, who *does* prescribe these things for her? It's so terribly *dangerous* — and she had taken off all her *clothes*, my dear, probably hoping that Christopher would come round and fall in *love* with her all over again, and they took her off to St Mary Abbott's hospital.'

'Is she all right?' I asked.

'Well, I think you must *ring* and find *out*. She wasn't *dead* exactly, but they weren't very *hopeful*.'

I went to the hospital, near Kensington High Street, the next day. Although he had refused to see my mother and had barely even spoken to her on the telephone since the divorce, my father accompanied me for moral support. He lived just around the corner. We walked to the hospital in silence and then waited on a bench outside the ward. We had been told that although she was still alive, her life hung in the balance.

I had become exhausted with listening to how unhappy she was. I found the stress of never knowing whether she was drunk or not too much to take. I had my own enormous emotional problems to deal with, and just hearing my mother's voice on the phone sent my adrenalin soaring into a panic attack. I felt faint and numb, like a blinded elephant, barely knowing my own name, crashing around in a maelstrom of anxiety.

I prayed that she would not pull through — for her sake as well as for mine.

Finally, a kindly matron came up.

'It's all right, dear, your mother's fine,' she said — and must have been surprised when I burst into floods of tears.

I remember screaming: 'But she doesn't want to live, she doesn't want to live!' as the walls seemed to whirl around me. 'She never wanted to live. She's not living.' I rocked to and fro like an Eastern widow, wailing. I could hear my cries echo round the hall, boomeranging back at me. My head felt as if someone had cleaved it with an axe and the two halves were lying at my feet beside me like halves of an orange. What was peculiar was that I didn't feel anything at all. I heard myself keening as if the sound came from another person.

'But she's *going* to live, my dear,' said the matron, thinking I had got the wrong end of the stick. 'Everything's *all right*.'

When I had pulled myself together, I went into the ward to see her. Her false teeth had been removed, her dyed black hair was a mess, straggling over her pillow, her white face was greasy and hollow.

'Mummy?' I said. She turned over and gave me a ghastly smile. With a strange kind of energy, she hoisted herself up, clinging to my arm.

'Am I dead?' she asked me, eagerly. 'Am I dead?'

'No, Mummy, you're not, you'll be OK.' I tried to sound like a cheerful nurse.

My mother fell back with a haunting groan of disappointment.

As we went back to my father's house, I clung to my father's arm. Hearing that my mother was going to live made me feel rather as a prisoner must feel when he hears his appeal has been turned down. The possibility of freedom made the return to what I felt was my cell even more intolerable. I turned to speak to my father, but to my horror I saw he was crying.

'What's the matter?' I couldn't believe he felt anything about my mother's suicide attempt.

'She wanted to die so much and she's alive,' he said, brushing his tears away. 'And Robin wanted to live so much and he's dead.' This was a man who never cried, who was humorous and cynical about everything. Not only that, he was crying in the street.

It meant nothing to me that I was only twenty-four and at the heart of swinging London, with a flat in Chelsea and a job that made most girls cry with envy. True, I had given up writing about pop for the *Daily Mail* — I packed it in when William Mann declared in *The Times* that 'The Beatles are better than Schubert'; my only interest in pop was that it was subversive and rebellious, and now it had been endorsed by the establishment, it no longer interested me. But I had switched to writing television reviews and entertaining end pieces for *19* magazine with cheery titles like 'How to Catch Your Man!', 'I was a Needle Addict! My Love Affair with Stitching!', 'Generation Gap? What Generation Gap?', and even one which declared: '"Is there a God? No!" says Virginia Ironside!' It all sounded as if I were leading a wonderful life. Woodstock was happening and hippies were dancing in the street with flowers in their hair. The truth for me was that most of the time I sat alone in my flat, worrying about my mother.

I felt unable to lean on my father, who was not only understand-ably preoccupied with his new family, but also, apart from that one show of emotion in the street, appeared to have that male ability to cut off completely from his past. If I ever mentioned my mother to him, he would simply shrug. 'She was terribly nice and bright and funny,' he would say, as if she had already died, 'but totally hope-less when it came to men and drink. Pity, really.'

My name is
VIRGINIA
IRONSIDE
I'm 24 and
not ashamed
to ask the question:

WHAT
generation
GAP?

THE ONE THING that brought me down about Danny the Red coming to England was not, like Mrs Whitehouse, that he'd be 'propagating ideas hostile to the interests of the nation,' but that the old argument about the generation gap had once more been resurrected.

My grandmother lived in a mansion block down the road and, although sympathetic, she was unable to be any support. She had her own anxieties – loneliness, age and forgetfulness – and although she had plenty of theories about the Mind of a Murderer, she had no clue about addiction and depression. Dressed in hat, coat and gloves, and now using a stick, she liked to buy me lunch in a hot, dark, smelly pub on the corner of the Earl's Court Road called The Hansom Cab.

'But *why* does she drink?' she would ask me in a puzzled way over potted shrimps and ham salad.

'She's depressed,' I'd reply.

'But *why* is she depressed? She has you, she has a nice young man, and everyone admires her . . . Of course, she should never have left Christopher. Do you know *why* she left?'

These pointless conversations caused me nothing but pain and I soon tried to change the subject to a happier one, like the motives of the latest serial killer.

I became suicidally depressed.

After consulting a variety of doctors, none of whom seemed to know anything about depression, I was sent by my GP to a psychiatrist, a Dr Peter Dally. His consulting rooms were at his home at 13 Devonshire Place, an elegant Georgian house reputed to have been occupied by Emma Hamilton, Nelson's mistress. Its high-ceilinged reception rooms were built for grand parties, the ceilings were by Adam, and huge mahogany doors led into his room.

Dr Dally and his wife, Dr Anne, had had five children. They were separated; he lived in a mews house at the back, and Anne lived in the main house. He practised as a psychiatrist and she as a psychotherapist. This pair were to look after my own mental health for the next few years, with little success.

Trying not to overburden my mother, who was now recuperating in Herefordshire with her parents, I wrote her cheery letters about my visits to the psychiatrist.

I saw Dr Dally the other day who was quite nice and put me on slightly different pills, Parnate and Neulactin (mean anything to you?)

with a Valium at night if I can't get to sleep which I can't. God the whole thing is a drag. I'm not so much gloomy these days but can't stop feeling incredibly tired round about six and having to go and have a kip for about an hour and a half; now the pills that he's put me on keep me perfectly okay during the day, but keep me tossing and turning at night. Admittedly I haven't started the Valium yet so it'll probably be okay, and presumably there's an in-between anyway. What a drag to be such an old nutcase. Dally, the poor wretch, is obliged to see me for around an hour to give his money's worth and he spends his time literally dredging up questions about my life and my past and surreptitiously looking at his watch and dragging out the knowledgeable 'Hu-u-ums' for five minutes at a time. I do sympathize with him; as a journalist I know that feeling so well.

But I expressed my real feelings in my diary. 'If I ever commit suicide,' I wrote, 'I want no one to feel unhappy. I didn't fit into the world at all. I am different from everyone else. I don't want to get on in the world and yet I don't want to fail. I care about nothing and nobody, even talking is strange, words are peculiar, I don't fit into life. When I talk it isn't me speaking it's someone else. I'm just a misfit, I appear to fit, but I find everyone I meet strange, because we can't communicate. I feel too lonely, just being me, to continue. I've lived for so many years and living hasn't really worked out very well so I'm longing for a change. I'm going to wait till I'm thirty and then kill myself if I don't feel any better. Life, I feel, is like a job and I've just got the wrong job.'

I moved into a flat in Royal Crescent, Holland Park. This was the first flat that I owned. I had saved up since I was fourteen. I used to put all my birthday money into a post-office account, and the rent from a lodger that I had at Draycott Place went into the same fund. Slowly I accumulated £2,000, enough for the deposit on a ninety-nine-year lease. When my mother had come round, puffing up the stairs, she gave my sitting-room one of her looks. 'Hmm,' she said, staring at the William Morris fabric that covered the sofa. 'Very nice. A pity that the green in the Morris does rather clash with the leaves outside the window.'

At the same time as I moved in, my mother's lease on Stanhope Gardens was running out. Soon, she would have nowhere to live. Anxiety consumed me like poison. If I didn't find somewhere for her, I would crack up. My mother was in no condition to look for flats herself, John was busy working as an interior designer, and it was up to me to find her somewhere she would like. I wanted her to be close to me, so that I wouldn't have to make long trips to visit her — the ideal scenario would be to have her near enough for me to pop in for the odd quarter of an hour — but everywhere in the area was prohibitively expensive.

I wrote a letter which said: 'To whom it may concern: I am desperately looking for a house or flat for my mother to live in in this area under £10,000. Please contact me if you have anything available.' I distributed this by hand to what seemed like every house in Holland Park — and to my surprise received one reply. There was a small workman's cottage for sale for £8,000 in Queensdale Place, just round the corner from me. It had a tiny garden and though it was run down, John would be able to redesign it all so it would be pretty. My mother was delighted — or as near as anyone depressed can be delighted — and bought it immediately.

While she was briefly working in India – she had got a small job designing clothes for a factory which hoped to sell clothes to Europe – John and I moved her things into Queensdale Place. For a while it was a mass of packing cases, but eventually we sorted it out and when my mother returned, she made it look beautiful. Every tiny room in the house was painted white and furnished entirely in black and brown. In the sitting-room, the big leather sofa was covered with crimson and scarlet embroidered cushions; on the walls hung William Daniell prints of India, and two beautifully mounted brass Tantric heads stood on the polished butler's tray that she had brought with her from Neville Street.

For one year, my life improved. The man I had been in love with on and off since I was seventeen, the funny, clever, good-looking and sweet Robin Grove-White, came to London and we lived together in my flat in Royal Crescent. He then went to Canada in order, I seem to remember, to 'find himself'. So upset was I by this move that I promptly fell wildly in love with his best friend, Paul McDowall, the lead singer with the band, the Temperance Seven, whose record I had so fiercely rejected when my mother had tried to foist it on me years before. But six months later, Robin returned from Canada. Whether he had found himself or not I don't know, but he was now desperate to marry me, while my complete misery over his leaving had turned me against the idea of accepting. I became so confused I couldn't make any proper decisions. He made an appointment at a Register Office for us to wed, but the moment I got married, on a freezing morning in 1970, at the same Register Office at which my mother herself had got married, I felt I had made the most terrible mistake. I wrote: 'Before you're married you have

Robin Grove-White and me just after getting married, outside
the same Register Office in which Christopher and Janey
married forty years before

getting married to look forward to, but once you're married, you've only got breaking up to anticipate. A doomy view, but true.' It could have been Madre speaking.

After marrying, my depression returned. I was tearful all the time, and every weekend Robin and I had long discussions about whether we were right for each other. I became obsessively jealous of other women – although I was sufficiently sane to realize that this was totally irrational – and once spent a whole day panicking that if Robin ever met Germaine Greer, he would want to run off with her. These tortuous thoughts became obsessive, until I felt like screaming with the pain of them. In my mind, I was left for another woman, again and again and again. I could not even walk down the street for seeing women that I was convinced Robin would find more attractive than me – not only would he find them more attractive, but he would find them far, far nicer. When I mentioned this to him much later, he was astonished, particularly about Germaine, whom, it turned out, he had met once but had never even considered as a girlfriend. Anyway, the thought of running off with anyone at all had never crossed his mind. He loved me very much, but I was never reassured of it. He only had to finish talking to me and then pick up a newspaper and start reading it for me to know that it was all over, that he had finally understood how utterly horrible I was, that he hated me.

My mother was in no position to reassure or comfort me. I was the one who had to comfort her. Very occasionally we would discuss her problems with alcohol. 'Ma was pathetically apologetic,' I wrote after I had once berated her about drinking again. '"The thing is I am an alcoholic and I shouldn't drink," she said. "But I find life isn't worth living without it." I was stumped as to what to reply, although I muttered firm, resolute things.'

It occurred to me that my mother's depression and mine might be linked. Since I was experiencing the most horrible feelings of being so removed from the world that I wondered if I wasn't dead inside, like a hollow tree, I rang her to see if she'd ever had the same feelings. She hadn't, but now I mentioned it, she told me she did have moments when she realized she had absolutely no clue who she was and, when she felt this, she hurriedly got up and had a glass of (here she hesitated) water and did something to take her mind off it. She told me, too, that she thought she had been born with a splinter of ice in her heart. This reference was to the story of the Snow Queen in *The Pink Fairy Book*, in which a looking-glass made by an evil hobgoblin shattered into billions of pieces. Some people got a splinter in their hearts, and that was dreadful, for then their hearts turned into a lump of ice. There were days when my mother couldn't bear to look at herself in the mirror and face the stranger who stared back at her. No, she had never felt 'herself'. When I told her that I had felt 'myself' briefly about five times in my life for an hour or so, she asked rather pathetically: 'Was it nice?'

Dr Dally tried to help, but when I told him that I couldn't bear to watch violent films and kept bursting into tears for no reason, he said, according to my diary: 'Aha, you are repressed and inhibited, and you should let your hair down and remember that life isn't a bed of roses, and for the sun to rise, the moon must set and into some life some rain must fall and you must face up to facts and stop featherbedding your existence if you don't want doom and disaster to descend.' After which he told me I was looking extremely well and that every cloud has a silver lining, charged me twelve guineas, accompanied me to the top of the elegant staircase, waved me farewell and retreated into his great room. Christopher said that everything he said was Freudian rubbish. Far from feeling a million dollars after seeing Dally, I felt more like jumping out of a window than ever.

I tried hard to make a go of things. Convinced that everything was my fault, I went to yoga classes, exercised, even visited the Spiritualist Association — but nothing worked. My depression was made more difficult to bear because people didn't seem to notice how wretched I felt; I was, and am, capable of putting up a game and entertaining front. One of the few friends in whom I could confide my real feelings was Diana Lisle, a younger journalist friend of mine who felt exactly the same way as I did. She would come round with a large bottle of wine and we would discuss depression endlessly, often cracking black jokes about the horror — and especially the horror of the Dallys, Diana also being a patient of Peter Dally.

'I think Peter is rather sexy,' said Diana in her deep, humorous voice. She came from a grand Scottish family. 'With his little crooked smile. And he's a friend of Alison Lurie. Isn't it odd?' Neither of us could reconcile Peter with the trendy American writer. His amazingly large family ('Rather disgusting, isn't it?' he had once said, wryly, to Diana) and his secret intellectual life made him a darkly fascinating figure. Diana, like a lot of his patients, was half in love with him.

Naturally I considered a change of career. Change your job, change your luck. I felt, completely irrationally, that Robin despised me for being 'just a journalist' and that if I were better educated he would like me better. I had worked to support Robin for a year because, having failed his degree at Oxford — he spent too much time drinking and acting in satirical reviews — he was determined to retake his finals. Now he had passed his degree with flying colours and was working for the Council for the Protection of Rural England. Trying to keep up with his serious and noble intentions — barely anyone knew what the environment was in 1971, let alone had any idea about how to protect it — I took a leaf out of his academic book, took two A-levels at a crammer and applied to go to university, while still freelancing for the *Daily Mail* and teenage magazines.

After one term as a mature student at Bedford College at the ripe age of twenty-eight (I studied history, of all subjects, the one I am least interested in), I found I couldn't cope. I simply could not understand why whoever it was introduced or reformed or repealed the Corn Laws, and I cried all day and every day. Robin was making new and radical friends, who had anarchist views, and they came round to the flat, sneering at the fact that I wrote for the *Daily Mail*. Robin, who had given up drinking when he came to London, became attracted to a somewhat ascetic life and began to talk about the merits of giving our television set away, doing without the car, stopping smoking, riding bicycles, becoming vegetarian and joining a commune.

Ever since my early experiences at Haverstock Hill, the word 'commune' has terrified me, and I imagined my fragile world collapsing — a world which was only kept going by the presence of our cat, my tidy kitchen, our dinner parties and cosy evenings in front of the box. I thought I would be forced to live in a tent, never allowed to read, let alone write for, the *Daily Mail* again, and I imagined, whenever I opened my mouth and revealed my accent, being sneered at daily by young anarchists from the Angry Brigade with greasy hair and bombs under their jackets, for whom I would be obliged to stew lentils over a wood fire.

As a result, my anxiety increased tenfold. I began to feel I was possessed by the Devil, who was sitting on my shoulder in the shape of a bird, grinning gleefully. I was terrified and didn't dare tell anyone, hoping that in time it would go away, but the evil bird was constantly close to my cheek, sneering and cackling in my ear. If I sit very still even now, I can sometimes feel his dark shadow. What I was suffering from was not simply a conviction that I was worthless – a feeling reasonably easy to bear – but a conviction that I was truly evil.

One day, I was in the kitchen chopping up some carrots. I had put down the knife on the draining board and was rinsing my hands under the tap. When I heard Robin come and say, in a friendly way, 'Oh, hullo, what are you up to?', I was suddenly overcome with an almost overwhelming urge to pick up the knife, turn round and plunge it into Robin's chest. I put my hands to my head and started screaming and crying. As Robin put his arms round me, trying to comfort me, I distinctly heard the Devil's voice, a real voice, speaking to me out loud: 'I will never leave you. I am always with you. Heh heh heh!'

A month later, I was no better. On Christmas Day in 1971, staying with Robin's parents in Anglesey, I wrote:

This afternoon I was half contemplating taking my pills into the woods and simply laying down my head and dying. I try to read the Bible; in church when praying I get a certain relief, but none of it lasts. I have no depth, no fundamental, no truth in me at all. And as for how other people operate, it's a closed book to me. I copy them up to a point but that's all. I don't know how to be a friend to anyone except out of a textbook. I don't know how to love or hate.

I became so freaked out that I went to stay for a few days with Christopher and Jean in Abingdon Villas – on a camp bed in the sitting-room – and spent most of the time weeping or asleep.

From then on, my days took a familiar form, waking up terrified and despairing, dragging through a morning feeling as if the Third World War was being fought in my head, sitting on the sofa while Christopher worked, and occasionally saying to him, just as my mother did to me: 'Christopher, do you think I'll *ever* get better?' He would look up and say: 'Of *course* you will' and go back to working. I wondered if he secretly felt as despairing about my condition as I did about Janey's.

Jean would call us for a simple lunch – perhaps cold ham and a tomato salad – in the basement. I would try to make conversation, and then, after another hour's screaming and moaning, while Christopher patiently tried to explain that I had no reason to feel as I did, I would fall asleep on one of the children's beds, my rest punctured by unnaturally vivid dreams. Then I woke up to give a rather feeble impression of my natural self – whatever that was – throughout the evening. Just before bed-time, Christopher and Jean would say brightly and hopefully: 'Well, you seem much better now!'

and I went to bed knowing that the whole cycle would repeat itself the following day.

Eventually I could go on no longer. Christopher and all the family were due to go down to a house he had bought in the country, leaving me in London. A few hours before they were due to leave, I was startled to feel the hand of Death touching me on the shoulder. I was convinced I was going off my head. I could hardly stand or think. Christopher kindly stayed behind while I somehow hammered out a television review – and, through a blinding headache, a cheery article for *19* on 'Man Made Pick-ups' ('Asking a man in the street where he got his scarf/tie/jacket from "because I want to buy one for my brother" is okay if you then insist that no, you don't know where Harrods is, could he show you on your map, perhaps he's walking in that direction himself . . .').

An emergency meeting with Dr Dally got me into Greenways nursing home, the same place in which my mother had been incarcerated a few years earlier. 'I got the horrors that she'd come and visit me, slightly drunk, stroking my hand at the end of my bed and looking at me, murmuring "Oh, Pinny Bean, Pinny Bean",' I wrote

VIRGINIA IR●NSIDE

One girl's week Man made pick-ups

In these enlightened days of emancipation you may have a job, blow up your own tyres on your bike, and even have an odd drink in a with the man downstairs is the occasional irritated bang on his ceiling/my floor with a broomhandle when my Elvis Golden Hits get too much for him.

In my time I've tried out several gambits. I've tried that risky. But you can't just stare at a man in a tube train in what you think is a particularly seductive and come-hitherish way and expect him to even raise his eyes from his crossword puzzle.

get out as you have no idea where it is. Hopefully, if he is nice (and if he's not, who cares), he'll lean forward and tell you to get out at the same stop as him, whereupon you must sit next to him and engage in my diary. 'The irony of the situation became so great that I resolutely made up my mind that she wouldn't get a chance to visit.' In the event, she seemed very relieved not to have to make the trip.

Eventually Dr Dally suggested that psychotherapy sessions with his wife would be a good thing. Anne Dally wore a bun and appeared to be a stout and sensible lady ('Keeping the money in the family, I see,' commented Mummy, sourly) but despite her ministrations, I was no better the following year. If anything, I was worse. Robin was in despair.

'I am very unhappy though I can't feel it. I cry every day now. The flatness gets flatter,' I wrote.

> I feel as if I'm two people locked back to back and one, the real one, is facing the wall and the other, the false one, is facing the outside and I've got to turn round. I am lost and always have been. I remember before I went to Greenways the feelings, the intense feelings. Then the sudden feeling of being in the same room as someone else, suddenly we were together, we were two people in the same room, like ordinary people are, it was wonderful. But all that seems to have gone now. Even the hatred of the carving knife, the menacing feeling of cunning destruction, the devils, the feeling of clashing rocks in my head that made me want to scream — all that has gone and left me only with deadness.

Three times a week I lay on Anne's couch not knowing what to say, while she pronounced that I had a 'false self' and that I was full of hostile feelings. I felt very guilty about these hostile feelings and tried hard to be more 'good' when I was with her. I had no understanding of how psychotherapy was meant to work and Anne, being the silent sort of psychotherapist, did not appear to be prepared to elaborate.

'How does this therapy work?' I'd ask, crying.

And she would reply, coolly: 'Why do you want to know?'

My mother was now under the care of the psychiatrist Dr William Sargant, the man responsible for the perfectly valid idea that most depressive and anxious states have chemical rather than psychological roots. He told my mother that he thought Anne was hopeless, and that psychotherapy was no good for people like me: a couple of reds, two blues and a few Surmontil and I'd be right as rain. But Anne said I shouldn't leave her at this stage: if I did, I might never get better.

'Your mother couldn't stand terrible blows against her, like your saying you wanted to leave,' said Anne, mysteriously, 'but *I* can.'

My father had become even more unapproachable since he had had a heart attack in 1971. Because I was so emotionally blank, I didn't feel anything at all about this, but I visited him in Winchester Hospital where he lay in bed with a hairy tweed jacket over his pyjamas, philosophical and humorous as ever. 'I really don't mind if I die,' he said. 'I'm not thirty-seven, I'm fifty-seven. I've had a good run. It would be awful for Jean and the children, but purely selfishly, I don't mind.' I noticed that how I might feel myself and my own grief, were he to die, did not seem to enter his calculations.

Month after month, year after year, I felt continually depressed. One of my old boyfriends had jumped off a roof to his death, and when my friend Diana Lisle once dropped in on us on a whim at six o'clock, I asked where she had been going.

She tucked her legs under her on the sofa, swigging from a large glass of red wine. 'I'd been planning to drive to Brighton, check into a hotel room — I thought the Grand Hotel would be nicest — and kill myself,' she said.

'What!' I couldn't help bursting out laughing. 'Not *really*?'

'Oh yes, I've got all the pills,' she said, giggling and producing a bottle from her handbag. 'I've been saving them up for weeks. And I've got this rather nice ring to wear so that when I check in they'll think I'm a respectable married woman.'

Diana was so young, funny, and full of energy and warmth, it sometimes seemed incredible even to me that she suffered from such black despair. I wondered whether I myself didn't present to the world a similarly cheery front.

'Well, I hope you've changed your mind and will stay to have supper,' I said, getting up to put my arm around her awkwardly. 'How lucky that we live on the way to Brighton. If ever you think of doing it again, you must promise just to pop in here first. Poor, poor you.'

Out of the few scraps I had in the fridge, Diana constructed a delicious tomato soup out of tomatoes, lemon and marjoram (when I make it today, I always think of her) and, after Robin had gone upstairs to work, we ended up drinking lots of red wine and laughing about the whole mad situation. Months later, Diana did succeed in killing herself. She left a note to Dr Dally, saying she was sorry and would he 'please look after Virginia'.

I read later in a book by one of the Dally daughters, Emma, that not only had the children once been looked after by a housekeeper who whirled them around the room by their ears as a punishment, beat them with wooden coathangers and threw their dog out of the window, threatening that they would follow if they didn't behave, but that one of the children became so depressed in later life that he killed himself, and Emma herself was on antidepressants and having psychotherapy.

On my twenty-ninth birthday, I wrote:

Soon I'll be thirty and will be able to commit suicide. I'm so withdrawn, I can't feel or see or hear or understand even the simplest things. I am very unhappy and confused. I spent this afternoon asleep in bed. A typical day. Sometimes I can only keep awake by watching television or reading letters in the *Radio Times* or colouring in pictures in ads with a felt pen. I've never known reality. Never in my life. I've had feelings but they've been cockeyed feelings, just random crushes, crying at movies, but never real feelings. I don't think I'll ever be able to jump into life. I just want to stay curled up asleep in a corner of my mind while the rest of me continues in this bleak way. I don't think I'll ever get better. I sit here in the drawing room with all this furniture I can't see, when people are here they seem like the furniture, except they move, and I'm like the furniture except I sometimes have a dull nerve where I normally have a migraine. I sometimes look at people and they look as if they're at the end of a long telescope they're so far away. As if we're blocked by sheets of thick glass between it. As if I'm invulnerable. And horrible. I am. The only way I can get through a day is by doing things from a list. Can you imagine that? Just look at a piece of paper and see what my orders are. I'm so alone. I'm even alone from myself. I have a banging in my head, it's like a person tied down by thick ropes trying to get free or like the Loch Ness monster trying to escape from a great web of staked ropes. I am not well at all. I wish

I'd had more good fairies at my christening. I just feel clobbered. I can't even cry at films now or songs or anything. I just sit and stare at my watch to count the hours away or just sleep.

A few years ago, I took advantage of the Data Protection Act and asked to see my doctor's medical notes. I found that one psychiatrist I had consulted had written: 'It is very interesting that Miss Ironside feels a whole person only when she has some other very dependent, sick person to care for, but as her husband becomes more and more independent, so she feels more and more threatened with illness. It would not surprise me if she ended up by killing herself.'

I have to say I wouldn't have been very surprised myself.

I could not commit suicide at thirty as I had promised myself, however, because although I was still extremely depressed, I now had a baby, William. Although I found it hard to feel anything for him when he was tiny, and was sometimes convinced that I was such a terrible mother that he would be better off either dead or in care, I did experience an extraordinarily strong connection with him, as if we were one.

When Will was eighteen months, Robin and I split up in circumstances too painful to describe. I behaved appallingly. Suddenly and uncharacteristically, having been completely faithful during my married life, I had sex with a different man every day for a week. Robin went berserk. Our relationship had been so 'civilized', it was hardly surprising that we should both, in our last week, go completely off the rails. Our marriage exploded like a nuclear bomb.

Carole Latimer

Me and Will

Robin remained in the flat, full of rage, while I ran, with Will, to my father's house. I was told after three days that my staying with him was, sadly, 'slightly inconvenient' in view of his young family, and he asked me to find somewhere else to go. So much, I felt, for being number one in his life. In retrospect, I think he felt tormented by what he saw as conflicting loyalties to me and to Jean. He was so intensely bound to both of us that having us together in the same house put him under intolerable stress. After a few weeks, Robin moved out and I was able to return home.

The brake that my son's existence put on my capacity to commit suicide, much as I longed to, made me wonder how on earth my mother could have tried to kill herself when I was around. Perhaps she felt no obligations towards me because she knew that I was unable to love her. Still, dutifully I popped round and did everything to try to make her life happier. But while I had to go on operating for the sake of my son, my mother seemed to have nothing to live for. She wrote her autobiography (at exactly the same age as I am writing this book myself), she worked for a while as a part-time advisor to the Fashion School at Bradford School of Art and even at St Martin's, and eventually she lived on a small pension from the College, engineered for her by one of her only remaining allies, the registrar John Moon.

I visited her in her beautiful house every other day, hoping that she was happier — but she never was. She could not even really respond to Will. When he toddled up to the table on which stood her brass Tantric heads, she became nervous and twitchy, frantic with worry lest he should touch anything or leave a fingerprint behind him.

She became fat, slow and dazed with antidepressants prescribed by Dr Sargant, and spent her time sitting at home, her neck swaddled in a bulky scarf, eating sweet biscuits and drinking tonic water all day. When I came round, she stared at me with howling damp eyes, sucking me in. Her shoulders were tensed, her hands trembled — probably because of the medication. She was hiding somewhere inside that hunched figure and I would look for her slyly, pretending I was doing something else. But she never appeared, except occasionally, as if she had moved away from a distorting mirror to wave briefly to a friend.

Sometimes she said, pitifully, her eyes rheumy with unhappiness: 'Darling, do you think I'll ever get better?' and I would reply: 'I promise, you will get better. Believe me.' Sometimes she asked the impossible question: 'Darling, it would be best if I died, wouldn't it?' And I would say, 'No, no, not at all', but deep down I knew it would have been a relief for all of us, including herself.

For months, I saw her into waiting-rooms, questioned doctors, talked at the end of a telephone, consoled, helped, reassured, encouraged, promised, but there was no reaching her. I arranged for her to have acupuncture, hypnosis, yoga, hormones, spiritualist sessions, massages, self-help books, even electric shock therapy. Nothing helped.

Then I got a phone call. My mother had attempted suicide again. She had collapsed outside her house and had been taken to hospital. When I went to collect her nightdress and washing things, there was a half-empty bottle of whisky on the table, around which were scattered hundreds of white pills. Under the whisky bottle was a note, written in a shaky hand: 'Pin. I'm sorry. I just can't face any more. I do love you. Mummy.' I didn't feel a thing. I gathered up the pills and put them into a small plastic pouch lying nearby, in case she wanted to try again, and put them in my bag.

I remember very little about this suicide attempt. I remember that my mother discharged herself early and, taking a taxi home, stopped briefly outside my father's and stepmother's house. She got out of the taxi in her nightdress, stared wildly through the window, and then, forgetting what was going on, was returned by the taxi driver to the hospital. I remember the anxiety, such anxiety that I couldn't even think. My head was filled with white noise. I remember bringing her home from hospital, and how she found it hard to negotiate the steps to her house, and I remember the sound of her feet dragging on the ground, like a baby's nagging cry.

For the next few months, she could hardly look after herself, so I went round nearly every day to help. John did his best, but he was working hard. She rarely dressed, she slept as long as she could, waiting for the days to pass; eventually she hardly spoke. She watched me attentively, limpid eyes scavenging my face for hope and finding none. Sometimes I thought that we both sat there in that immaculate drawing-room, both scouring each other's faces for a sign of life or support, both desperate in search of an answer.

One morning shortly after the suicide attempt, I was glad to find her dressed at least. She was sitting on the sofa in much the same place that she must have sat when she had taken the overdose. When I sat down, I pulled the chair close, just to change the position of one piece of furniture in the room. She sat, swollen and slumped. Her hair was thin and hadn't been washed for days; her skin was beige-coloured and there was a ladder in one stocking. But her eyes were bright, almost starting from her head as if she'd had a lot to drink. She had tried to do something with a streak of smudgily applied lipstick and she had painted her nails, though some of the nail varnish had gone on her fingers.

She looked at me intently. 'Darling, were there some pills left over?' she said. She crossed her legs quickly; her eyes were sharp and interested. She looked as she had looked long ago, her face lively and mobile. She was sitting bolt upright now, straight and eager.

'Why?'

She giggled uncharacteristically.

'You didn't throw them away, did you?'

'No, why?'

'Oh, darling, thank you!' she said. Her voice hummed with life, a tone higher than usual. She smiled at me gratefully. 'Where did you put them?'

'Oh, somewhere,' I said. I knew they were in my bag at the time. I knew also that she shouldn't have asked me and I shouldn't have told her.

'Do give them back, won't you?' she said. 'They are mine, after all.' She licked her lips nervously.

'You'll only try again.'

'Oh, no, darling, I won't. I don't want to upset you again, you've been through so much . . .' Her words came out in an enthusiastic gabble. 'Oh, please, you know you can trust me.' She sidled seductively along the sofa, put her hand over mine, stroked my cheek. 'Darling, you will give them back, it's not to try again, I've learned my lesson. It's just, well, you know, they're sleeping pills, just occasionally, I can't sleep, they won't prescribe any more like that. After I've been so silly. They'd just keep me going, the odd occasion, hardly ever, I won't take them . . . Where are they? Are they at home now?' Her voice was pleading and wheedling.

'They're in my bag,' I said.

I remember her hand leaping out from her sleeve like a snake from the undergrowth. I stopped her, pulling the bag to me.

'I can't,' I said. 'I'd never forgive myself.'

She clasped her hands tightly in front of her, staring at me. Her hair stuck out at all angles, her skin shone and her lipstick was all licked off.

'Please, darling.' Behind the panic, there was a note of hatred. I was keeping oblivion from her. 'Give them to me,' she suddenly snapped between clenched teeth.

I reached into my bag. The pills were white, still in their pouch. There must have been at least a hundred there. I handed them over.

'Oh, thank you!' she said. She was childishly delighted. 'I'll never use them, I promise,' she said, fondling the packet as she looked at me, 'except to sleep. Oh, darling, I've been so worried someone might have thrown them away. I should have known I could rely on you. Oh, thank you!'

I left her sitting on the sofa, the bag of pills in front of her like a treasure trove.

My big mistake was in telling my father what I had done. I sat having a cup of coffee with him, in his sunny Kensington drawing-room. He looked uncharacteristically rattled.

'You should *never* have given them back to her,' he said, quite severely. 'If she did try anything again, you'd never forgive yourself.'

'Yes, I would,' I said. 'She's desperate to kill herself. You don't know how unhappy she is.'

'I see your point,' he said, looking rather glum. 'But even so, you shouldn't have done it. Quite apart from anything else, it puts you in an *appalling* position legally.'

So the next day I rang to find out when she would be out and then went round and raided the house.

She had left a fire on, and a light. Yesterday's newspaper was on the table, unopened. I felt like a burglar, guilty and secretive. But I had to find the pills. First, I looked in all the bathroom drawers, and the little pots on her dressing-table in the bedroom. No luck. I looked under the mattress, behind cushions, at the backs of cupboards, even in the flower pots in the garden. But just as I was giving up hope, I noticed a blue and white Chinese jar in the sitting-room. I reached down inside and at the bottom was the crunchy feel of pills in plastic. I took them out and went upstairs, threw them down the lavatory and flushed the chain. Then I heard my mother come in and I started to go downstairs. She stood below me, swaying. Her clothes were awry, her tattered basket empty except for a carton of milk. She looked at me like a stranger. I wished I could have run into her arms and told her what I had done and asked her to forgive me. I wanted her to put her arm around me, console me, just for five minutes, just to give me a break; but the last time I had cried in front of her, she had shrunk away from me. 'Don't be upset, darling,' she had begged, 'I can't bear it when you're unhappy. You make *me* so unhappy. Please cheer up for my sake.'

My mother looked at me blankly. There was blood on her leg.

'What is it?' I cried.

'Oh, it's you, darling,' she said, turning to the wall. She had fallen in the street, blood was pouring from her knee. She was taking so many antidepressants and tranquillizers, she could hardly walk. I dabbed her wound with cotton wool and Dettol, made her a cup of tea and left her sitting alone at the table, staring into space. I knew she was living in a void that had no beginning and no end. Coming into the house, I had felt like a murderess, but as I left, I felt that I had murdered any kind of hope for her. I wished I could die for her. I have never forgiven myself for getting rid of her pills. I always cry with guilt when I think about it.

Later in the week, I had a worried phone call from her. 'You didn't see my pills, darling, did you?' she asked. Her voice ached with depression.

'No,' I said.

'They've disappeared. Or maybe I put them somewhere. I've forgotten.'

'Well, it's probably for the best.'

'I don't know.'

I don't know who was more relieved, my mother or myself, when it turned out that she had developed breast cancer.

twelve

NEGLIGÉE   *A soft, feminine wrap worn over a nightdress; may be loose or sashed and is more glamorous and more casual than a dressing gown.*
  Janey Ironside, *A Fashion Alphabet*

When I took her to her GP for the verdict after a biopsy had been done on the lump on her breast, Janey had difficulty in getting up from the waiting-room chair and into his surgery. She was still fat with antidepressants, sleeping pills and tranquillizers, which slowed her up and bludgeoned her into a drugged stupor.

'It looks like cancer,' the doctor said when we sat down. 'I prefer not to beat about the bush.' I remember that although he had cared for my mother for years now he seemed unfamiliar and remote, like a doctor one might stumble across on holiday. He seemed to have forgotten to travel into work that day, left himself at home.

'However,' he added, pushing his blotter to one side about a centimetre and a half and closing one eye to see if it was now parallel with the sides of his desk, 'you shouldn't worry too much. A lot can be done for it these days.' His shifty eyes told me that a lot couldn't. 'I am referring you to a colleague of mine who is excellent, and I shall suggest you see him tomorrow.'

My mother had stumbled up from her chair and was already on her feet, holding out a trembling hand. She hadn't been listening to what he had said.

'Thank you,' she said, slurring the words as if she were drunk. It was the effect of the pills. 'The dentist, you say.'

'No, Mrs Ironside, a consultant, a *cancer specialist*.' The doctor leaned forward and mouthed it carefully.

'Oh? Oh, cancer.' My mother smiled broadly. 'Oh, thank you.'

She stood on the Turkish carpet in front of his desk, on a patch worn bare by other patients who must have stood in that very spot, perhaps patients full of terror, or patients brimming with gratitude. She swayed slightly, twisting her hands, and then adjusted the scarf round her neck. She seemed to find a little piece of food lodged between her teeth and her probing tongue distorted her mouth.

'I'll talk with the doctor while you wait outside,' I said in a loud voice.

'Mmm.' Janey staggered slightly and I got up and put a hand under her arm to help her to the door.

When she had gone, I sat down.

'To be perfectly blunt,' he said, 'she hasn't got long to live.'

'But how long?'

'A year? A year at the most. Possibly weeks, months. A year at the most. That's it, I'm afraid.'

There was a silence.

'No, she's not a happy woman,' he said curtly. He shut her folder. 'It might be for the best.'

I remember then the mixture of relief that rushed over me. I imagined life without her. I saw myself running out to greet a new life, tumbling into the open fields, arms spread wide to catch the sky. This feeling was naturally swiftly obliterated by a huge black dollop of guilt.

'I'll fix an appointment with Dr Foder now,' said the doctor. 'He's excellent.'

In the cab back, Janey asked vaguely: 'What did he say?'

I remember that journey so clearly. Outside the window I could see ripples of shadows and sunlight. A woman walked down the road trundling a small child in a pushchair, as my mother had once pushed me. The child had a sunhat on and was munching crisps from a packet. I could almost feel the rumble of the wheels underneath me, the railings flashing by at eye-level. On a tree, a blackbird sang. I thought: doesn't it look good out there? And then quickly, my eyes filled with tears. Who could comfort me? I had to comfort her. My tears dried up instantly.

'Oh, you know, cancer. But they can do wonders with it these days.' I pulled a smile across my face like a curtain in an effort to make it good news. My voice resonated with the most awful certainty around the cab's walls, like an actor's. I adjusted my body language so that I seemed relaxed and carefree. 'I won't let them do anything awful, I promise. Perhaps it's not even cancer. They'll have to do proper tests tomorrow. Oh lord, more hospitals.' Trivia poured out of my mouth like breakfast cereal out of a packet. 'Poor Mummy. But I'll come with you.'

'Mmm.' Janey stared ahead. She twisted her bag nervously on her lap, and moved back into the black seat. 'You're an angel to take me, darling, for taking me together, I mean for taking me today.' Blank, Valium-glazed, large-pupilled eyes turned on me.

I stared unfocused at an advertisement for typewriters on the back of the seat opposite. If I didn't look at her, I could feel something warm and sad stirring inside me. My mother reached out and put a cold, old hand on mine. It felt like a leech. I flinched, and tried not to withdraw.

I talked energetically.

'We're going to the radiotherapy department at the hospital tomorrow,' I said. I had to crank my mouth into action. 'To see everything's OK.'

'What?'

'Tomorrow!' I said loudly. 'We'll go to the radiotherapy department. We have an appointment. I'll take you.'

My mother's face suffused with panic. She took a little book from her bag. 'I have a hair appointment,' she gabbled, leafing through it with trembling hands, 'And I have to do the shopping because John and I haven't got anything for supper.' I looked too, but it was her address book.

'You're not doing anything,' I said, when I found her diary. The pages were blank except for a spidery line of writing: 'Cat to vet'. Ten years before, her hand had been round and firm; now it was cramped and nearly illegible.

'I must have my hair done before going to the hospital,' said Janey. There was fear in her eyes; she cringed away from me as if I were a jailer. 'I can't go like this. Will I have to take a suitcase?' Her hands twisted together in panic, old knuckles moving through shiny skin.

'We are simply going for an appointment.' My voice was reined in, squeaky. 'You're not going in. I promise. Don't worry.'

'Mmm.' Janey pushed her diary into her bag under mounds of filthy tissues. I thought: who is this woman? My mother was beautiful, clever, amusing, she smelled of expensive scent. This woman is nothing to do with me.

At the hospital the next day, we sat for an hour in a dusty waiting-room. In the middle of the small table in front of us was a dying plant. A few bits of an old jigsaw had been cleared up into the saucer in which it sat. There was also an ashtray full of stubs. On the yellow walls were travel posters of Switzerland – and yet most of the people who arrived here would probably never travel again. My mother stared into space; I read some women's magazines which were ten years out of date and smelled of other people's hands.

Finally, a middle-aged man in a white coat appeared and pumped Janey's hand.

'I'm Dr Foder,' he said, and the beam that he gave her hung like a Christmas garland suspended from each ear. His teeth sparkled and his eyes twinkled. Behind the cocktail party exterior he had summed Janey up, but I couldn't quite spot when. He shook my hand as well. He led us to a small cubicle and waved us into seats opposite his desk. I wouldn't have been surprised if he had offered us tea and cucumber sandwiches.

'How nice to meet you,' he said, relaxing into a swivel chair opposite. His voice was like an actor's talking to the gallery, deep, fruity and confident. 'Do take your coats off. What a chilly day! But it's so hot in here. The heating is all controlled by a central system

over which we have no power.' He turned to me to include me in
the conversation, smiling, as if I were a special guest in a theatre box.

Janey smiled vacantly at him, clutching her bag. 'Mmm,' she said,
staring at his desk.

'My sister was so thrilled to hear I was going to meet you,' he
said, jotting a few notes with one hand and looking up cheekily. 'She
makes pots. Actually we've just come back from New York, seeing
a Clarice Cliff exhibition. What a delight! Have you heard of her?'

'Heard of Clarice Cliff!' said Janey, suddenly lively. 'Of course
I've heard of Clarice Cliff! Who hasn't heard of her!' She looked
quite sharp and spiteful, like she used to. It was as if inside her a
couple of torn wires had briefly connected by accident. 'Personally,
I always think she was rather overrated.'

'*Do* you?' Dr Foder looked interested. He put down his pen and
stared at her, folding his arms. He was trying to say: 'Don't worry
about cancer. Art is more important. Relax.' What he did say was:
'Why do you find her overrated?'

'Awful colours,' said Janey, pointing rudely at one of the pots on
his desk. 'Rather like . . .'

'Mummy! His sister made them!'

'They're very colourful, perhaps not to everyone's taste,' said Dr
Foder tactfully, 'based on a visit to Japan and local peasant craft.
Wonderful sense of *colour*,' he said. 'And a *superb* sense of *line*.'

'Those aren't Japanese colours,' said Janey, contemptuously.
'More South Sea islands.'

Dr Foder guffawed and turned to me as if to say: 'What a card
she is!' But he said: 'Well, we all agree that your mother has the most
marvellous taste! Such a talented woman. What a pity you're not

still at the Royal College of Art. The standard isn't the same these days.' He looked at his notes, and wrote something down. 'I had another patient in the fashion business.' He mentioned a woman's name. 'Immensely talented.'

'Never heard of her,' said Janey.

'She came to me ten years ago. Same problem as yours,' he said. 'She's now in South Africa. Five years ago I last saw her. Absolutely marvellous. On top of the world.'

I wanted to say: 'Get on with it.'

Dr Foder noticed my impatience and drew his files nearer.

'Well, our X-rays,' he said. 'Down to work. We can't sit about all day chatting. Unfortunately!' he added, suddenly looking up at both of us with a warm, glowing smile.

The central heating was pulling at my skin and making my nose ache. I was sweating. And yet if I took my coat off, I thought, I might never get out of the hospital.

'I'll just examine you, if I may,' said Dr Foder, rising slowly from his chair. 'But before we go any further, may I say you have nothing to worry about. These days, one can do wonders with pills with no side-effects whatsoever. Slip your clothes off, would you mind, just your top, and I'll take a peep.'

'I'll go outside and wait,' I said.

'Don't leave!' cried Dr Foder. 'I'm not going to do anything that can't be seen! There's no reason to go at all.'

But I didn't want to stay and see my mother's white shoulders, her unshaven armpits, her weak breasts, her waistband digging against her white skin. I wanted to hide my eyes. Outside, I stood against a fat pillar, heavy and warm with yellow gloss paint. Nearby, a nurse stared at a screen; a round red light flickered nervously above a double swing door with curtained windows. An Indian sat in a wheelchair, covered with a cellular blanket.

Finally Dr Foder came out from his room, an optimistic spring in his step.

'Come in! Come in!'

'Can I see you alone?' I asked, in an undertone.

'There's no reason,' he said, loudly, but then he shouted at my mother: 'Won't be a minute, Mrs Ironside!' and shut the door behind him quietly.

We went next door into a room full of white machines, filing cabinets and odd office chairs. Dr Foder looked at me sorrowfully, rubbing his hands.

'Oh, I don't like seeing patients' relatives alone,' he said, smiling reprovingly. 'It gives the patient a feeling that they're being kept out of a secret.'

'But you can't tell me in front of her. What do you really think?' I asked.

He was silent, and stared at the floor. Something behind him hummed and whirred.

'Well, not too good, but there again, it could be a lot worse,' he said. I remember noticing how reluctant he was to talk about it himself. He not only wanted my mother to believe in a miraculous recovery but he wanted to believe it himself. Probably he wanted me to believe it, too. 'But I can't of course say how long she's got.' His voice had become softer and more human. 'Some patients come to me in the same state as your mother and a week later . . . well . . .' He shook his head. 'Others come and are still alive and well today, ten years later. And I mean well, living a fit and active life. Oh yes. Jogging! Playing squash!' I couldn't imagine my mother playing squash. 'It so much depends on the attitude of the patient.'

'Yes.'

'To have a positive attitude is half the battle. And that is why we don't like talking to patients' relations in private. She must believe she will be cured. She must fight. All around her must go along with the same thing,' he added. (I wondered if I, so befuddled with ambivalent feelings about her future, could possibly manage to 'go along'.)

'I suppose you know that a few weeks ago she made an unsuccessful suicide bid,' I said. 'Nothing to do with cancer. To do with clinical depression. She doesn't feel like fighting.'

Dr Foder shook his head. He hadn't heard what I said. It didn't suit him. 'You see, all this is so much more the reason to get her feeling better, feeling positive,' he said, looking into my eyes, the old smile returning, cheerleader tones creeping back into his voice. 'Doing things. Going to the theatre.'

'But the treatment? Radiotherapy?'

'Oh, no,' he said. 'Not in this case. Simple pills. Simple hormone pills. Rather like the Pill. No side-effects.'

'Your hair drops out and you get fat . . . ?'

Dr Foder laughed reassuringly. 'No, no way, no way,' he said. 'Those are the cytotoxics. Only used in final stages. Other times for general treatment. But happily, not in this case. I certainly hope in this case we won't have to use them.'

'You won't let her suffer? Long ago, I promised her . . .'

Dr Foder leaned forward, with a broad grin on his face.

'No problem,' he said. 'You see, we doctors are in the business of prolonging life, not prolonging death. That's what it's all about.'

'You haven't mentioned the word "cancer". That is what it is, isn't it?'

'It's not a very nice word, so we don't use it,' said Dr Foder, not using it. 'It has all sorts of connotations we don't like. Not every patient dies by any means. We must go back now or your mother will be getting suspicious.'

Back in the office, he dispensed more reassuring grins with a low, rumbling laugh. Janey looked sorrowful.

'I don't think your mother approves of my furniture,' he said jovially to me with a broad wink at Janey. 'When I do my office over, I shall get you in specially to choose things for it,' he said. Janey smiled. 'And now,' he said, picking up the telephone receiver, 'I'm going to ring your own doctor. We'll put you on pills with no side-effects and you could be on them for years and years with no problem.'

All the time he was dialling the number. (I could imagine him talking at cocktail parties: 'What I always do to reassure my patients,' sip, 'is to *ring* up *their* doctor, *in front of them* . . .')

'Dr Fox? Foder here. I've got Janey Ironside here *with me*,' (said in case Dr Fox shouted anything tactless down the other end) 'and she's doing absolutely splendidly. I'm putting her on Tamoxifen and she'll be right as rain in no time, everything under control. Oh, yes, me too . . . That was bad luck. Incidentally, yes, John – what a dirty thing to do. Typical *BMJ*, of course. Can't trust these journalists –' (here, he gave me a knowing wink) 'I know. Well, they invited me to go on that committee, but honestly . . .'

During the long conversation, I smiled encouragingly at my mother. I put my hand out and patted hers.

She sat so vulnerably, a baffled little person on a hospital chair.

On the way back, she said: 'What a *ghastly* little man! I didn't want to hear about his other patients. And those dreadful pots of his sister's!'

'"*Wonderful* sense of colour!"' I said, imitating his voice. '"*Superb* sense of line!" And he was so dreadfully cheery!' We laughed together and for a moment I heard her giggling properly, just like old times. 'John would *hate* them,' she added. Then: 'Too cheery,' she said, gloomily. 'I don't trust him.'

'Oh, I think he's OK,' I said. I had no idea whether he was or not. 'I mean, they do their best, don't they?'

'Darling, you are an angel to take me.'

'Of course. I couldn't do otherwise, could I?'

In order to make ends meet, I had taken in two lodgers. One told me, the moment he arrived, that his father had kicked him out of his last flat as a result of his burning it down because he had a habit of leaving lit candles around at night; the other liked me to believe he played some glamorous role in the drug world. I don't think he did, but he spent a lot of time at the Sun in Splendour in Notting Hill Gate and reading *Lord of the Rings*, and telling me: 'If the fuzz ever come round, just don't let them look in the suitcase on the top of my cupboard, right?'

Robin came round on Saturdays to take Will out, but we were still unable to speak to each other. When he rang the bell, I went into the corridor, opened the door a centimetre, came back, put Will in the corridor and shut the sitting-room door. At about six-o'clock, Robin returned him into this no-man's land.

Determined not to get a job that would mean I would have to leave my son in the same way my mother had left me, I contrived to scrape by on what I earned from the lodgers and from a ten-pound-a-day stint at a basket and kitchen shop called Graham and Green in Notting Hill Gate. I worked there on Saturdays, when my husband looked after my son. I had also managed to secure four columns: a book-review column for *Girl About Town*, a free magazine, and another for *Woman's World*, a weekly column for *19* magazine and one for *Rave* magazine called 'Who Cares?' Every month, I addressed some subject like ill-treated donkeys, lepers, shy people − I would scour lists of charities, get them to send me the facts, and then churn out yet another tear-jerking piece.

On top of this, I wrote anything anyone asked me to do. 'Ten Tips on How to Get Your Man', 'Ten Tips for a Stress-Free Christmas', 'The A−Z of giving a Party', 'Would you Rather your Partner Fell in Love with Another Woman or Slept with Her?', 'Would You ever be Unfaithful?' ('NO!' says Virginia Ironside, 'YES!' says someone else.) 'Jealousy − the Green-eyed Monster', 'Is Marriage Going out of Style?' ('"YES!" says Virginia Ironside − but we want to hear YOUR views') and I also wrote as many serials for teenage magazines as I could.

Having finally managed to dump Anne Dally, I jumped from the frying pan into the fire. Twice a week, I went to an analyst most inappropriately called Dr Wright, who insisted I lay on a couch while he sat behind me. There was a horrible greasy smell in his basement rooms, and given that they were located in my least favourite part of town, North London, it wasn't surprising that I felt gloomy when I visited him and even gloomier when I came out. Dr Wright very rarely said anything.

What surprises me now is that it never seemed to occur to anyone that I was depressed simply because of my present hideous circumstances. My mother was severely depressed, dying of cancer; I was a single parent and broke as well; and despite the fact that John Wright was living with Janey and was amazingly kind and helpful, he was working all day, so I felt total responsibility for her welfare.

This feeling of responsibility for everyone else's miseries, the endlessly caring role that I was forced into, must certainly have contributed to my sense of fulfilment in becoming an agony aunt later on. I must have felt at some unconscious level, that constantly striving to make others feel better, happier and less erratic would result in my feeling less guilty for whatever nameless sin I must have committed to make my mother so unhappy, and if my caring worked, it might result in being better cared for myself. I have learned that almost everyone in 'altruistic' professions, from doctors to nurses, is also prompted by the same fundamentally selfish urge – if I can cure this person, they may look after me; if I provide help and comfort for this person, I shall get off on some of my own kindness and, like lighting a fire for a freezing man, I may find that some of the warmth may come my way as well.

In order to give my mother and me something to talk about on those many miserable afternoons when I would pop in to find her white-faced and dismal on the sofa, I sold a publisher the idea for a book set at the time of the Indian Mutiny. After reviewing so many bad books for women's magazines, I realized that I, too, could write a historical novel fairly easily. Unfortunately, I had time only to ask her what a banyan tree looked like, what exactly was the sound of a hoopoe bird and what was the role of a punkah wallah, before it became clear that Dr Foder's optimistic prognosis was hopelessly wrong. My mother lost weight dramatically, and eventually became so ill that an ambulance took her to hospital. I was called, urgently, by the Sister, who asked me to come as soon as possible.

I rushed to her house to pick up a few things for her, drove to the hospital and took a lift to my mother's ward — a great ballroom of a lift designed to accommodate horizontal bodies — and, under a bright neon light in the corridor leading up to the ward, found two nurses gossiping, their friendly Irish voices a contrast to the surroundings. I paused, waiting for the conversation to end. They continued talking. Behind them, in a darkened room, an Arab with an eye-patch sat in a wheelchair, his figure outlined in white flickering light from a huge black-and-white television set. He was thin and gaunt, as if he were being eaten up from the inside.

I stood some time longer, more and more irritated by the nurses. Finally, one must have been struck by my impatience, because she turned.

'The Sister rang me an hour ago,' I said. 'She said she wanted to see me about Mrs Ironside.'

'Oh, good Lord,' said the other nurse. 'Sister's having her tea break. Are you a relation?'

'Her daughter.'

The other nurse turned to go.

'Well, perhaps you'd like to see your mother?'

I started to cry.

Perhaps it was the strain of the whole day or perhaps it was the ward; everything seemed too much to bear. The Sister having her tea break was the final straw.

'No, I want to see the Sister first. When — when will she come — come back from her tea break, the Sister, I mean?' By now I was howling and I knew my face was like a child's when it's upset, mouth gaping and gasping, red-cheeked, gulping for breath. I wanted the Sister *at once*. It was terribly, terribly important.

The other nurse said: 'I'll get Sister,' and went away, while the first nurse guided me into the television room where the Arab still sat, staring at the screen. 'Would you like a cup of tea now?' she said, kindly. She held my hand. I started to pull myself together. I found myself becoming overbearingly in charge. I thanked the nurse with a duchess-like condescension born of trying to keep control.

'Thank you so much for being so sweet,' I said. 'You *are* kind.'

The Sister was big, with large breasts, and she wore a blue uniform with a small blue and white cap on her misty white hair. She was like a wooden figure on the prow of a ship. She drew up a chair and sat down.

'Don't you upset yourself, dear,' she said, kindly. 'Your mother's alive. Don't worry at this stage.' (At what stage? I wondered?) 'You need a word with Doctor perhaps. I'll get him on call. You know what it is, don't you?'

'Cancer,' I said. Now the Arab seemed to be listening hard. 'The, ah, disease . . . ?' I corrected myself.

The Sister nodded. 'She's collapsed. She's very anaemic. But don't lose hope. Maybe something can be done. Certainly, in some cases . . .'

'Oh, yes.' I wished I had enough kindness in me to be able to look up at her gratefully, to thank her with my eyes; but confusion made me short and selfish. We got up and went down a corridor to a door with a window and a small curtain over it. I went in.

There, in the bed, was my mother, though it was hardly a bed and she was hardly my mother. She seemed to have deteriorated horribly in the space of a day. She was lying with her eyes closed, gasping heavily, on a drip, emaciated and worn, with a cracked mouth and hair glued down to her scalp with sweat.

Then the Sister shouted at my mother. 'Your daughter's here, dear, a nice surprise for you, feeling better, are you?' She bustled over to the window and opened it. She fiddled about with the bed-rest and heaved my mother forward.

'Don't . . . don't torment me!' My mother didn't know where she was.

'Feeling more comfortable, are you, dear?' shouted the Sister, above the noise of a disc jockey on a radio that was being piped into the room. 'Have a glass of water, dear, that's good. What a pretty negligée!' She shook what my mother and I would call a nightdress out of the suitcase I had brought. 'And a *lovely* new toothbrush! Soon you'll be back to your old self. I'll leave you two until the doctor comes.'

She bustled out of the room, shaking thermometers and checking them on the way. I sat down beside the bed.

'Mummy?' I said, pressing her hand. It felt warm and sad. I wanted to cry when I looked at her. I ached for her, but more, I ached for myself. The responsibility I felt was too much. John was a support, but he was as baffled by the situation as I was, and I knew that he would hate to take any major decisions about her treatment. 'Mummy? It's me. Are you all right? Can you hear me?'

She turned her face towards me as if she heard me. Then she opened her eyes very slowly and her pupils contracted as she focused on me. A spectre-like smile crept over her face. I remembered a picture of a witch in an old book of fairy-tales. I had always turned the page quickly when I got to it. I wanted to turn the page now. Then she looked hopeless and resigned.

'Why can't I die?' she asked in a rasping voice. She relapsed again into a wheezy sleep. I got up and turned off the radio. My hand was shaking and my palms were slippery.

'You'll be all right,' I said. I leaned over the bars and kissed her cheek. It was cold, covered with a gluey sweat.

The Sister knocked. 'The doctor is here,' she said.

Dr Foder came in, his foot springy with confidence. He was wearing tinted glasses and gold jewellery peeped out from under the cuffs of his white coat.

'Well!' he said, rubbing his hands together and smiling. His voice was as resonant and well-oiled as ever, as if he'd just had it serviced. 'Mrs Ironside! Janey!' (I thought: if he calls her 'Janey', she must be dying.) 'How good to see you looking so well! Much better than this morning!'

My mother's head rolled to one side and she gave a pitiful little smile. Her eyes nearly opened, then sank back. She was hunting desperately for a compliment.

'We'll have you out of here and right as rain in no time,' he

boomed. 'You've done marvellously well, marvellously! You've
pulled through! You're remarkably strong!'

'Can I talk to you?' I asked. I was begging.

'Nothing that we can't talk about in front of your mother!' shouted
Dr Foder jovially. Behind his eyes, I could see he was saying: help
me keep up this act, for God's sake, for your mother's sake. And I
remembered that sometimes my mother had been charmed by him.
'Ghastly little man,' she'd say when we left his surgery. 'Awful short
legs. Why are they so unattractive? How can his wife bear to go to
bed with him?' But when he told her she was looking wonderful –
'Wonderful! Are you sure I haven't got your age wrong in the notes?'
– she would simper suddenly and give him a warm smile full of
promise.

I started to cry again. The doctor put his arm around me, grip-
ping hard. 'We'll be back, Janey!' he said, steering me out of the
room and into his office, a tinted glass box down the corridor. On
the walls were abstract paintings; on the desk, many peculiar paper-
weights and ashtrays, gifts from grateful patients – or perhaps the
grateful relations of dead patients.

'I'm sorry about this, my dear,' he said, sitting in his chair. The
office resounded with his voice. 'I must admit something to you,
something that, I might add, I never admit to my patients.' He gave
me a well-used smile and I wondered how many times he'd used
that phrase to the relatives of other patients. 'I feel upset. Because
this was a failure. A failure on my part to realize how far the disease
had gone. However, there are other pills that can help. She can be
promised, certainly, another three months if not a great deal longer.
Of course, I have to say it, there are side-effects. They can be

painful. And of course her hair will go. But I know your mother is courageous . . .'

I felt like someone watching helplessly as a foreigner who has asked the way drives off in the wrong direction.

'I've promised her I'd never let her suffer side-effects like no hair and weight gain,' I said. It was true, but my voice sounded mechanical, as if I were lying. 'She has always been depressed. As you know, she tried to kill herself even before all this started. You can't rescue her to go on living the way she has been living. And with no hair. That's cruel!'

'People ask for promises to be put out of their pain when they are healthy. When it actually comes down to it, very few people want to die. As for hair, there are always wigs . . . Just because you find it hard to cope with your mother now doesn't mean . . .'

'Look, she's never been happy.' There was an urgency in my voice. 'She's been under psychiatric treatment for the last ten years. She is an unhappy person who wants to die.'

The doctor shook his head and picked up a marble egg from an onyx ashtray, tossing it from palm to palm. 'You don't have the right attitude,' he said. 'We don't believe in dying, here. We believe in living.'

'But *she* believes in dying!' I argued. 'It doesn't matter how good the pills are. She'll still be depressed. And if they have side-effects . . . I couldn't do it to her.'

'She's got everything to live for,' he said. Then he leaned forward, placing the egg back into the dish. 'And not *least*, a marvellous daughter like you.'

I forced a smile at his cruel flattery.

'And of course she is the most original, talented woman, the most attractive, fascinating woman . . .'

I was attacked by a familiar dart of jealousy.

'. . . afraid of this disease. And yet there's no reason,' he continued. 'It carries a dreadful stigma. Everyone thinks you die of it. Why, half the people you see walking around on your way home probably have it and will live as healthily as you or I. Chances are more likely they'll be run over by a bus than die of it!' He fingered his digital watch. It started to squeak.

'Why do you never use the word?' I asked again.

'What word?' he countered. 'No, look. I rely on you, you and I together, to restore your mother's faith in life . . .'

After a transfusion the next day, my mother became more of her old self. She recognized me and John, and she could talk, though we never spoke of personal things, nor about her cancer. Over the next few weeks, she might sometimes come home for a couple of days, but she would always have to go back. Now, myself nearly the age that my mother was at the time, I would behave completely differently, but I wasn't old enough then to have the courage or knowledge to realize that it is actually very easy to talk to people about death.

As time passed, the effects of the transfusions wore off more quickly. She lost all ability to speak coherently. She would talk as if she were talking normally, but utter rubbish came out.

'What raspberry, darling?' she said, back in hospital, when I visited her.

'Raspberry?'

She laughed, shaking her head. 'Rather, raspberry,' she finally managed to say.

'I don't understand, Mummy.'

She smiled, shook her head and tried again. 'Today. Raspberry. Then in here.'

I stroked her hand and looked into her face, with its huge mouth trying to form words. 'Oh Mummy, I'm so sorry I can't understand you. Are you all right?'

She nodded, and I started talking.

'You'll never believe what we're selling now at Graham and Green.' I said. 'Egg-cups with legs! They're selling like hot-cakes!'

My mother smiled. 'Very watch!' she might say. 'Watch . . . I mean . . . watch. No, Selo . . . selo . . .'

'Sellotape?' I said.

My mother shook her head, sadly.

When I left, John took over and sat with her. I knew he was extremely worried, but he was a very shy and silent Northerner who rarely expressed his emotions. Certainly, I never liked to confide too much in him my feelings about my mother because, caring for her and admiring her so much, he would probably have felt disloyal even listening to them.

The problem was that they couldn't start the new pills until she had 'stabilized' and she refused to stabilize. After a few weeks, it was clear that she was dying, that she was making every effort to die, that everything was heading towards death; it was only the transfusions that held her back. This time, she had been in the hospital for ten days, her longest stay yet. Her shrunken figure was shoved awkwardly into position against large pillows like a fragile present packed for the post. Her hair was thin and her white scalp showed through the black strands; her shrivelled arms were taped to drips and another tube hung out of her mouth. Her eyes stared open, starting from their sockets. All over her body, she was starting to bleed from strange cracks that had appeared; she looked as if she had been cut all over with tiny razors. Her nails seemed to be the only thing growing, as if they had a life of their own. They looked like talons.

'Uuu . . . ooo arring,' she said when I went in on the tenth day. It hurt her to speak so she only mouthed strange vowels.

'Are you all right?' I always said this. I didn't know what I wanted her to say.

'Oh . . . oh . . . oh . . . ell . . . me, ell . . . me . . . peese . . . hhelp . . . me . . . aahling!'

I sat with her for a bit, holding her gummy hand, staring into her terrible face. Then I had to get up and go into the corridor to breathe. A nurse was in the corridor and when she came up to me she looked upset. She took my arm and guided me into a side room. She stood there, gabbling at me.

'. . . forgive me, I'm a Catholic, you see.' She was shaking her head, patting my arm. 'But this is not right, not right. Oh, I have experience in these cases, God help me. You know what your mother has got?'

'Cancer,' I said, staring at her. It helped me to say the word.

'Yes, cancer. She's got cancer.' The nurse seemed relieved at hearing the word, too.

'There are things the doctor can do . . . to relieve the pain . . .' She hesitated . . . 'if you know what I mean. I shouldn't be . . . but you don't know what pain your mother is in, mental pain it is, isn't it?'

'Yes.' She actually understood about my mother. I listened intently to what she said.

'It's terrible to see her anguish. The good Lord Himself, He would not wish her to suffer like this. We see this . . . Doctors don't. Yesterday when you were gone . . . Oh, it was terrible what she went through. I have seen some sights here, my dear, God have mercy on me, but I never . . . Oh, please, I'm a Roman Catholic, but she mustn't be in such pain . . . It is only kindness . . . and love, my dear . . . and what is being offered her? A month more? In mental torment?' Her voice trailed off as if she were ashamed of what she had said.

But what *had* she said? I thought I had understood an underlying message – but had I? I felt that she knew that I knew that she knew that I knew . . . but what if she *didn't* know that I knew? Or what if I only thought she knew? How could I answer her?

'But I've asked the doctor already!' I said, desperately, without saying what I'd asked him. I've spelled it out. How can I ask him again? I would be nagging at him to . . . I would . . . I would seem . . . It would be, he would think I was a . . .'

'But I beg that you do just that,' she said, holding my hands in her two hands and looking into my face. She looked pure and good, like a mother. 'I tell you, I'm a Catholic. But please, do the right thing by her. Ask the doctor again. There is no hope for your mother, dear. Only another few months of agony.'

I said I would try again, but I didn't know if I meant it. As I left the nurse, Dr Foder walked by in the corridor, as if the meeting had been pre-arranged. He asked me into his office.

He sat down and shot his white cuffs from under his white coat.

He made a joke to a houseman who was sitting silently beside him. Then he turned to me.

'We'll start the treatment tomorrow, now she's a little stronger. Only an outside chance, of course, of it having an effect. But you never know . . . I think it's worth a try myself.' The young houseman stared at the notes and nodded his head like an automaton.

There was a silence. I read his unequivocal statement as a question. I cleared my throat.

'My mother tried to commit suicide twice before she got cancer,' I said. 'She has been talking of killing herself for years. She longs to die. She has always asked, begged me not to leave her in any pain, mental or otherwise.'

My voice sounded as if it were on the radio, measured and smooth. I continued evenly.

'I gather she is considerably anguished here.' I heard myself using the strangely formal vocabulary that people sometimes employ when overcome with emotional pressure. 'I can witness she is physically ill. For the last year, since she has developed cancer, she has been talking constantly of death. She longs to die. We are not discussing the situation of a happy woman with a will to live here. We are discussing my mother . . . my mother who wants to . . .'

But my control snapped. I dropped my head into my hands and sobbed. Even now, I wonder whether I meant it or whether I was acting a part. Was I genuinely upset or not? I felt so confused. It was the pain of the confusion that made me cry, not the idea of my mother dying.

The doctor coughed. Then he said in a different voice that seemed closer to my face: 'Well, of course, before this treatment

. . . and in view of this . . .' (As if it were the first time I'd mentioned it to him.) 'Well, not in view of this . . . we would have to do this anyway . . . but of course what you have said . . .' He seemed very confused. 'What do you say we give her a strong pain-killing injection and see how that goes for a while?' His houseman nodded. But what was he agreeing to? The doctor pulled a notepad towards him and started writing. Then, everything in the room seemed to relax. Even his desk seemed to sink into the floor a few millimetres, with a creaky sigh. The doctor rang his bell. A chain of flat gold links fell against the hairy back of his hand.

'Let's do this right away, eh?' he said, as if he were in a hurry to get it all over with. A nurse came in. 'Ah, nurse. This is the injection for Mrs Ironside. I think we'll see how this goes, eh? Now I must get on . . . Best of luck, my dear . . .' He got up and bent over his desk to shake my hand. Was it my imagination, or was it, in fact, a farewell squeeze? As our fingers touched, I had the strong feeling that he was a kind man doing a terrible job.

I stammered out my thanks. But then I thought: what is this injection? Had he really understood what I'd meant? Maybe it was just a temporary painkiller. Maybe my mother would be relieved of her pain, then recover, and who knows, be off playing squash or whatever ghastly activity that he had predicted. I said goodbye and followed the nurse into my mother's room.

My mother was in the middle of a spate of hysterical activity and talking nonsense. 'Keep me in here, in 'ell, at the round of devils . . . you bitch, go home, go home . . . Oh, darling,' she said when she saw me. She was trying to pull a drip from her arm with a hand like a claw; her nails dragged against her paper-thin skin. She was restrained by the nurse. 'Going home . . .' she said. She tried to get out of bed and the tube fell from her arm.

The nurse shouted in a loud voice: 'Just an injection, Mrs Ironside, just an injection.' She settled my mother, turned her over: the houseman hurried in; a needle sank into her flesh. Then the nurse drew the window curtains. 'Get a bit of sleep now, Mrs Ironside,' she yelled. 'A bit of sleep.'

She went out of the room and I was left alone with my mother. I clicked down the metal rack that propped up her pillows and settled her head so that it was flat. My mother smiled. She curled into a foetal position and took my hand. I pulled the bedclothes over her with the other. I sat beside her and stroked her hand. She looked so scraggy and brittle, like a little new-born fledgling dropped from its nest, feathers still awry and staring in all directions.

'Mummy, Mummy,' I said, leaning close to her. I was filled with a mad kind of certainty built on desperate hope. 'Don't worry. Everything is all right. I promise now. I have organized it. There is nothing to worry about. Just oblivion. It's just oblivion. You will go to sleep and never wake up. Don't worry. You won't have any more pain. I'll stay with you until you go to sleep.'

She leaned forward and with her dry, cracked lips, she kissed my hand. 'Thank you, darling,' she said, and her voice was warm and clear. Then she fell asleep and I sat there for an hour as her breathing got heavier and heavier until eventually she fell into a deep sleep.

The next morning, the Sister rang me to say that, on 7 April 1979, at the age of sixty-one, my mother had died in the night.

thirteen

CRÊPE   *Crêpe is a lightweight silk, cotton or wool fabric with a wrinkled surface obtained by twisting of yarns, or chemically. Wool crêpe is a soft fabric with irregular surface originally used for mourning clothes.*
  Janey Ironside, *A Fashion Alphabet*

Before I visited the undertaker the next day, I had to collect a chit from the Sister to reclaim my mother's clothes from the office on the ground floor of the hospital. As I stood in the queue, I saw the houseman.

'Oh, hello,' he said. 'I thought you'd like to know, by the way. We opened her up. It turned out that your mother was riddled with cancer. She wouldn't have lived.'

Did I detect a kind of relief? Or was it my imagination?

'Oh, good,' I said. 'But that injection . . . if I'd had it, I wouldn't have died, would I?'

I think I was hoping that he might say: 'Oh, no. It was just a painkiller. Delivered to a healthy person like you, it would have done

absolutely no harm at all. But sometimes if someone is dying already
. . . then . . .'

But he didn't say that. He looked uneasy. He coughed. He said
absolutely nothing.

I went home with his silence ringing in my ears.

I wished I'd never asked him. I wished I'd left it vague.

My next stop was the undertaker. He wore a greasy suit and wrote
in biro at a collapsible desk in what appeared to be the living-room
of his home in the Uxbridge Road. I imagined him folding everything up at night and, in the evening, watching television with his
family in the same spot I was sitting in at the time.

He was as polite and kind as possible, but he had said it all too
many times to sound sincere. He had even adopted a special low
voice for talking to his clients. He called my mother 'mum'. Finally
he said, staring at my neck through unfocused eyes: 'We shall be
collecting mum tomorrow before the cremation service, and if you
would like to see her beforehand, you can visit her at our office in
Fulham Palace Road at any time on Friday, when she will be waiting.'

'See her?' I said, feeling rather baffled. 'Why should I want to
see her?' Hadn't I seen enough of her? I was utterly blank and numb.

He stared at the form in front of him. 'Some people like to see
their relatives. It gives comfort. It is quite understandable if you
don't. Many people don't. Many people do. It is part of our service.'

'What do you do?' I was curious. 'Make them up to look good?'

I thought: my mother would have gone mad at the idea of anyone
touching her face with make-up she hadn't chosen herself. 'Frightful
green eye-shadow, so common . . . can't possibly put on foundation
and powder, so ageing.'

The undertaker smiled. 'Oh no, not like in America. It's not like that here. Well, not if you don't want it like that. No, nothing distasteful. It's up to you. Think it over.'

'No, *thank* you!' I said, shuddering. Peering at the dead was not part of my family's culture. If anyone died, we'd groan and say 'How *ghastly*!' and pick straws for who was to go to the funeral. My mother would have hated the idea. 'What's the point of seeing a dead person? How ghoulish. Ugh!' she would have said.

I didn't want to take my mother's bag back to her house – John was still living there, distraught with grief – so I took it back to Shepherd's Bush, where I picked through her pitiful things. There were her nightdress, her toothbrush, her dressing-gown, her half-finished paperback, an Erle Stanley Gardner. Only ten days ago, I'd guided her last shuffling steps to the hospital, held her arm to help her to the lifts; and yet that day I had walked boldly out of the hospital with nothing but her absence, a bag full of her belongings and a bit of paper in my hand. There weren't just my mother's 'effects' in that plastic bag; there was something almost tangible which was 'not my mother' as well. The glimpse of her black embroidered Kashmiri dressing-gown poking out of the top of the bag was a reminder. It was like looking at life in a black-and-white negative; my mother seemed like one of those white shapes, all shadows in reverse. Print it up and there is a sparkling, smiling figure against a pale background; but in negative, the background is black and the person is only defined by shadows of absence. But still there. Not gone.

That afternoon, I went to see my father. ('Ah, well,' he'd said, when I'd told him she was dead. 'Best thing, really. What a business.'

Then he had picked up the *Evening Standard*.) When I asked him about seeing Janey in her coffin, he agreed it would be a tremendously bad idea. 'A frightful mistake,' he said. Almost as he spoke the words, I perversely changed my mind and decided I would see her. After all, I would never have a chance again and I'd always wanted, from schooldays, to see a 'dead person'. And I could show my son, Will, who was only four, a 'dead person' too and it would be good for him to take death in his stride.

I also, privately, wanted to be sure she was really dead. At the back of my mind I had a troubling thought that perhaps she was being kept in some underground wing of the cancer hospital so that they could experiment on her. Or maybe one day I might meet her accidentally in a lift and she'd say: 'Oh, *darling*, you couldn't possibly . . . just for me . . .'

I rang the undertaker to say that I had changed my mind and he said I could spend the whole morning with her, but as I had spent enough mornings with my mother, staring at her lifeless face, when she was alive, I said no, I just wanted a peek. He didn't feel comfortable with that word.

When we arrived, the road was cast in watery April sunlight. The glass of the undertaker's window was dazzling and looked like mirror until you moved closer. The interior was shaded by exotically draped yellow and orange curtains. There was a dead fly in one of the folds. We went inside and a woman popped out of a door. She had a cup and saucer in her hand and a biscuit in the saucer.

'Be with you in a minute, dear,' she said.

A few minutes later, she looked out again. 'For Mrs Ironside?' she said. 'Through here, dear. And the lad?' She led us into another room across the hall, which was bare except for a long, high table covered with a drape. She pulled back the drape and underneath was a coffin.

'There you are, dear,' she said, pulling back the hinged lid of the coffin. 'There she is. I'll leave you for a while, dear. Just tell me when you leave, won't you, so I can pull it to.'

'Thank you,' I said.

She left, closing the door behind her. We moved closer.

There, inside the coffin, was my mother. Or at least her head and shoulders, for nothing more was visible. I thought: 'Probably her body has been mangled up by the post-mortem.' Her head lay on a silky cream-coloured cushion; her hair had been combed, not as she would have liked it, but not unpleasantly. She had on some kind of garment . . . nothing you'd notice. A white shift of some cheap man-made material that came up to her neck. And her face was quite white, untouched by any undertaker's brush, except, perhaps, for a discreet dusting of light powder. Will, completely unfazed by this occasion, pointed out that the reason she looked so strange was because her red lipstick was gone; her lips were pale, like the flesh of a white fish on a slab.

Then I realized why seeing her seemed so peculiar. She was dead. And I was struck again by a huge sense of not misery, but absence. It was as if I'd come into the room looking for my mother and this woman had shown me a wooden box and a pile of old clothes and I had said: 'Oh, no, that's not my mother, my mother is, you know, a person, surely you know what people are like, you know, people, human beings . . . this is just a pile of things.'

Then I thought: 'How ridiculous to feel anything unpleasant or sad when looking at her body. Better to feel happy that she is indeed dead, and happy that if she is dead, she must have gone somewhere else.' Even 'somewhere else' seemed a bit strong.

She was cremated at the Mortlake Crematorium but, rather oddly, looking back, I didn't go to the service. My uncle did, and he left me a note before he returned to Scotland. 'Hope you had a good day,' he had written. 'The funeral was just as you'd expect. They called her Janet Ironside (not Janey) which she would have loathed. I asked for her ashes to be scattered in the Garden of Rest (sic) as don't imagine you want to go down and look at the urn. Hope she's happier wherever she is. You have been marvellous. Don't lose touch. All the best. Ant.'

I went over and over her death in my mind. I wanted to discuss it with other people, but whenever I got to the bit about asking the doctor to give the pain-killing injection — by far the more *interesting* bit, I thought — they mostly said: 'Ugh, don't go on, don't think about it!', which made me feel like a cold-hearted freak. I wanted to discuss with someone how very easy it must be to kill someone you love when they are in pain – for this is how, in my confusion I interpreted what had happened – and yet, how painful and how hard it is to kill someone you wish dead, out of a sense of duty.

I received piles of condolence letters, which I read in the mornings, wearing my mother's black Kashmiri dressing-gown. 'I know how much you must be suffering': 'She loved you so much': 'Our hearts are with you in this painful time'. I felt angry as I read the notes from people who had absolutely no idea how I was feeling. I was feeling crazed, relieved, bonkers but not in pain. And with what resentment I read the letters from her students: 'Without your mother

I would have been nothing'; 'The award meant everything to me'; 'Your mother was an icon, there is no other word for it'; 'If it hadn't been for your mother giving me my first chance . . .'; 'I owe everything, and I mean everything, to your wonderful mother'. There was nothing, naturally, from Robin Darwin.

It was odd, pottering about in her dressing-gown. At one point, I suddenly felt as if I was my mother. My body was her body. I had her limpid eyes, her wide unmanageable mouth, her long red nails and her hands, with the pale skin on the back just starting to wrinkle. I could feel her tongue in my mouth, I could smell her old gorgeous smell. Her plaintive voice quivered in my throat. I looked down at my feet expecting to see her sheer dark stockings, the elegant ankles and black heeled shoes. But I saw only my red slippers. As I climbed back into myself, I felt a surge of loneliness.

'Your wonderful, wonderful mother. So sensitive . . . talented . . . gifted . . .' I read. And then my old resentment returned.

After her death, John had gone away to Yorkshire for a break, so I went round to my mother's house to clear away some of her things. He had found the process unbearable, so I had agreed to throw out the things we wouldn't want and keep anything I was uncertain about until he got back. I put the key in the lock, went into the dark hall and shut the door. Her black coat still hung on the peg as she had left it on the day I had taken her to the hospital. I touched it. When I took my hand away, one of her hairs was on my hand, black, with a tiny, greasy, white root. I shivered and shook it to the floor.

I turned to go into the sitting-room. I steeled myself. I expected to see her on the sofa. I could imagine her with a drink in her hand, swaying slightly. She would be wearing her dressing-gown and there would be white yoghurt stains down the front. 'Hello, darling,' she'd say in a dull voice. 'Have a drink.'

I put my hand on the door and pushed it slightly open. The room was empty. That meant she really had died.

No one had opened the windows for days, so there was a hot stuffiness inside. I could almost smell her. But everything was tidy and in its place – the brown leather sofa from the Bath Club, the two Tantric heads staring out of their brass eyes, the long, white curtains. It all looked polished and plumped up.

I went upstairs and started to open the drawers in the chest in her bedroom and took out her clothes, stuffing them with great energy into big plastic sacks to take to a charity shop. I could have used them. I never had qualms about wearing my mother's clothes. But now I just wanted to get rid of everything. Her sighs were all around me, clouding the air; there was an ache in the room like a tune. I stripped the sheets and blankets off her bed and took her skirts out of the wardrobe in big clumps of threes and fours.

On the way down the stairs, I plucked the pictures off the walls, like picking apples. I cleared out the kitchen cupboards, the desk drawers, the broom cupboard. At the back there was a trunk of memorabilia. Inside were the first locks of my hair in an envelope: 'Pinny's hair' she had written on the front. Her writing was firm and courageous then. My first birthday card to her was there and a tiny pair of my first shoes, red leather, with little buttoned straps.

There was also a collection of photographs. One showed her face full of life, laughing, one lip just slightly catching on a side tooth as if she had just said the sound 'or'. Perhaps the photographer had said: 'Let's have a lovely smile now, Janey, imagine you're in the country, relaxing, surrounded by lovely grass, sheep, the smell of fresh air.' And perhaps my mother had replied, giggling: 'I can't *bear* the country! It's a healthy grave, as Sydney Smith said. And anyway, air shouldn't *smell*, it should just be there, like water.' And she would have laughed at her own remarks, not at the idea of being in the country. Her eyes sparkled, her face was fizzing with life. She was wearing a black-and-white-striped scarf tucked into the neck of a crisp black dress. It seemed as if she were smiling directly at me. I could almost feel her closeness. I could hear the tone of her voice as if I'd picked it up on a radio transmitter, rather far away, just the odd word. 'Darling,' I could hear her say: 'Darling. Sweetie. My poppet.'

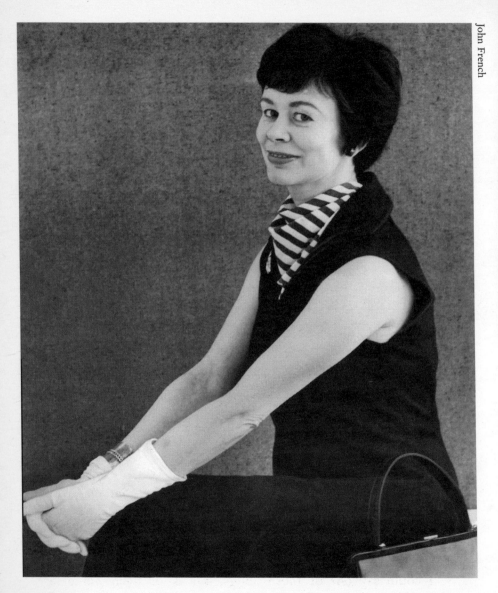

Janey

epilogue

Now my mother has been dead for over twenty years, I wish I could say, as do many of the authors of books like these: 'Ah, well, when I look back on it all now, I forgive my mother, I realize I loved her dearly after all.' I wish I could say: 'I realize now that as a parent I'm not so hot myself, and the sins of the fathers are borne by the sons and on it goes for ever.' Or I wish I could say: 'Writing this book has been a cathartic experience. Now it's done, I can put everything behind me, I can draw a line under everything, and emerge, at last, as *me*.'

I could say one of those things, but all of them would be completely dishonest. The truth is that little has changed. I suppose I feel that my mother wasn't the uncaring person that I used to think she was sometimes – she was funny, brilliant and damaged, and did her best. When she wasn't drinking, I could feel affectionate towards my mother, fond of her, but I wouldn't say I ever loved her.

The truth was that my mother was an icon. An icon is not really a person. An icon is something sparkling and brittle. If you are an icon, you just cannot, I think, be a mother. The qualities that make an icon – qualities of style, cool, remoteness, glamour – do not sit well with waiting by the Round Pond with a pushchair in the pouring rain while your child fishes for minnows, or finding the thought of putting ghastly pieces of pottery made by your child in the centre of your mantelpiece irresistible, however frightful they may look compared to the rest of the room Not only do the qualities not sit well, they do not sit at all.

Having written this book, I realize, too, that my relationship with my father was not as simple as I had thought. It was, to start with, like that of the two parents of a wayward child – my mother; then like two lovers without the sex; then, when my mother left home, like an old married couple. When my father died, in 1992, it was a faithless husband that I lost, not a father.

No, I'm still here, just the same, in the same Shepherd's Bush house that I was living in when my mother died, living alone with a lodger upstairs and trying to keep depression at bay, mostly reasonably successfully. I get up in the morning, read the papers over tea and toast with Marmite, spend the day pottering about, changing lightbulbs, shopping for food, writing, washing, phoning, reading, until the evening, when I go out. Pretty much every night.

I sit at a desk I inherited from my mother in a chair given to me by my father. On the floor is one of my mother's Indian carpets and in a cabinet looking straight down at me are photographs of my father and mother, of Robin and my two grandmothers. I am wearing colours that my mother adored — red and black. As I write, I am wearing a cardigan designed by Marion Foale, one of my mother's students, and a skirt designed by Paul Smith, who, although he wasn't taught by my mother, is married to Pauline Denyer, one of her ex-students, and claims that his wife influenced him greatly. I sometimes think that, now I am nearly the same age as my mother when she died, that the clothes her students design, her furniture, her Indian Moghul paintings and the portraits of her by my father all comfort me in the same way as the piece of my mother's black felt hat used to do when I was tiny.

Try as I may to establish some kind of identity for myself, I am always drawn back to my parents. That is not so awful or so surprising, but I think I hug them closer to me than most other people hug theirs.

When I once went into a craft shop in Suffolk, determined for once to buy a picture that was something *I* had bought, not something by my uncle Robin or a watercolour by my aunt Rene, or drawings by my father or mother (her pictures of evacuees are, of course, framed on my walls), I noticed a picture of an embroidered boat under which swam embroidered fish.

That, I said to myself, is pure *me*! I am making a completely individual choice, in no way connected with my parents. When I told the person I'd been staying with that I had bought it on my way home, she wrote back and said that she knew the artist and had told her that I had bought it.

'Not Virginia Ironside, daughter of Christopher?' the embroiderer had exclaimed. 'He was my tutor at Maidstone and he taught me everything I know!'

Despite the fact that both my parents are dead, I feel their presence curling around me like wood smoke.

I feel connected, too, to all their friends, to their world. I still see John Wright, who lives with his new partner in London and Norfolk; sometimes I dine at the Chelsea Arts Club and think how much my mother would have enjoyed it and how much my father would have hated it. Every year, I am kindly asked to lunch at the Royal College Common Room, where the present Professor of Fashion, Wendy Dagworthy, introduces me to the winner of the Janey Ironside Travel Award, which was set up by John and myself after her death. The painters are no longer at the painters' table. But the beautifully designed salt and pepper sets still sit, brightly polished, on the chic leather-covered tables.

Although I have never actually taken a bottle of vodka wrapped in a nightdress to drink in my room when I go away, I have often considered it. The Janey in me says: 'Go on . . . there'll be nothing to drink there and you'll have to wait till dinner till you get your first measly glass of wine. It'll be ghastly, you'll go absolutely mad!' The Christopher in me says: 'For Christ's sake, don't be a chump! Use your loaf! Once you start behaving like that, you're on the road to cardboard boxes under Waterloo Bridge!'

Christopher wins.

There are two areas of my life, however, in which my mother and I differ completely. When it comes to Will, my maternal instincts leap into bloom, though heaven knows where they came from. I cherish him above all else. Ever since he was born, I have made scrupulous efforts always to take him to and pick him up from school. One of the most flattering things he has ever said to me was: 'When I was young, mum, I never really realized you worked at all.'

I have fried more fish fingers, made more bowls of spaghetti and bought more packets of Angel Delight than my mother could ever have imagined. I have cheered my son on at swimming races, rung up his teachers to fulminate about unfair detentions. I have even, to help him through his history exams, rowed him across the sitting-room floor in order for him (William the Conqueror) to attend the battle of Hastings, and then I've fallen down in a heap, yelling, as he shot me (changed from an oarsman into Harold) in the eye.

When my son says he's going to the theatre, I try to say not 'How ghastly!' but instead: 'Lucky you!'

And knowing how dreadful it is for children of divorced parents to experience the brutal separation that my own parents inflicted on me, both my ex-husband Robin and I have bent over backwards to deepen, rather than lessen, our friendship. He is now Chairman of Greenpeace UK, and I regard his new wife and their three children with almost as much affection as if they were my own loved family.

One day last year, I returned to Varengeville-sur-mer in Normandy with a friend. We stayed at the same hotel that my mother and I had stayed at, Les Terraces. Like my mother and I, we peered over the cliff before supper – luckily no dead horses to be seen – and walked down to the beach, stumbling down a broken path. As we looked into a sunset, glowing pink and red against the grey-white cliffs, I could imagine why my mother found the whole place so romantic. I felt so sentimentally close to her, I found myself thinking: 'If only I could bring Will to this place!'

The dining-room had changed, but we had the most wonderful supper of *moules marinières, porc au cidre* and *îles flottantes*. The hotel was run by a family: the proprietor was the son of the original family who had been there when I was small. When I revealed the momentous news that I had stayed there as a child, his response could not have been more Norman. He and his wife shrugged their shoulders and hurried into the kitchen to chop up some wild mushrooms, not remotely interested.

In the reception area there were photographs of the place as it had been before it was modernized, and I felt charged with that choking, exalted, sickly (and fundamentally inauthentic) feeling of nostalgia – the same antique feeling that some people get when listening to great music, or sobbing over Princess Diana's death, a feeling that they wrongly mistake for something genuine.

The following morning, my friend and I went to the little church where the funeral had been, on the top of a cliff. We bought postcards of the Braque windows. Later in the afternoon, we went around the Lutyens house and, in the sunlight, soaked up the Gertrude Jekyll-designed gardens. We both wished we were staying another night.

Ever since I had discovered, in my mother's papers, an account of our holiday together in Varengeville (she had written about it as a short story, starting: 'We had gone to Varengeville, my eight-year-daughter Alice and myself, after my husband had died . . .'), I had been longing to rediscover Pierre. Since she had mentioned his

surname in the story, discovering him, if he were still alive, became
a real possibility. Underneath my sensible 'research' exterior, I was
confused by irrational feelings both of wanting to find him and kill
him, and to find him and have an affair with him, just to pay him
and my mother back. However, I did imagine that if I could meet
him I might get something sorted out in my head and find a kind of
peace. I wrote a letter to everyone who had his surname in the French
phone-book (luckily only thirty of them, but none of them with the
initial 'P'.)

Nobody replied for three months, until one night, as I was sitting
at my word processor, a deep male voice came on the line. "Allo?
C'est Mme Eeronseed? *C'est* Pierre.'

I was going to stay in Grasse the following month, so when I
was there I drove over to the run-down little port in which he now,
aged well over seventy, had a tiny one-roomed flat, the front door
of which was wedged between two shops, Zazi – Modes pour les
Dames, and Lingerie Lola. He had been married but was now single,
and through his bony features I could just make out the remnants
of the good-looking young boy from the Varengeville dining-room.
Although he was once rich and his family owned pictures by Picasso
and Matisse, he had become an ascetic recluse, keeping his only
possessions in two wooden crates. He remembered the affair he had
had with my mother as a turning-point in his young life and said,
rather apologetically, that he hoped I hadn't been upset by it,
reminding me that he was only about eighteen at the time.

Most of his career had been spent as a biochemist, but now he
had given all that up. Like Mr Casaubon in *Middlemarch*, he was
preoccupied with writing a book 'that will encompass everything

about life, from science, to biology, to religion, society, to psycho-
analysis, war, genetics, love, hate . . .'. He sat in his little room alone,
writing and writing, day after day. 'Sometimes I write thousands of
words in one day and will keep nothing but one word,' he said, his
eyes glittering obsessively. 'Who knows when I will finish it? Perhaps
never.' Strewn around his room were old bits of printed paper with
various sentences highlighted in pinks and yellows. He was just as
selfish as I remembered him. I didn't like him then, and I didn't
exactly take to him when I met him again. But when I mentioned
my mother, his eyes took on a far-away look and he smiled. '*Elle
était si belle, une vraie femme . . .*'

His remark reminded me of something one of her students had
said about her. 'We all admired Janey so much,' said Sylvia Ayton.
'She never really said anything, she just was. She made it all happen
just by being there. We all wanted to look like her — we made white
paper collars, wore red lipstick and dyed our hair black. We all
wanted to be like her when we grew up.'

I do my best *not* to be like her now I am grown-up, although occasionally, through the adult mask of sensible Christopherishness, she
slips through, with surprising flashes of intense and unsuitable sexual
desire (thoroughly bludgeoned down these days, of course), waves
of giggles, the accidentally released bitingly acid remark, or deep
pits of depression.

When John and I organized a memorial service for her at St
James's church in Norland Square, it was presided over by the then
vicar, a man my mother despised, having insisted she once saw him
kicking a dog under his cassock in the street when he thought no
one was looking. (Though I have to say the story seemed unlikely,

since he was very kind and helpful with the service). I have no idea why we decided to have it in a church, except that it was the done thing then. My mother had no more faith than I or my father. When she was sixteen, she'd written in her diary: 'I try not to think about God now, it's too frightening. Sometimes I believe and then sometimes I feel a sort of cold light and I say to myself: "Yes, but what is he, how can he exist?" Then I stop thinking and sing or walk about quickly.'

The whole service was completely inappropriate. We asked Sir Hugh Casson to deliver the eulogy. Considering this was a man who had had an affair with her when she was married and a man she had described as stabbing her in the back, I cannot think what got into us. It was probably because he was famous and had known her from when she was quite young. I asked to see his address so that I could look it over before he delivered it, but when I made a couple of corrections, he snapped at me on the telephone: 'Who's giving this speech, duckie? Me or you?'

Because the vicar had insisted on something religious, I rustled up the views of a vicar friend, who suggested a passage by Thomas Traherne, probably because it had the words 'clothes' in it.

The dust and the stones of the street were as precious as gold: the gates were at the end of the world. The green trees when I saw them first through one of the gates transported and ravished me, their sweetness and unusual beauty made my heart to leap and almost mad with ecstasy, they were such strange and wonderful things. (The Men! O what venerable and reverend creatures did the aged seem! Immortal cherubims! And young men, glistening and sparkling!

Angels and maids, strange, seraphic pieces of life and beauty!) . . .
Boys and girls tumbling in the street and playing, were moving jewels
. . . The streets were mine, the temple was mine, the people were
mine, their clothes and gold and silver were mine, as much as their
sparkling eyes, fair skins and ruby faces. The skies were mine, and
so were the sun and the moon and stars, and all the World was mine;
and I the only spectator and enjoyer of it . . . So that with much ado
I was corrupted, and made to learn the dirty devices of this world.
Which now I unlearn, and become, as it were, a little child again
that I may enter into the Kingdom of God.

Reading the passage back now, I don't think she would have liked
it that much either.

Before the service, I dressed carefully. At home, in my bedroom,
I had put on a straw hat, and I wore a red jacket, a white top, a
yellow skirt and pale tights. But as I left the house and closed the
front door, I felt uneasy. Something was wrong. I unlocked the door
and went upstairs. I looked again in the long mirror — the same
mirror that my mother had looked at herself in every morning and
every night. Was it my pale tights? They didn't look right. I changed
into a pair of darker ones. That was better. But my yellow skirt?
No. It was too — well — too yellow. I took a black skirt from the
wardrobe and put it on. And that white top would have to go, too
. . . I looked in the mirror again. God, the hat looked silly. I took
it off. Now, add some black and white bangles on my arm . . .

When I surveyed the final get-up in the mirror, I saw myself with
short dark hair, pale skin, a jagged slash of a red mouth, a red jacket
over a black top and skirt, with dark tights and shoes.

'Oh, *darling*!' my mother would have exclaimed with a sudden smile, looking me up and down approvingly. 'Oh, *darling* — you *do* look nice!'

picture credits

p.169: Cartoon by Osbert Lancaster, by kind permission of John Murray Publishers Ltd

p.183: Photograph of Janey by kind permission of Eric Wilkins

p.185: Photograph of Virginia by Peter Laurie

p.190: Photograph of Ossie Clark's show by Annette Green
© Condé Nast Publications Ltd

p.238: Photograph of Robin and Virginia by David Ash

p.251: Photograph of Virginia and Will by Carole Latimer

p.294: Photograph of Janey by John French, by kind permission of the Victoria & Albert Picture Library

Cuttings: kind permission of Associated Newspapers Ltd, Express Newspapers Ltd, Telegraph Group, Ltd.

Endpapers: Pictures of Virginia by Hans Wild